American Nature Writing 1999

American Nature Writing 1999

Selected by John Murray

Oregon State University Press

Corvallis

The paper in this book meets the guidelines for permanence and durability of the Committee on Production Guidelines for Book Longevity of the Council on Library Resources and the minimum requirements of the American National Standard for Permanence of Paper for Printed Library Materials Z39.48-1984.

ISBN 0-87071-550-X
© 1999 John Murray
Printed in the United States of America

Oregon State University Press
101 Waldo Hall
Corvallis OR 97331-6407
541-737-3166 • fax 541-737-3170
www.osu.orst.edu/dept/press

for Barry Lopez

I support a positive philosophy of life and art. Wherever this leads me, I am sure it is further than were I a practicing pessimist! I frankly profess a somewhat mystical concept of nature; I believe the world is incomprehensibly beautiful—an endless prospect of magic and wonder.

— Ansel Adams

Commencement Address, Occidental College (1961)

Contents

Preface

American nature writing is energized by our most urgent social and political relationships: how to live in right relationship. In learning to pay respectful attention to one another and plants and animals, we relearn the arts of empathy, and thus humility and compassion—ways of proceeding that grow more and more necessary as the world crowds in. I'm trying to say nature writing is in a period of great vitality because it is driven by a political agenda, as good art always is.— William Kittredge

With this volume the *American Nature Writing* annual series, published for the past five years by Sierra Club Books, begins a new association with Oregon State University Press. Much about the series will continue unchanged. Each anthology will feature a diverse selection of some of the best current nature writing, a geographically representative selection of American authors, and an alternating sequence of male and female voices to provide a natural rhythm that will hopefully add to your reading pleasure. In this volume the writings range geographically from the Tibetan Plateau (Natasha Ma) to the Mexican Baja (Bruce Berger), from the woods of New England (Franklin Burroughs) to the wilds of northern Alaska (Carolyn Kremers). Some of the authors are well established (David Petersen), others are just becoming widely known (Susan Tweit), and at least two are being introduced to a national audience for the first time (Jeff Ripple and Ken Lamberton). All have mastered their voice and craft and have something compelling to say about nature.

Readers familiar with the 1998 volume will note an essay with a similar title here: "White Poplar, Black Locust" by Louise Wagenknecht. Last year's essay, "White Poplar," was a brief three pages long. The version in this volume is considerably expanded in both length and scope.

More so than in past volumes, this new series will be committed to the writing of emerging writers—to those who have perhaps not yet published a book but who have demonstrated the clear potential to join the ranks of the most stellar authors. In this year's annual, two-thirds of the contributors have not yet published their first book, although many surely will in the next few years. These annual collections provide the opportunity to showcase the work of this important group of writers, to offer visible encouragement to them through publication, and to share their often extraordinary talents with a larger national constituency. Their essays and books will be sorely needed in the environmental battles of the twenty-first century.

Next year's volume is already being planned. If you have a selection or know of a selection that you believe would contribute to that anthology, by all means send it to me at P.O. Box 102345, Denver, CO 80250. 1 am particularly interested in nature writing (i.e., writings of any genre with a strong natural content) from the following groups: (l) writers known only locally or regionally but with national potential, (2) writers from the Midwest, Northeast, and Deep South, (3) writers with experiences in nature abroad, (4) writers concerned with nature in an urban or suburban context, and (5) writers from ethnic groups offering alternative perspectives on nature (such as African American, Asian American, and Native American). Working together—readers and editor—we can continue to build anthologies that, like this one, hold both literary excellence and thematic and stylistic diversity as the standard.

The *American Nature Writing* series is designed not only for the general reader interested in enjoying some of the finest current writing in the genre, but also for teachers, students, and practitioners of the nature essay. For teachers in particular, the anthology can be helpful in writing workshops, contemporary literature courses, composition and exposition classes, literature seminars, interdisciplinary environmental studies courses, and field study courses. Although several fine anthologies representing the better-known nature writers are available, this is the only series to consistently feature the work of the younger, emerging nature writers. In that sense, it holds a particular appeal to those just learning about the genre, or about prose writing in general, as well as to those who delight in discovering fresh new talents.

I would like to thank David Spinner and Jim Cohee of Sierra Club Books for their many years of warm and faithful friendship, and Warren Slesinger of Oregon State University Press for his enthusiastic support of the series.

Introduction

Our village life would stagnate if it were not for the unexplored forests and meadows which surround it. We need the tonic of wildness. . . . We can never have enough of nature. We must be refreshed by the sight of inexhaustible vigor, vast and titanic features, the sea-coast with its wreckes, the wilderness with its living and its decaying trees, the thunder-cloud, and the rain which lasts three weeks and produces freshets. We need to witness our own limits transgressed, and some life pasturing freely where we will never wander.

—Henry David Thoreau, *Walden*

i

Although several important works of American natural history were written before and during his lifetime, Henry David Thoreau is traditionally credited with having created the modern nature essay. After a series of promising early essays, including "A Winter Walk" and "Natural History of Massachusetts," Thoreau produced, after seven years of concentrated effort, the world's first unified collection of nature essays in *Walden: or, Life in the Woods.* The book chronicled his two-year stay on some forested lakeside property owned by his friend Ralph Waldo Emerson. His essay "Civil Disobedience," based on the teachings of Christ, later served as a primary source document and philosophical inspiration for twentieth-century social reformers such as Mahatma Gandhi and Martin Luther King. When Thoreau died at the age of forty-four, Emerson observed that "the country knows not yet . . . how great a person it has lost."

The three major themes of *Walden*—communion, renewal, and liberation—continue to pervade the genre even now, at the dawn of the twenty-first century, and are evident in the eighteen nature essays featured here. By far, the most prevalent theme is the first, communion, which involves the intimate sharing of the human spirit with the natural world. Naturalist David Petersen, for example, takes us to a high mountain trail in Glacier National Park where grizzly bears are often seen. Here he is treated to an epiphany:

> I whoop and Neal joins me, and for the next several minutes we watch the [grizzly] as it feeds among the quiltwork of tiny meadows . . . melts into then reappears from dense copses of subalpine spruce and fir and otherwise indulges and enjoys its wild and fierce freedom. . . . Here, I reflect, is the flesh-and-fur incarnation of the wildness in which Thoreau advised resides the preservation of the world. The preservation of my world, at least.

Similarly, Bruce Berger describes one of his favorite "getaways" in the world—a Steinbeckean village in the Mexican Baja—in his essay "Under the Cypress." It is a quiet, pastoral realm where the beleaguered spirit is free to mingle with a lovely, humanized parcel of the natural world:

> I never ceased marveling at the sheer abundance. In the vegetable garden were onions, garlic, chiles, hops, potatoes, celery, peppers, cabbage, parsley, cilantro, and a variety of greens for spice, salads, medicines, and herbal teas whose English names I didn't know. Overhead hung bananas, papayas, pomegranates, dates, and citrus crosses of Hector's devising. Spiking the greenery were zinnias, marigolds, roses, hollyhocks, and cosmos, and the balance of the property drifted in grapevines.

Bruce Berger reminds us that for many, perhaps most, nature is a lowercase noun—the tame world of backyard gardens and village or city parks. A communion with nature in this context is just as valid, in some ways just as ancient, as a communion with nature in more remote areas.

A second theme found in these essays is renewal, the rejuvenation of the fatigued spirit, heart, and body through contact with the regenerative forces of wild nature. Although present to an extent in all the essays, the theme is strongly evident in two selections. Susan Tweit's essay "Sanctuary," from her memoir of life in the Chihuahuan Desert, comes to mind first, as she writes about tuberculosis victims traveling to the Southwest for the healing effects of the arid mountain air:

> *Tuberculosis was big business for the desert Southwest, ranking equal in its economic benefits and in the number of new residents that it attracted, say historians, to agriculture and mining. Towns competed to attract lungers, advertising their healthful qualities. . . . Doctors moved in by the hundreds. . . . The hotel and boardinghouse trade boomed.*

Later in the essay she and her husband discover a different sort of healing "sanctuary"—a rare desert spring on the side of the rugged Organ Mountains near her former home in Las Cruces, New Mexico. Here the afflicted human spirit may be restored as much as the ailing body was in the desert sanitoriums of an earlier age.

Physician Glen Vanstrum, who works near death and suffering every day, regularly seeks renewal and solace in the undersea kelp forests and abalone beds near his home in La Jolla, California:

> *There is something both peaceful and exhilarating about swimming along thirty feet deep in the quiet Pacific at night. The warm glow of the torches limits one's visual field and focuses attention. Daytime fish like garibaldi and bass disappear, and a new shift of characters, octopi, crabs, and eels, comes out to explore and feed. To me it was sheer wilderness joy, the same feeling found, say, hiking in Alaska's Brooks Range—only this joy was just a few feet from my urban home.*

In his writing, and passionate love for the sea, one is reminded of the work of Rachel Carson. Both Venstrum and Carson see the ocean as a place of natural wonders—a realm in which to rediscover the pure joy of childhood—and also as a source of personal renewal.

The theme of liberation—which often involves the sense of being disencumbered and quite literally freed from some internal or external burden—is evident in the selection by Teton forest ranger Susan Marsh. Attending a field study class presented by the Yellowstone Institute, Marsh hikes into the mountain forest with a length of twine, forms a circle with the string, and then intently studies everything within the circle. Gradually she begins to see the natural world through a different prism and is "liberated" from traditional perceptions:

> *Sitting on a boulder in a far corner of Yellowstone, I collect myself. I pick up my twine and sweep it over the nodding grass. It loops across the goldenrod and gentian gone to seed. The morning is almost gone. I want to stay in the space encircled here, made precious by my hours of attention. I realize that my simple act of noticing, alert to this moment with all its beauty and quiet, is more important than whatever I achieve.*

Natasha Ma (pseudonym) reminds us, in her heartfelt essay about the plight of Tibetan plateau fauna, of the moral responsibility that we all have to free wild nature wherever she is threatened and abused. Despite threats of Chinese retaliation the author speaks out on behalf of the voiceless:

> *I have been called in to be reprimanded by the head of [The Tibetan Academy of Social Sciences]. He tells me I must stop asking my students to write essays about how their land has changed since the "Chinese liberation." I tell him that I saw a tiger pelt and horns of the endangered Tibetan antelope in the marketplace yesterday. This is wrong, I say. Your people must stop this before everything is destroyed.*

Thoreau would be proud of this young woman, who is fighting so earnestly for the rights of wild animals in a distant land to a life of dignity and freedom. In her actions and words she is honoring the finest and oldest traditions of the genre.

ii

When the twentieth century began the best-known nature writers in America included John Muir, Theodore Roosevelt, Mary Austin, John Burroughs, and Ernest Thompson Seton. A similar list compiled at the beginning of the twenty-first century would include such figures as Edward O. Wilson, Peter Matthiessen, Barry Lopez, Terry Tempest Williams, and Rick Bass. In examining the differences and similarities between these two groups, one can appreciate how far American culture has advanced in the short span of one hundred years. During the era of Roosevelt and Muir, a postfrontier extractive philosophy dominated public land administration, and wildlife management was controlled by what environmental historians now call "predator prejudice." Today, both points of view have significantly evolved. The National Park Service, Bureau of Land Management, and Forest Service now strive to manage public land units as unified "ecosystems," and major predators—grizzlies, polar bears, black bears, wolves, lions, coyotes, jaguar—are considered by land managers as essential elements of the natural landscape and are protected by strict federal and state laws.

American nature writers have grown considerably with the times, as well. Their writing has become more overtly political and more personal (at times even confessional) and is more consistently concerned with the nuances and rigors of true literary craft. One of the finest books of the 1990s—Terry Tempest Williams's *Refuge*—exhibits these dramatic changes perfectly, as the author writes about her mother's death from ovarian cancer. As a parallel metaphor, she also narrates the death of a wildlife refuge near her home in Salt Lake City, Utah. One hundred years earlier, Theodore Roosevelt fled to his North Dakota ranch following the death of his mother and wife, and yet the many books he published about the ranch made no mention of these highly personal experiences. Because of the literary and social conventions of the time, Roosevelt deeply submerged his intense pain in the ranching and hunting narratives, where it appeared only briefly now and then in death motifs. A reader today cannot help but think that Roosevelt would welcome these healthy changes in the genre, which allow authors more political and personal freedom of expression. As a result, writers can achieve greater personal catharsis in their work and also have the opportunity to communicate more openly and honestly with readers.

The primary cultural trend throughout this century—and nature writing reflects this at every stage—has been toward the progressive liberalization of American society. It is no coincidence that in the same year that women were given the right to vote (1920), Congress also passed, and the president signed into law, the act officially founding the National Park Service. There is often a parallel between how a society treats its women and how it treats nature, and in the United States, at least, we have seen that as more rights have been conveyed to the former, the latter has benefited proportionally. Because so many of these changes have become institutionalized politically and socially and gained historical momentum, it is likely that the situation will continue to improve in this regard. Nature writers such as John Muir, Aldo Leopold, Robert Marshall, Rachel Carson, and Edward Abbey are at least partially responsible for this small but significant bit of human progress.

iii

What will happen to the genre in the twenty-first century? Because nature writing is currently absorbed in its social responsibilities, it would appear the form is approaching its maturity. No evidence of senescence is yet manifest—it has not exhausted the idiom, become institutionalized, fallen into the hands of unskilled practitioners, been rejected by a younger generation, or lost its readership and hence the capital that supports it in the publishing world.

If anything, the genre is gaining in appeal. The sheer exuberance and optimism of nature writing has already gone a long way toward reversing the urban skepticism that had pervaded Western culture since the end of the Romantic Age. The resanctification. of the Earth evident in nature writing also reverses a trend of secularization that began with the Renaissance. Both reflect good and healthy changes in literature and society. Future literary historians may view nature writing as the major nonfiction genre of our time, and they may also see it as a vital force that helped to revivify both lyric poetry and the social novel.

At its best, contemporary nature writing is capable of achieving the qualities of all literatures that endure: universality, a high level of craft, depth of feeling, stylistic innovation, and personal revelation. Nature writers such as those gathered in this volume are more than interpreters and commentators. They are highly skilled artists creating with deceptive simplicity in a form that is not close to being exhausted. Since the times of Moses and Christ, the wilderness has been a place of vision, inspiration, and insight, and these modem nature writers are descendants of those earlier thinkers. They are also political—in the tradition of Thoreau—and attempt to be critics of society in the best sense of the word. These writers are trying, above all, to transcend a cultural alienation from nature that in Western civilization goes back to Biblical times. In the centuries to come, their efforts will only become more essential as humanity strives to preserve the natural beauty of this world.

Sanctuary

Susan Tweit

*All landscapes have a history . . . There are distinct voices,
languages that belong to particular areas. There are voices
inside rocks, shallow washes, shifting skies; they are not silent.*
—Joy Harjo, *Secrets from the Center of the World*

This is a sacred place, please behave accordingly.
—Sign in the Cathedral of Saint Francis, Santa Fe

In Memory of Elsie Johnson (1915-1994)

On the first of April in 1918, Robert Lewis Cabe boarded a train in tiny Hampton, Arkansas, bound for Crossett to see a doctor at Crossett Hospital. Reverend Cabe, a circuit-riding Methodist preacher, had been ill for months. His parishioners, concerned about his deteriorating health, had convinced him to see a doctor and had taken up a collection to pay for a two-month recuperative vacation.

After what Reverend Cabe's journal describes as "a most extremely thorough examination," Dr. J. E. Sparks of Crossett Hospital delivered the verdict: "Tuberculosis in a very active form." His advice: "Go West at once if you expect to live." The doctor recommended New Mexico. Although the elegant script in Reverend Cabe's journal does not reveal his feelings, the diagnosis—essentially a death sentence—must have stunned him. He was in his thirties and his life was going well; he loved his work. He and his wife, Sarah Della Hope, who was then six months pregnant, had five young children and a comfortable house with a big garden and a cow.

Reverend Cabe took the 5:30 a.m. train home to Hampton the following day. Two weeks later, at noon on Thursday, April 18, having sold their house and most of their belongings, the family boarded a train "in a great downpour of rain," on their way to the desert Southwest. The following night, my husband's grandfather and his family reached El Paso, Texas, in the Chihuahuan Desert where Texas, New Mexico, and Old México meet. There they stopped.

The remaining daily notations in Reverend Cabe's journal, written in a sprawling and feeble hand, are brief and poignant. Saturday, April 20: "Ill day at the Hotel." Monday, April 22: "Too ill to write, but hunted for a house." The following Sunday, his terse note reflects his depression at having no spiritual flock to tend for the first time in many years: "A lonesome Sunday." Monday's entry is no better: "Nothing worthy of note." The diary ends two days later on Wednesday, May 1, with these words in a barely legible hand: "For the past month I have been so ill that nothing was of interest to me. I hope this month to be better." Reverend Cabe's hopes did not come true. He died of tuberculosis in El Paso three months later on August 13, 1918, leaving Sarah Della Hope on her own with seven children, including two-month-old twin boys, one of whom is now my father-in-law.

Until Richard was offered a teaching job in Las Cruces, we had paid little attention to Cabe family history. We did know that Richard's grandfather was buried in El Paso, Texas, just forty miles south of our new home, but we didn't know why. On a visit to Arkansas before we moved, Richard questioned his parents: Why was his grandfather buried in El Paso when his father had grown up in Arkansas? How long had the family lived in the Chihuahuan Desert? What had taken them there, so far from home? (Sarah Della Hope packed up the children and their belongings and took the train home after Reverend Cabe's death, and there they stayed. Arkansas remains home for this branch of the Cabe family.) In answer, Richard's mother dug out Reverend Cabe's diaries. Richard stayed up long after bedtime turning the pages of the clothbound ledgers, reading the faded handwriting: lists of sermons prepared and the dates they were used, columns of expenses, and page after page, book after book, of daily entries in neat handwriting on thin blue lines—the details of the life of a circuit-riding Methodist preacher. I was fast asleep long before he read the last few pages with their poignant story of Reverend Cabe's diagnosis and the family's desperate flight to the desert Southwest. I woke when Richard crawled into bed next to me, his face wet with tears. I held him close as he told me the story of the grandfather that he never knew, the man who died when Richard's own father was just an infant.

After we moved to Las Cruces, I read Reverend Cabe's journals again. Reading of the Cabe family's journey made our own difficult move to the desert seem infinitely easier. It put my acute feelings of dislocation and discomfort in perspective. Imagine how it felt, I thought, for these Arkansas natives, used to trees and rain and green, to be plunked down in this endlessly tan desert landscape. How in their dry-as-dust yard could they plant the huge garden that had fed them in Arkansas? Did Sarah Della Hope miss her flowers? Imagine them learning to cope with the musical cadences of Spanish instead of familiar Arkansas accents, with a culture as much Mexican as American. Imagine Sarah's feelings of despair as she gave birth to twin boys and cared for her ailing husband and their other five children while Reverend Cabe, her partner as well as her means of financial support, sank closer to death. The fact of their journey and their months in El Paso made our own move easier. Richard's family left footprints for us to follow. Reverend Cabe's grave down the valley gives us roots here—tenuous roots, but roots all the same—making this foreign landscape seem more like home.

When Richard first read his grandfather's journals, we wondered at the odd coincidence that sent the Cabe family to the same part of the Chihuahuan Desert where we settled seventy years later. Actually, their story was a common one. Reverend Cabe and his family, like hundreds of thousands of people suffering from tuberculosis, came to the Southwest in search of a health sanctuary in the hope that the dry air and mild climate would perform miracles that medicine of the day could not deliver.

For generations born after antibiotics revolutionized medicine, it is hard to imagine the magnitude and effect of tuberculosis. Dubbed the "White Plague" for its virulence (in contrast to the Black Plague of the Middle Ages), tuberculosis was the leading cause of death in nineteenth-century America. By 1890, tuberculosis killed 150,000 Americans each year: or about 1.5 people out of every thousand. (By comparison, AIDS in 1990 killed almost one per ten thousand.) Medical historians estimate that, for every death, there were ten to twenty others seriously affected by the disease. At its height, tuberculosis claimed one-third of all Americans who died between the ages of fifteen and forty-four.

Tuberculosis is caused by a tiny, airborne bacterium, a parasite on human cells. As the bacteria grow and reproduce, they burst the walls of their host cells, forming lesions. In the most prevalent form of tuberculosis, the bacteria infect cells of the lung linings, causing the lungs to fill slowly with fluid. Soon the sufferer is literally gasping for breath, her or his lungs barely able to absorb oxygen. The common name of tuberculosis, "consumption," reflects the result: without oxygen, food cannot be metabolized and the victim simply wastes away; flesh is seemingly "consumed" by the disease. Until the discovery and widespread use of antibiotics in the middle of the twentieth century, there was no cure. Some consumptives recovered. But in many cases, a diagnosis of tuberculosis condemned the sufferer to a slow, lingering death.

When Richard's grandfather was diagnosed with tuberculosis, the most promising treatment was just what Dr. Sparks of southern Arkansas's Crossett Hospital prescribed: Go West at once. Altitude Therapy, as this regimen was called, relied on the thinner air at elevations several thousand feet or more above sea level to give sufferers' afflicted lungs a rest, and on arid climates to dry out the tubercular lesions. The healthy air, reasoned adherents, would allow sufferers' lungs to heal. Fresh air was considered crucial. Patients spent hours at a time outside in all seasons, often lying on chaise lounges—hence the popular phrase, "chasing" the cure—and even slept outside. (The fashion for screened porches dates to the rise in popularity of altitude therapy.) The mild climates of the southern Southwest were thus especially popular destinations for tuberculars. Dr. Sparks most likely aimed Reverend Cabe and his family toward New Mexico because of the hundreds of tuberculosis sanatoriums that had sprung up in the state and because of glowing recommendations from tuberculosis specialists like Dr. J. F. Danter, a Toronto physician who visited New Mexico territory in 1891. Danter grandly reported that New Mexico was superior "to any other part of the United States or the world in helping to cure the consumptive."

Claims like these propelled hundreds of thousands of "lungers," as tuberculosis sufferers were called, west. The flood of health-seekers began around the 1880s after the railroads made Western travel more comfortable and affordable, and continued until the 1940s, when antibiotics began to be widely distributed. One of every eleven New Mexicans in the early 1900s came to the state seeking a cure for tuberculosis, according to Dr. Ernest Sweet, author of a U.S. Public Health Service study published in 1913 and quoted in *Doctors of Medicine in New Mexico,* by Jake W. Spidle, Jr. (Family members accompanying health-seekers, such as Sarah Della Hope and the couple's seven children, swelled that number considerably.) Like my husband's grandfather, most of the health-seekers were in their twenties or thirties, and most were also men. Dr. Sweet surveyed a thousand health-seekers in El Paso and found 715 men and 285 women. The disease wasn't prejudiced. Women were just as likely to contract tuberculosis as men, but their roles as mothers, wives, and daughters kept them tied down, less able to move west to chase the cure. If Sarah had been the one diagnosed with tuberculosis, would the Cabe family have come west? Most likely not, since that would have meant sacrificing Reverend Cabe's livelihood. But since it was Reverend Cabe who was ill, his income-earning potential was already lost, and so the family might as well chance the move west. They had nothing left to lose.

Tuberculosis was a big business for the desert Southwest, ranking equal in its economic benefits and in the numbers of new residents that it attracted, say historians, to agriculture and mining. Towns competed to attract lungers, advertising their healthful qualities. Hospitals, convalescent, homes, and sanatoriums sprang up to serve the flood of lungers. Doctors moved in by the hundreds (incidentally, according to Spidle in *Doctors of Medicine in New Mexico*, greatly improving health care for all New Mexicans). The hotel and boardinghouse trade boomed; rental properties were jammed; lungers even sought sanctuary in auto courts (early motels) and hastily erected "tent cities." According to Sweet's study, anywhere from twenty to eighty percent of the households in New Mexico towns sheltered a tubercular boarder in the early 1900s. Moving and storage companies sprang up to serve the consumptive migrants, as did other businesses including, of course, funeral homes. Even colleges jumped on the health bandwagon: Our own New Mexico College of Agriculture and Mechanic Arts, now New Mexico State University, advertised "Health" as one of three reasons to attend the school. In an 1899 advertisement, the school boasted that its site in southern New Mexico was "the healthiest locality in the world," drawing "hundreds of invalids" each year. Indeed, the college's first president, Dr. Hiram Hadley, came to Las Cruces to visit his ailing son and stayed to lead the fledgling college.

Sadly, the outcome of the Cabe family's journey west was also common. Going west was not an infallible cure-all. Between 1903 and 1912, 1,419 people in Albuquerque died of tuberculosis, according to Spidle, at a rate nearly ten times the national tuberculosis death rate. (Albuquerque's total population at the time numbered just ten thousand people.) Ninety-one percent of those deaths, according to Dr. Sweet, were lungers who had recently emigrated to New Mexico. In other words, for many people like my husband's grandfather, going west was futile. Still, the lungers kept coming. Before antibiotics, no other treatment promised so much hope.

After antibiotics became widely available in the late 1940s, the tuberculosis boom fizzled and was quickly forgotten. Tuberculosis sanatoriums closed their doors or converted to other uses. Doctors specializing in the lunger trade retired or changed their practices. Hospitals converted tuberculosis wings to other purposes. Towns no longer touted themselves as sanctuaries for health-seekers.

One of the first sanatoriums for tuberculosis sufferers in southern New Mexico was established at Dripping Springs, a canyon in the Organ Mountains visible from our house. It is a beautiful site for a health sanctuary. Named for the spring itself, which slides down a smooth channel worn in a rock wall at the canyon's head, Dripping Springs is one of the largest canyons cutting into the Organ Mountains. At its upper end, where the spring is, its bare, red-purple rock walls rise steeply above a narrow valley bottom studded with short, twisted hackberry trees and evergreen oaks. The spring, a gush of water after summer rains or rare winter snows, a clear trickle the rest of the year, is one of only two year-round water sources on the west side of the Organ Mountains. From the cool shade of the valley, some two thousand feet above Las Cruces, the hot desert seems far away.

Dripping Springs has served as a sanctuary of sorts, a refuge from the searing heat of the desert, for millennia. Tools, pottery, and other evidence show that people have sojourned in the Dripping Springs area since at least forty-five hundred years ago, during the time that the pharaohs in Egypt were building the first pyramids, according to Mike Mallouf, Bureau of Land Management archeologist. But as far as we know, says Mallouf, there were no permanent settlements in the valley in the 1880s when Colonel Eugene Van Patten, a Las Cruces businessman and community leader, began to build Mountain Camp, a summer place, just around the corner from where Dripping Springs splashes into the valley bottom.

What Van Patten planned for Mountain Camp is not clear. Starting out as a summer retreat for family and friends, it was later advertised as a tuberculosis sanatorium. But Mountain Camp soon evolved into a different kind of sanctuary, an outpost of elegance and generous hospitality in the harsh expanses of the Chihuahuan Desert. By the early 1900s, Mountain Camp had become a gracious resort, one of the places to see and be seen in southern New México, far west Texas, and northern Chihuahua, México. It boasted a lovely stone, two-story hotel and a cluster of more rustic tent cabins, which housed tuberculosis sufferers and their families. The hotel included over twenty guest rooms, a dining room large enough to double as a dance hall, and shady, wraparound verandas. A contemporary photo of the dining room shows a linen-draped table set with silver, china, and crystal; in the background is an upright piano; above hangs a chandelier. Beautifully landscaped grounds surrounded the hotel and cabins with green lawns, flower beds, an orchard, and even a wrought-iron bandstand. Entertainment included concerts at the bandstand, ballroom dances, and Indian dances by residents of nearby Tortugas Pueblo. The *Rio Grande Republican* carried weekly news about Mountain Camp: details of improvements and additions, reports on weddings and other social functions held at the resort, and names of vacationers and visitors—México's Pancho Villa and Sheriff Pat Garrett of Billy the Kid fame among them.

Franklin Hayner, a Las Cruces lumber magnate who later built his own summer retreat in the lower part of the Dripping Springs valley, recalled Sundays at the hotel, when it was fashionable for "belles in flowing skirts and beaus in flowing whiskers" to ride several hours up from town just to take Sunday tea in the dining room with three or four hundred other guests. Van Patten's, Hayner said, was "the showplace of the country side," attracting local and El Paso guests plus "wide-eyed Easterners." Mountain Camp was a favorite destination for students and faculty of the New Mexico College of Agriculture and Mechanic Arts as well. References to "pik-nicking at Van Patten's"— poems, stories, reports of group outings—crop up regularly in the *Collegian*, the college magazine, and the *Swastika*, the yearbook, from the 1890s until the World War I years.

Unfortunately, greed shattered the idyll and, in the end, caused Dripping Springs to be closed to the public for many decades. During the resort's boom years, Dr. Nathan Boyd, a physician and officer of an English company that was organized to build a dam on the Río Grande, summered at Mountain Camp with his wife and family. In 1904, Boyd rented a side canyon from Van Patten to establish his own tuberculosis sanatorium and cash in on the lunger boom. Van Patten built Boyd's sanatorium—perched on stilts because of the steepness of the canyon— a house for his family, and supplied meals from Mountain Camp's kitchen. Then Dr. Boyd discovered that the land description on Van Patten's title erred—it included neither Dripping Springs, Mountain Camp, nor the side canyon containing Boyd's sanatorium. Boyd immediately filed a claim to the whole area. Van Patten refiled. Boyd sued for ownership. The dispute went through the New Mexico courts and all the way up to the United States Land Office and finally the secretary of the interior—twice. Although each jurisdiction reaffirmed Van Patten's ownership of the property, the final time in 1909, Boyd refused to budge or to pay his debts to Van Patten. Finally in 1917, the year before my grandfather-in-law and his family came west, Colonel Van Patten, eighty years old, broke, and worn out, sold out to Dr. Boyd for the sum of one dollar.

Neither elegant resort nor antiseptic sanatorium survived much longer. Boyd, nearly bankrupt from the failure of his dam company, sold Dripping Springs and his sanatorium in 1922. The new owners allowed picnickers for a fee and rented summer cabins, but Mountain Camp never regained its former glamour, the sanatorium closing for good. In 1940, the 242-acre complex went up for sale again. A group of forward-thinking Las Crucens tried to raise the four-thousand-dollar asking price, hoping to open the area as a public playground. Their ambitious plans included restoring the buildings, and constructing picnic units, foot and saddle trails, tennis courts, a swimming pool, and a golf course. They failed to raise the funds. As the tuberculosis boom faded from popular memory, so too did the memory of Mountain Camp and the tuberculosis sanatorium. During World War II, the whole area was leased to the army as part of White Sands Proving Ground, now White Sands Missile Range, and officially closed to the public.

Closed to the public it stayed, until the Nature Conservancy, a nonprofit organization dedicated to preserving plants, animals, and natural communities, bought the whole valley in 1988 and traded it to the federal Bureau of Land Management, which manages the surrounding public land including much of the rest, of the Organ Mountains. The Bureau of Land Management had spent the previous decade futilely attempting to find a way to protect the Dripping Springs area—then part of the Cox Ranch, a large family ranch—and reopen it to the public. Finally, with the Nature Conservancy's help, the bureau succeeded. The same qualities that had drawn others to Dripping Springs for millennia also attracted the bureau and the Nature Conservancy: its rare permanent water source, high elevation, and rocky remoteness make this valley a sanctuary far removed from the harsh desert below and from the metropolitan area creeping near. Not just any sanctuary either, Dripping Springs shelters eight kinds of plants and animals found nowhere else in the world.

The geography of the Organ Mountains is part of what makes Dripping Springs so unusual. Just eighteen miles long by one ridge wide, the Organs are not a big mountain range. Although small in area, they loom large. The Organs are the tallest mountains visible from Las Cruces, rising five thousand feet above the surrounding desert to peaks as high as nine thousand feet above sea level. Their soaring height transforms the Organs into a world far removed from the hot, dry landscape below. Since the average air temperature drops about 4°F with each thousand-foot elevation gain, when the thermometer in our backyard records 106° on a sizzling June afternoon, the mercury is not likely to rise much above 90° in the Dripping Springs valley. At the site of Mountain Camp, tucked in the narrow upper canyon around the corner from Dripping Springs itself, the temperatures are moderated further by the shade and thermal mass of the towering rock walls.

Height also equals more moisture. As moisture-laden air rises in order to pass over the range, the air cools and drops some of its water. The Organs thereby snag precipitation that never reaches the lower desert. Las Cruces averages just under nine inches of precipitation per year, while Dripping Springs averages more like fifteen inches. The high ridges above Dripping Springs catch even more, funneling moisture down the chute that feeds the springs. With cooler temperatures and increased moisture, mountain ranges such as the Organs, isolated by the formidable expanses of desert surrounding them, indeed merit the name sky *islands.*

Geology is the other reason for Dripping Springs' uniqueness. Born of a volcanic caldera, the Organs are a bipolar range, split into dramatically different north and south halves. The south part of the range is formed of rock layers spewed forth when the caldera exploded several times some 34 to 33 million years ago. The violent explosions built up layers, two miles thick, of dark, reddish-purple rhyolite and orange-red tuff, which now form the skyline of rounded, hump-backed ridges that characterizes the southern part of the Organs. The north half is as different as can be: a fluted skyline of pale gray rocky pinnacles, the "organ pipes" for which the mountains are named. This half of the Organs is comprised of a nubby kind of granite with large quartz crystals formed when the magma was trapped deep underground and cooled slowly. Its geological split personality gives the Organs a wide variety of soil and landform types in a relatively small area, resulting in lots of different niches for many different kinds of plants and animals.

Some of the species that live on sky islands like the Organs are relics, survivors of more temperate climates during the ice ages several tens of thousands of years ago. As climates warmed and dried, these species survived only in the more clement environments of the mountain slopes and canyons. Over time, some, isolated by the miles of desert between sky islands, evolved into unique species, known only from their own particular island mountain range. Most of these endemic species are plants and small animals. (Large animals and birds are more mobile and therefore less likely to be stranded, more likely to be able to migrate from island to island.) The Organ Mountains, although small in area, are home to an unusually large number of such endemic species: two kinds of land snails, a subspecies of the Colorado chipmunk, a small clump-forming cactus, a nodding cliff daisy, an aster, a figwort, and a spectacular evening primrose.

If I were to pick one plant to epitomize the magic that attracts people to Dripping Springs, it would be this last, the Organ Mountain evening primrose. Found nowhere else in the world, these perennial plants epitomize life's astounding ability to adapt to changing conditions. While most desert plants evolved water-saving adaptations as climates dried out, Organ Mountain evening primroses instead staked their survival on growing where the water is. This raises problems. For one— and it is a big one—water is in extremely short supply, even in the Organ Mountains. All of the "streams" draining the Organs, even Dripping Springs downstream from the springs itself, barely deserve that title. They only flow above ground after summer rainstorms or occasional winter snows. But many drainages carry water below ground throughout the growing season. Organ Mountain evening primroses have adapted to take advantage of these underground streams, growing smack in the channels of the half-a-dozen or so larger drainages, between about 5,500 and 7,500 feet elevation. The scarcity of appropriate habitat limits their numbers; the entire population of Organ Mountain evening primroses totals only around two thousand plants.

Not only is water in the Organs, as in all desert mountain ranges, limited, but the supply is erratic, oscillating between long drought and sudden deluge. After months of no rain, intense summer thunderstorms may drop as much as four inches in an hour, transforming the dry stream channels where Organ Mountain evening primroses flourish into roaring flash floods carrying a deadly slurry of rocks, mud, and boulders. Such catastrophic floods alternately scour streambeds to bare rock or bury them Linder several feet of debris. Most plant life is uprooted or smothered. But Organ Mountain evening primroses survive. Their above-ground parts, mounds of numerous flexible stems, may be ripped off, but the perennial part of the plant lives on under the surface of the stream channel, protected from the catastrophic floods. After a flash flood passes and the channel dries out, the roots simply sprout a new crop of above-ground stems.

Their ability to thrive in the catastrophic environment of flashflood channels is not Organ Mountain evening primroses' only magic. These plants look quite ordinary for most of the year, forming green mounds up to three feet high and twice that across, tinged with rust from a sparse cover of sticky hairs. Then, after the first summer rains, each mound of stems sprouts an abundance of long, pointed flower buds. The buds burst open by the hundreds after dusk on summer nights, revealing huge, lemon-yellow, fragrant flowers. But that is not all. Organ Mountain evening primroses have evolved a food-for-sex partnership with two species of giant night- flying moths.

Plants go to great lengths to avoid inbreeding. Unable to wander around freely and thus to find sexual partners to whom they are not intimately related, plants have evolved a wide variety of tricks to accomplish sex while maximizing the mixing of their gene pool. For instance, evening primrose flowers, including those of the Organ Mountain evening primrose, are designed to prohibit self-pollination. The stigma, the sticky tip of the female sexual part that collects pollen, protrudes above their stamens, the pollen-carrying organs. The heavy golden pollen grains cannot make the upward leap from stamens to stigma. Organ Mountain evening primroses take the prohibition against self-pollination one step further: they are self-sterile. Fertilization only occurs with pollen from a different Organ Mountain evening primrose plant. Since the blossoms open in the darkness of late evening and each lasts only one night, this makes exchange difficult. Hence, Organ Mountain evening primroses, like many flowering plants, depend on a partner to ensure reproduction.

In order to entice partners, Organ Mountain evening primroses offer food. Like all evening primroses, they have evolved nectar glands, deep inside the flower, that secrete a sweet, honeylike fluid much sought by insects, hummingbirds, and bats. When these nectar sippers visit the flower to drink, their bodies touch first the protruding stigma, depositing pollen grains collected at other flowers, and then the pollen-laden anthers. As the diners fly from blossom to blossom, they crosspollinate the flowers.

How do airborne diners find night-opening Organ Mountain evening primrose blossoms? Smell and sight; the flowers broadcast a sweet, come-hither fragrance on the night air. And the blossoms' light color makes them visible in even the faintest moonlight.

Unlike other evening primroses, Organ Mountain evening primrose nectar is not available to just any nectar feeder. These unique evening primroses have evolved a pencil-thin, seven-inch-long floral tube, the longest of any evening primrose. A pollinator must possess a very long tongue indeed to reach the sweet food at the base of the tube. Although other nectar feeders attempt to drink from these primroses, only two kinds of night-flying sphinx moths—big ones—have evolved tongues long enough to sip at the nighttime feast provided by Organ Mountain evening primroses.

When Richard and I learned of the partnership between the rare evening primroses and the giant sphinx moths, we determined to watch this example of evolutionary magic. Thus, one Friday night in early July found us driving out of town and up the creosote-bush-clothed bajada sloping steeply toward the base of the Organ Mountains. Past the gravel quarry and around the north side of Tortugas Mountain, its grassy slopes tinted pale green with new growth, and then onto the washboarded gravel road where the pavement ends, we headed up, up, and up through the desert toward the spare slopes of the Organ Mountains and Dripping Springs. The sun slanted low by the time we reached the preserve gate, which was locked now for the night. The caretakers let us in.

We parked the car in the empty gravel parking lot, unpacked our picnic dinner, walked over to the botanical garden in front of the visitor center, and settled ourselves on a low rock wall next to a spring sprouting two huge mounds of Organ Mountain evening primrose. Our perch gave a splendid view westward over the Chihuahuan Desert. Below us, the bajada sloped downhill, stippled with olive-green creosote bush, its even expanse broken only by the rounded, tortoiselike hump of Tortugas Mountain. At the base of the bajada, the Mesilla Valley cut a wide north-south swath through the desert, checkered with farms and orchards. The town of Las Cruces sprawled across the valley, edging toward the glimmering thread of the Río Grande. Past the valley, the desert took over again. Cumulonimbus clouds above West Mesa, across the valley thirty miles away, leaked lavender streamers of rain. A hint of cool breeze trickled down the Dripping Springs valley behind us, heralding the beginnings of night.

The two nearby mounds of Organ Mountain evening primrose, each five feet across and three or so feet tall, bore hundreds of thumb-length, slender, sharply pointed flower buds poking up through their leafy canopies. Each bud looked ready to pop. The previous night's flowers were wilted into wads like so many wet tissues.

The air was still warm, the early evening light still bright. Crickets chirped nearby. The humming of honeybees filled the air as they traveled from wildflower to wildflower, their hind legs trailing yellow globs of pollen. Black-chinned sparrow and canyon towhee songs echoed from all around. The sun slipped out from behind the lower edge of the storm clouds to the west, tingeing the slice of sky below the clouds ruddy red.

We watched for the opening of the first blossom, betting on the flower buds closest to the ground, where pools of shade merged. Soon, a lengthwise slit appeared in one bud near the ground. Moments later, the case suddenly split, as if slit by an invisible zipper. One edge of a lemon-yellow petal, freed from its tight spiral in the bud, peeked out like a miniature flag. In a minute or so, the force of the unfurling petals flexed the bud case downward, like a banana peel pushed back. I grabbed Richard's hand and pointed at the bud. He turned to look just as the petals unfurled—the flower was open! Its four lemon-yellow petals slowly unwrinkled and spread into a wide, flat, cross shape. Eight golden stamens with pollen grains hanging off them stuck up from the center, and a sticky stigma protruded above. Fascinated, we watched for more opening blossoms. Soon, buds were unzipping all over. Within fifteen minutes, we counted seven dozen open blossoms on just one plant!

We were so absorbed by the primroses that we forgot to watch the larger view. Richard looked up just as the sun began to slide below the distant horizon, throwing one last beam of light on the thunderclouds towering over West Mesa. At his exclamation, I looked up just in time to see the sun's orange edge disappear. We turned around as the huge silver disk of the moon rose over the head of the valley. We were silent, awestruck.

One by one, the birds quit singing, replaced by hundreds of chirping crickets. Soon a big sphinx moth appeared. I heard it before I saw it. Its two pairs of long, wide wings produced a hum so low it was barely audible as it hovered near my car. The moth was bigger than I imagined, the size of a small bat. The moonlight picked out the dark, treebarklike marbling on its slowly beating, chocolate and silver-gray wings, and the fur mantling its stout, cigar-shaped body.

The big moth flew slowly over the now-hundreds of open Organ Mountain evening primrose flowers, feeding systematically. It hovered about three or four inches above the center of a flower, its long wings bearing to hold it in place in the air while it carefully positioned its wire-thin proboscis, a hollow tongue not much bigger than the diameter of a human hair. The moth aimed the delicate proboscis down the narrow floral tube, then dropped itself down, still hovering, its wings now raised in an acute "V," until part of its weight actually rested on one tissuelike petal. It remained thus, hovering and drinking, for what seemed a long time but was probably actually only ten seconds. Having drunk all it could, the big moth rose ponderously, retracted its foot-long proboscis until only a few inches hung down, and then flew gracefully to the next flower and repeated the whole process. Then on to the next flower and the next and the next. Soon the front of its dark body was dusted with golden pollen. As it hovered and lowered itself over a new flower, its furry body contacted the stigma, delivering its gift of pollen.

According to Katie Skaggs, former Dripping Springs naturalist, four species of sphinx moths visit the unique primroses. After many nighttime pollination vigils, Katie concluded that only the two largest species—the rustic sphinx moth and the tomato hornworm moth, both dark-colored sphinx moths with wingspans measuring around five inches—possess proboscises long enough to reach the nectar gland at the base of the Organ Mountain evening primrose's elongated floral tube. Smaller sphinxes try to reach the nectary, but cannot, and so quickly fly on. But the rustic sphinx and tomato hornworm moth can sip the flower's nectar, Katie thinks, and therefore also successfully cross-pollinate the primroses. It is an unlikely partnership.

Indeed, hovering sphinx moths seem improbable. Their wings do not look big enough to lift their stout, furry bodies. Powering their long wings and keeping their heavy bodies aloft require an enormous amount of energy, and hence their need for high-sugar food like flower nectar. However, hovering raises an even more difficult problem: heat. Sphinx moths' massive flight muscles cannot operate if they are too cold but, once airborne, the activity of the same muscles generates enough body heat to cook the moth to death. This paradox stumped scientists who once thought—as we all learned in school—that sphinx moths and all other insects are polkilotherms, "cold-blooded" animals that cannot regulate their body temperatures internally, as we mammals do. Scientists speculated that since sphinx moths couldn't warm or cool themselves, perhaps they solved the paradox by flying at dusk or at night when temperatures are warm enough for their wing muscles but cool enough to keep them from stewing. A neat explanation, but it doesn't fit. In summer, late evening air temperatures in the desert are still warm enough that the big moths would quickly overheat when hovering.

Intrigued by the mystery, entomologist Bernd Heinrich attached tiny temperature probes to flying sphinx moths and found that they can indeed regulate their own body temperature. Before taking to the air, sphinx moths shiver by firing the synapses of their flight muscles synchronously so that the wings work against each other, resulting in a great deal of heat but no flight. This warms their flight muscles up to the critical 95°F internal temperature. In flight, when their body temperature quickly rises over 110°, sphinx moths circulate heated blood through their large abdomen, which dissipates heat to the outside air. Heinrich's discoveries forced scientists to reevaluate their perceptions of insects as "primitive," simple life forms. Life is more sophisticated than we think.

A cool breeze blew downhill past Richard and me in the now-dark garden next to the Dripping Springs visitor center. As the color in the western sky faded to dusky purple, bolts of lightning zigzagged through a distant thundercloud. Another big moth flew in to hover over the evening primrose plants, stopping at one flower to drink, hovering, and then carefully withdrawing its proboscis and moving on. Coyotes yipped and howled from the ridge behind us. Mosquitoes whined around our cars until a small bat fluttered past in pursuit. Poorwills' low voices called monotonously. A nearby owl hooted softly. A third big moth joined the first two over the blossoms. Darkness claimed the landscape, but still the flowers glowed, lit by the moonlight, and the three big moths flew from flower to flower, continuing the slow dance of life with the Organ Mountain evening primroses.

Fortunately for the sphinx moths and for all of us, Organ Mountain evening primroses are protected by Dripping Springs Natural Area. When the Nature Conservancy helped the Bureau of Land Management acquire the unique sanctuary that is Dripping Springs, the two groups agreed to an unusual joint management plan: The Conservancy would provide the biological expertise; the Bureau would be responsible for the day-to-day management. The two organizations, figuring that the best way to protect this one-of-a-kind area was to teach people about it and allow them to enjoy it for themselves, envisioned Dripping Springs as a new kind of sanctuary. A preserve open to the public, it would protect the unique human history and provide a safe haven for the endemic animals and plants.

Much has changed since the heyday of Mountain Camp and the lunger invasion that brought the Cabe family west. The once elegant hotel is now a roofless ruin; its crumbling rock walls still bear faded wallpaper. The lawns have long since died; the ornate bandstand has disappeared; only a tangle of raspberry canes hangs on as a reminder of the extensive gardens. Boyd's wooden sanatorium building stands empty, its windowpanes broken and its floors rotting, home now to pack rats and the occasional fox. But some things have not changed, for Dripping Springs remains a popular spot. The canyon resounds with the voices of some twenty-four thousand people per year, hikers and birdwatchers and picnickers and strollers, people of all kinds drawn to the verdant sanctuary high above the desert.

One hot spring afternoon, I hiked the preserve with Katie Skaggs, a biologist-turned-educator and the preserve's first naturalist. Katie, a bright, energetic, cheerful woman in her early thirties, had just finished a master's degree in biology education at New Mexico State University when the Nature Conservancy advertised for a naturalist for the brand-new Dripping Springs preserve. Tired of living in town and "teaching biology in a shopping mall," Katie jumped at the prospect. "I'm a field biologist," she said as we walked up the trail to Dripping Springs, a rocky gravel road that once carried stage coaches and wagon loads of visitors to Mountain Camp and patients to Boyd's sanatorium. "I'm happiest with dirt under my fingernails, working outdoors." So Katie and her family, her husband, Roger, also a biologist, and their two elementary-school-aged sons, moved into the small adobe house next to the visitor center at the lower end of the Dripping Springs valley, a dusty half- hour car ride from town. It was the sanctuary they needed. One day a week, the two towheaded boys would forgo the trip to town for school and help Katie with her work. Sometimes that meant helping to lead nature walks for school classes, sometimes assisting Katie as she studied Organ Mountain evening primrose plants. On her morning run up the valley, Katie said, she usually saw deer; at night, quadrillions of stars spangled a sky undimmed by the glare of streetlights.

For the preserve's first four years, until a school-teaching job lured Katie and her family back to the mountains of southwestern New Mexico, Katie was Dripping Springs' foremost evangelist. She led hundreds of nature walks and gave dozens of talks, and her contagious enthusiasm and love for the place enticed numerous volunteers to help study and protect the unique valley. Katie's vision of the new preserve was never a selfish one. It was not just her place. She saw Dripping Springs as a living sanctuary, not just for the Organ Mountain evening primroses, the sphinx moths, or for her and her family, but for everyone. Still, the number and variety of visitors surprised even Katie. At first, she said, the Nature Conservancy and Bureau of Land Management worried about the popularity of the place; they didn't want visitors to love it to death. "After all," said Katie, "it's a preserve, not a city park where you can do just about anything."

It turns out that the Bureau and the Conservancy needn't have worried. Despite its popularity, the preserve has remained pleasantly peaceful. I commented on how little trash I saw, surprising given how many people hike the trail. On weekends it carries everyone from serious hikers to families in their best clothes pushing baby strollers. "That's the magic of this place," said Katie, "people come up here with a good attitude. We rarely pick up litter. We have no paid clean-up crew, and we don't need one." "People," she added, "seem to love this place."

"Something that I have only realized recently," Katie said as we turned back toward the visitor center to see if the boys had arrived home from school, "is that people see Dripping Springs as a 'safe' place. It seems to be just wild enough to offer solace, but not wild enough to be scary. People who might not go to a 'wilderness' feel safe coming here," she continued, "especially women."

We walked quietly for a while. As we crossed the dusty parking lot to the visitor center, Katie said, "I think that people really do see Dripping Springs as a sanctuary."

While waiting for Katie, I thought about why we treat Dripping Springs as a sanctuary. Is it the rare occurrence of a permanent spring blessing the parched desert country with its water? Is it the rocky beauty of the place itself? Is it because of the unique species that live here and nowhere else in the world? Just outside the fence that encloses the Dripping Springs Natural Area, the desert grasslands are grazed to bare dirt. Beer cans and plastic bags litter the roadside. Subdivisions are popping up all over. Why don't we treat the rest of the desert as a sacred place also? I looked down the valley. Far below, the Río Grande shimmered in the intense sunlight. The birds were silent in the afternoon heat. The dry breeze ruffling my hair brought no answer.

Richard and Molly and I live in an ordinary subdivision in Las Cruces. Our house faces away from the subdivision's curving streets and the other houses, oriented instead to its large backyard and the view across a nearby field. In the background, dominating the eastern horizon, rise the rocky slopes of the Organs. Almost all of the glass in the house looks over the backyard and the view of the distant mountains.

Unfortunately, when we moved in, all the world passing by had a great view of us too. A cement-block wall surrounded the backyard but was too low to give us any privacy. Past the wall, the dirt road atop the irrigation ditch bank afforded strollers, runners, and bicyclists a panoramic view of our lives as we relaxed on our back patio, ate dinner, worked in the vegetable garden, lounged in the living room, hung out laundry. . . . We felt like an exhibit at the zoo. Beyond the irrigation ditch El Paseo's four lanes carry a constant stream of traffic from roaring semitrailer trucks to the thumping bass of Friday-night cruisers. (Our subdivision marks one end of the cruising strip.) Even without its noise, the unending stream of vehicles on El Paseo disrupted our peaceful view of the Organs.

Thus, we decided that one of our first remodeling projects would be to raise the backyard wall to gain privacy and quiet. But how high should it go? We didn't want to block the view of the mountains; we did want to remove the traffic in the foreground. After much experimenting with string tied at different levels to mark the top of the new wall, we decided to go up four feet. That would screen foot traffic on the ditch road, and would block out all but the tallest vehicles passing on El Paseo. We hoped that the mass of the cement block wad would also dampen some of the traffic noise.

The project succeeded in ways that we didn't expect. A stream of cars no longer passes in front of our view of the mountains; we see only the very tops of pickups and the occasional big truck. Passersby on the ditch road can no longer observe the details of our lives. The traffic noise is reduced to a steady background rumble. Best of all, though, is the intangible effect: our sprawling yard, once a fishbowl open to passersby, has become an intimate place. The curve of its tall gray walls hugs the enclosed space, inviting us outside to relax, to read, to garden, to entertain, to watch the sunset tint the Organs with a ruddy glow and the stars pierce the dark sky at night. We can hear the world outside, but it no longer intrudes. The quality of this outside space changed once we raised the walls.

Now the yard, intimate and protected, is a part of our house. We landscaped it to emphasize these new qualities. At one end of the backyard, where the curve in the wall is lined with a grove of six gnarled, drooping Mexican elder trees, we killed the bermuda grass lawn, rototilled the area, and scattered desert wildflower and grass seeds. For Molly, we hung a private reading hammock hidden by the drooping branches and the pale-green foliage of the Mexican elders. Now our "wilderness" sprouts wild flowers on its own, surprising us with its color and texture, and is home to an abundance of scurrying lizards, butterflies, and chattering birds. Walking paths will someday wind through the wild area, reaching a small patio enclosed by the grove of Mexican elders. Sitting on a bench there, with the flowering branches of the elders around and the hum of bees on the warm air, the rest of the world seems far away. The wild room is our home refuge.

What makes our yard—or any place, for that matter—a sanctuary is how we treat it. Because we raised the wall, the yard came to seem private, inviting, restful, a place to heal, to retreat from the frustrations and busyness of daily life. Once we saw its sanctuarylike qualities, we began to treat it as one. Soon after the new wall was finished, we held a celebrate-the-yard party, inviting all of our friends to come over for a potluck dinner and hand-cranked ice cream. Along with the crowds of friends and the abundance of food came their goodwill and enjoyment. The happiness of that evening and many subsequent ones continues to bless our yard.

Friends comment about the peace and tranquillity of our house and yard. Houseguests end their stays surprised at how restful, how healing, the time has been. We find ourselves spending more time at home. Our house and yard provide a quiet center for our lives, a place of refreshment, solace, with time and space for unhurried reflection, reading, relaxing. The yard, with its mix of wild and cultivated spaces, welcomes wild lives too, from spadefoot toads to roadrunners. What began as an ordinary suburban house and yard is now a refuge, an island sanctuary right in town.

In *The Thunder Tree,* Robert Michael Pyle's self-described "love song" to the irrigation ditch nearby where he grew up in suburban Denver, a linear stretch of urban wildness that served as a sanctuary for him and untold numbers of other lives, Pyle writes, "It is through close and intimate contact with a particular patch of ground that we learn to respond to the earth, to see that it really matters. We need to recognize the humble places where this alchemy occurs, and treat them as well as we treat our parks and preserves—or better. . . . Everybody has a ditch, or ought to. For only the ditches and the fields, the woods, the ravines—can teach us to care enough for all the land."

"There is a balm in Gilead," goes one spiritual, "to make the wounded whole." Gilead has no monopoly on balms. Every place is sacred. The qualities that make a place able to heal us, refresh us, and inspire us are part of every landscape; only our vision fails us. We cannot see the beauty, the sacredness in many landscapes, including this battered Chihuahuan Desert. We treat the Chihuahuan Desert as if it was indeed barren, wild, and worthless. It is easy to see the beauty in a place like Dripping Springs Natural Area, with its thread of water splashing down the dark rocks to green the canyon, its history, and its unique plants and animals. But it is harder to see the magic outside the fence that encloses Dripping Springs. Only if we set ourselves to learning its stories and searching out its beauty—the nighttime opening of *reina-de-la-noche*'s magnificent flowers, the petroglyphs etched on dark rocks, the emergence of thousands of chorusing spadefoot toads—do we come to recognize the Chihuahuan Desert as the sanctuary that it is. Until we do so, we will continue to litter the roadsides and arroyos, to squander the groundwater, to overgraze the once-fertile grasslands, to allow unwise development, to tear down the historical buildings, to ignore the stories and traditions of the viejos who came before us. As long as we treat this desert as a worthless place, its qualities as a sanctuary will elude us. Only when we begin to perceive its sacredness will we find the balm in this Gilead.

On my tour of Dripping Springs, Katie Skaggs led me through the gate at the side of the visitor center and along a path to where Dripping Springs' arroyo cuts below the old ranch buildings. She stopped me at the top of a steep flight of steps cut into the arroyo bank. Below us, a lichen-crusted cement dam plugged the arroyo bottom. A rusty galvanized metal swimming pool slide plunged downward in a graceful curve from the side of the arroyo into a stand of cattails. A diving board attached to the top of the dam poised over solid ground. Twisted old hackberry trees shaded new growth of willows, cattails, and other water-loving plants. What had once been a swimming pool ponded behind a dam was now a fledgling marsh, growing in layers of mud, gravel, and sand trapped behind the dam when the arroyo carries loads of rocky debris after summer thunderstorms. A verdant green tangle of vegetation now grew in the old swimming pool.

As Katie talked, I noticed a mounded green plant growing from the solid ground in the shade of the diving board. The plant was about two-and-a-half feet tall with wavy, narrowly oval leaves bearing a characteristic rusty tinge: Organ Mountain evening primrose. The plant was positively bursting with flower buds. I pointed it out to Katie. She nodded her head in recognition and grinned. I grinned back. One of the Organ Mountains' endemic plants was quietly reclaiming its own sanctuary.

from *Barren, Wild, and Worthless: Living in the Chihuahua Desert*

Under the Cypress

Bruce Berger

Citizens of San Ignacio work, beget children, pay taxes, even die, but so relaxed is their oasis that jokes about them have swept the peninsula. It is said that the cows wear sneakers so they won't waken their owners. Ignacianos are alleged to have altered their phones so that instead of ringing, they go "*pssst.*" They cut the vocal cords of roosters that crow them awake. To frighten away their ghosts, Ignacianos set out hammers, hatchets, rakes—tools of work. It is said that Ignacianos grease the palm leaves to soften the rustling and that they have replaced the bronze clapper of the mission bell with a duplicate of rubber. A 100,000-peso note is said to have floated toward an Ignaciano drowsing against a palm. As he reached for it the wind shifted, the note settled several meters away, the Ignaciano muttered, "Damn!" and sank back to sleep. One Ignaciano made it to the U.S. border, where all Mexicans are asked where they are from and whether they have a work permit. "Your permit," demanded the border guard.

"I don't have one."

"Where are you from?"

"San Ignacio."

"You're not going to work anyway," said the guard. "Go on through."

For many of the reasons implied by the Jokes, San Ignacio had been my favorite town in Baja California since I first saw it in 1968. Its palms beckoned like deliverance when it could only be reached on a one-lane track through hundreds of miles of volcanic rubble. I was afraid the highway would run roughshod through the middle, but pavement kept a thoughtful distance, respecting the two-kilometer approach to its plaza across the lagoon and through its greased palms.

I stopped whenever I could over the years, still taking one of the six rooms of Oscar Fischer's motel in back of town, and discovered my own palm to lean against. It swooped over the lagoon, inviting me to clamber backward along its trunk, libation in hand and binoculars around my neck, to settle where it curved in perfect lumbar support and extended a headrest. My gaze, cradled upward, met the top of a fan palm where finches and orioles nested. Coots, egrets, and pied-billed grebes paddled the lagoon around me; night herons flapped past, complaining "*gwork*"; least grebes, sleek as rodents, dived beneath me; and if a 100,000-peso note had floated toward me, a reach for it would have landed me in the drink. I wasn't the only outsider working on his indolence, for at Oscar Fischer's I met a Chicano who drove down whenever he could to unwind from tensions of life in a Los Angeles barrio. He reported knocking on the unmarked door of a haircutter, to be told she was asleep and didn't appreciate being roused. When he went out for his evening jog, an old man stopped him and asked what was the matter. On learning nothing was the matter, the old man suggested the Chicano slow down and stop setting a bad example. San Ignacio, lacking aerobics, is known for its centenarians. When I first arrived the oldest Ignaciano was 114, though by 1992 the quickening pace had dropped that figure to 105. It was said that Ignacianos who stayed home far outlived relatives who moved to the coast to fish or to Isla Cedros to work the salt company's fishing port.

I got to know a number of Ignacianos during early stays at a pension, and though there were stretches during the seventies and eighties when I didn't drop by for years, the familiars hadn't budged. Foremost of these was Héctor who, in 1969, had led a friend and me to a cave where *manos* and *metates* lay undisturbed on the bedrock. He also gave me a mail-order catalog in Spanish for a company in Brooklyn, a compendium of switchblade knives, Virgin Marys that glowed in the dark, pornographic playing cards, and spray cans of frankincense and myrrh. He counted out money to send for a paint sprayer, asking me to bring it in person the following year so it wouldn't disappear in the mail. Twenty years later, our friendship secure, he admitted that the sprayer worked on 220 volts and only dribbled paint on the 110 volts locally available, and I confessed that I had done better by the catalog, making quite a hit the Christmas I gave out spray cans of myrrh.

Héctor lived on several acres of agricultural land that had belonged to the family for generations. An alley off the plaza led to a slatted gate where the tiny dogs known in San Ignacio as "doorbells" announced visitors in yips that convulsed their frames. A scattering of small buildings shaped a courtyard of packed earth, shaded by citrus, a cedar, and three sprawling pepper trees of a sort I had not seen elsewhere. Their low branches were propped by stakes and suspended from them, singing and shrieking, were caged orioles, cardinals, assorted canaries, and a large magpie jay from southern Mexico, along with a clear Japanese fishing ball that bolts of sun turned opalescent. On folding metal chairs, Héctor and I sipped coffee and discussed international politics, paranormal phenomena, a new way of fertilizing grapes—whatever occupied Héctor at the moment. Angling a chair just right, you could glimpse whoever was leaving the plaza or case who was headed toward the gate. Often we were joined by Héctor's father, who followed the conversation keenly and sometimes took part. When Héctor once marveled in his father's presence how the ninety-year-old could still hear perfectly and read without glasses, I added, "And his brain is still intact."

His father looked at me sharply and snapped, "No, I'm not crazy yet."

Héctor was all the more rooted in his property for having sampled life away from it. During the long hiatus in our friendship, Héctor worked at many of the projects that had changed the central part of the peninsula. He joined the road crew that paved the Cuesta del Infiernillo, the Descent of the Little Hell, with its scenic, pan-banging dropoffs. As a landscaper at Hotel El Presidente, he acquired the pepper tree saplings whose shade we now enjoyed, and which were the only such trees in San Ignacio. When the mission underwent an extensive restoration, Héctor was enlisted as a stonemason. He endured several wind-blasted months at a fish packing plant on Isla Cedros, the island from which Exportadora de Sal dispatched salt to the world. Most adventurous of all, Héctor helped lay the grid of single-track roads over the Vizcaino Desert when Pemex prospected for oil in the seventies, tracks whose endurance I had witnessed by air. Groups of five or six men had worked as teams, were paid by the kilometer, and averaged a kilometer a day. Over dunes, through arroyos, maintaining straight lines whether nature flourished or languished, rose or sank, they cleared shrubberywith machetes, felled trees, and scraped the leavings from their path with a bulldozer. A Pemex functionary showed up every three days to check up; otherwise they were responsible for buying and preparing their own food and for packing medicines to cope with accidents, illnesses, and snakebites. Héctor thrived on camping out, loved exploring hidden parts of the peninsula, and despised the work. During those years it was considered a feat for off-roaders to reach Malarrimo, the scavenger beach I finally saw, after years of anticipation, on a pronghorn count. Of all the fabled treasures—ships' wheels, World War II cans of Spam, cases of scotch—the pièces de résistance were the glass floats for fishnets, clear or turquoise, known as Japanese fishing balls. While Pemex found treasure in its secret wells of natural gas, Héctor scored a Japanese fishing ball, and instead of maneuvering a four-wheeler over rocks and through loose sand, he rode to Malarrimo by tractor.

When I got back in touch with Héctor in the late eighties, I found someone who had seen enough of life beyond his property to be consumed by his land. He married late, to a woman past the age of childbearing, and his paternal feelings were sluiced onto the growing things around him. He referred to his land as a *huerta*, a word narrowly translated as "orchard," and Héctor's *huerta* was a compound of fruit trees, vegetable and flower garden, and vineyard. After we finished our coffee and caught up on the world and each other's lives, we always eddied slowly through the *huerta*, commenting on what was new or seeing how the old was coming along. I never ceased marveling at the sheer abundance. In the vegetable garden were onions, garlic, chiles, hops, potatoes, celery, peppers, cabbage, parsley, cilantro, and a variety of greens for spice, salads, medicines, and herbal teas whose English names I didn't know. Overhead hung bananas, papayas, pomegranates, dates and citrus crosses of Héctor's devising. Spiking the greenery were zinnias, marigolds, roses, hollyhocks, and cosmos, and the balance of the property drifted in grapevines. Overlapping leaves of so many shapes and shades caught the sun like stained glass.

Nothing lacked its purpose. When I asked what three large cans of dirt were for, Héctor explained that two contained soil from different arroyos, the third held loam from a hillside, and he was testing various combinations for ornamental flowers. The rusted cans were not litter, for Héctor tossed them into holes for new plants, believing they charged the soil with iron. He sliced off leaves from two aloe vera plants, one the commercial strain, one the wild original, and had me smell their gelatinous cross-sections: the wild was odorless and the commercial one stank. "Wouldn't you think they could improve on a plant without ruining the smell?" he asked. We would stop to inspect a giant four-clove garlic from a plant brought in from Tijuana, or a tangerine-mandarin cross from Héctor's endless grafting experiments. One year I noted an unlikely number of tomato seedlings and asked if he planned to market tomatoes.

"No," he sighed, "people will only pay for tomatoes that arrive in boxes from the north."

"But surely you can't eat so many."

"Of course not, I'll be lucky even to give them away. I just started planting tomatoes and couldn't stop."

As we paused by a mulch pile, Héctor would reflect on his attitude toward plants. Like most Ignacianos, he refused to use chemical fertilizers or insecticides, believing their avoidance was one reason for local longevity. "When you raise poison for other people," he says, "you wind up eating it yourself." It was important to factor in phases of the moon, and anything planted between the dark of the moon and the first quarter would come out weak. We moved on to the bird trap. With the passion for variety common to birders, but without their binoculars, Héctor reversed the process by bringing the birds to him. He had contrived a box of wire screens whose lid was propped open with a small stick. He rested a date on the stick, and when a bird landed to eat, the stick gave way and the lid collapsed on the bird. After Héctor had reached in for the cardinal or thrasher, looked it in the eye, and turned it to the light, he let it go. It frustrated Héctor that he knew only the local names of birds, which he didn't trust, and I understood the problem when year after year he referred to his magpie jay as a lark. At last I found him a Peterson's Guide in Spanish. The next year I asked him what happened to his lark. "That wasn't a lark," he said. "It was a magpie jay and it didn't belong here. I gave it to my brother in Ensenada."

On one of our strolls through the *huerta* I noted that the doorbell who trotted after us sported a collar of corklike projections between bits of metal. "An ornament for the dog?" I asked.

"It's to keep her from getting pregnant," said Héctor.

"How does it work?"

"The collar is made of sections of copper tubing for natural gas, alternating with slices of corncob. Male dogs can't stand the smell of it and stay away."

During early winter months Héctor spent his days at long waist-high tables covered with woven reeds, spread with dates drying in the sun. Beginning in November, five Ignacianos adept at tree climbing knocked down date branches for the whole town, batting them with extensions of the ropes that held them to the trunks. The golden branches were arrayed on the matted tables to bake for three or four days. The dates were raked from the branches with a device like a giant wooden comb, then sun-dried for another three or four days while the bad ones were weeded out. Cured but still moist, they were stuffed into polystyrene sacks that said things like "Wyoming Grown Cowboy Brand Twice-Washed Pinto Beans." What wasn't fit for human consumption got fed to the animals.

Every several days, all year long, came Héctor's turn to irrigate from a communally owned tank at one corner of the property. Some ten meters across, it dated to the time of the *padres* and received water from the spring that fed the lagoons, two kilometers away, by a system of *acequias*, or irrigation canals, also pioneered by the *padres*. Héctor opened the hole to his irrigation system by shoveling muck away from the tank's underwater hole, freeing the flow. Carp kept the tank clean and their droppings added to the water's nutrients. When I asked if the carp were also good eating, Héctor replied that they were but that Ignacianos had no tradition of eating them and so seldom did. The carp's most curious aspect, he added, was that every quarter moon they thrashed and roiled the water so violently that all the water outlets had to be cleaned the next day.

Life on the few acres, varied by invented fruits and new birds in the trap, was further livened by visitors at the gate. Neighbors showed up to buy dates, mostly in small bags for home use, or to buy small quantities of the two wines Héctor distilled from his grapes. Héctor was usually out of bottles, so people brought their own, or just a glass for washing down the next meal. Called *semiseco* and *dulce*, semi-dry and sweet, to my palate they were sweet and saccharine, and Héctor himself, otherwise a nondrinker, had only an occasional glass "after breakfast to settle my stomach." For a time the priest bought Héctor's wine to use for communion, then switched to another brand. Héctor also sold ornamental plants, along with citrus, mangos, melons, papayas, and bananas from his *huerta*.

Little money switched hands in these transactions, and Héctor often exchanged his products for whatever people showed up with. The versatility that enabled him to pave roads, landscape hotels, and pack fish also gave him trading potential for skills at carpentry, plumbing, even repairing TVs. A dentist from Tijuana, traveling with his instruments, got paid in fruit and wine. Ranchers traded meat and milk for produce and dates. There was no public newsstand, and a La Paz daily that home-delivered to known customers, insisting on cash, got no business from Héctor. One day when I arrived from the south, passing up the chance to patronize the El Boleo Bakery in Santa Rosalia in my eagerness to reach San Ignacio, a young salesman from El Boleo arrived at Héctor's gate. He was from Veracruz and knew little about his wares; I had the privilege of telling him he was peddling the best bread on the peninsula, made from recipes brought in by the French who started the copper mines. Héctor continued his education by advising him to handle the bread with tongs instead of his hands.

One morning a man in an ironed shirt and polyester pants was shrilled at by the doorbells and passed through the gate with five plastic bags of small packages. Héctor asked him to sit down, relatives gathered from the compound, and a couple of women followed him from the street. The stranger pulled out packets of herbs and spices—cilantro, cinnamon, bay leaves, tea of manzanilla, and cardon cactus—as well as various creams and unguents. Health and flavor were temptingly fused in his pitch. One woman raved how one of his teas "cleansed the grease from my blood" and helped her lose weight, and she bought more to finish the job. When I bought an ointment for an aching finger joint, the salesman pulled out another product for the same ailment, *aceite de vibora*, or snake oil. Never having seen the product so honestly labeled, I snapped it up. When the transactions were finished and the customers left, Héctor, the salesman, and I discussed global problems for nearly an hour. The salesman worried that Russia's economic weakness might tempt it to sell the bomb to countries like Iran and Iraq, though it seemed in general that the world was getting safer and governments were converging. Overpopulation was the world's great threat and religions shouldn't be permitted to undermine birth control programs. When I remarked on the power of the church, he replied that Mexico, though deeply religious, practiced a strict and sensible division between church and state, and as far as he was concerned, the only god worth respecting was reason. If this was snake oil, I was still buying.

Over the years I realized that I had become part of the view from Héctor's courtyard. Héctor asked for enlargements of my first photographs of San Ignacio, to show how extensive the family vineyards had been, and had me take new shots from the vantage of historic photos for before-and-after sequences. No one asked for tidings of the States, but I always stopped to and from the pronghorn census and was pressed for the latest numbers. San Ignacio had never been pronghorn habitat, but most older Ignacianos had seen them toward the coast and wanted to be assured of their well-being. Oscar Fischer, who had hunted them with his father as a young man, described migration patterns that were only theories to biologists. I left brochures at the little restaurant where I ate and one of the regulars, a doctor who traveled the coastal fishing villages we suspected of poaching, promised to dispense pronghorn lectures with his medicine. Most avid of all was Héctor's father, who rhapsodized over each of the markings on the folder—the horns, the face pattern, the little tufts of hair over the hooves—concluding, "They're so adorable and so delicious."

As a visitor, alas, I was as drab as the bread boy and the snake oil salesman. A man on a plateau over town saw a bright orange ball rise straight up, then shoot sideways out of sight. A woman saw an odd turquoise glimmer through the palms, thought it was an odd place for an American to park a trailer, and it soared through the fronds and vanished. The sightings were duly mulled in Héctor's courtyard and I had the impression that when local gossip ran thin, UFOs took pity.

The future was an occasional drop-in but it was the past, embodied in the mission, that dominated the town. In his vineyard Héctor spaded up a coin with the same schematic castle and lions rampant that appeared on the shield of the mission's facade, a tangible link with the founding Spaniards. Knowing the mission well from having worked as a stonecutter on the restoration, he began a tiny replica from similar lava, completing a tower with a raisin-sized wooden bell, and vowed to complete it when the *huerta* gave him time. The priest summoned him back to shoot a pair of doves that were nesting inside the church, strewing sticks, defecating on the pews, and frightening people as they swooped in and out of the door. Héctor questioned the propriety of shooting in church, but the priest insisted. Héctor's air rifle reported like a cannon in the old stone vault, but it did the job.

"Héctor," I said, pausing for drama, "you shot doves in church? You shot the Holy Ghost?"

He shrugged, expecting it. "It's what the priest asked for."

As a traveler Héctor had only gotten as far from San Ignacio as Tijuana and La Paz, and on the first trip he was so tormented by San Ignacio jokes that subsequently he said he was from Santa Rosalía. He had two younger brothers, one a store manager in one of the coastal villages, the other a traveling salesman who lived in Ensenada, bought cheap and often used merchandise in northern Mexico and San Diego, and sold it out of his car to isolated towns like San Ignacio. Both of them urged Héctor to travel more, to see something of the world, and they seized the opportunity when Héctor needed to spend ten days in Ensenada because of a stomach ailment. He stayed with his salesman brother, had only to report to the hospital for tests, and the rest of his time was free. The brothers wanted to show him the sights and they arranged phone calls in which Héctor's wife assured him she was feeding the birds and Héctor's nephew swore he was watering the plants. The only sight in Ensenada Héctor wanted to see was one they hadn't thought of, the bird market, and he demanded to be taken immediately back to the *huerta*. When I asked Héctor what he had seen in Ensenada, he replied excitedly that he had counted two hundred house finches on a single phone line and seventy starlings on another.

What Héctor's brothers took for terminal lack of curiosity was simply that cities effaced what he found of interest. He hadn't possessed a car in years, and when I suggested excursions he hesitated, claiming duties in the *huerta* while overcoming a certain shyness about occupying my time and vehicle. That barrier crossed, he became the eager explorer, alert to the faintest shifts in plants and rocks, a connoisseur of remote ranches. We pored over a limestone shelf where fossilized mollusks, clam shells,and sea snails lay embedded in blinding white rock. We scrambled through some scree where Héctor thought the Jesuits had quarried the stone for the mission. We bought cheese from an embittered man from Tamaulipas who had fled to an abandoned ranch where he would only have to deal with goats. I had read of a geothermal project at which the government hoped to tap underground steam near the still active volcanoes of Las Tres Virgenes. We followed a thirteen-kilometer graded road to a clearing with scattered machinery and I pulled up to the nearest idle man. He was the foreman and told me they had not reached the steam they expected; for now they were tending equipment while someone in Mexico City decided whether to send a bigger drill or give up. At the end of the exchange the foreman looked past me to Héctor in the passenger seat, rigid with his high-crowned hat and his features of the Arce family that dominated the mid-peninsula, and said, "Don't you speak Spanish?" Remarked Héctor as we pulled away, "It must be my pink complexion."

One year I suggested a jaunt to Rancho Santa Martha, where I had begun a mule trip to the cave paintings eighteen years before: I had heard they had opened a museum and I couldn't imagine it. Héctor lit up. Thirty years ago he had ridden there by mule with his father, a journey they had lingered over six days, and they arrived to be feasted royally by distant relatives. The people were wonderful and also they might buy some dates. Ten kilometers of highway and thirty more of bad ruts shrank the trip to three hours. A couple of men greeted us cordially while assorted people on porches glanced up and continued what they were doing. Nobody bought dates, though we bought goat cheese. At my request they showed us the small museum, a spread of arrows, metates, dried plants, kids' drawings, rocks and animal skins, a hobbyist's heap lit through the door, discernible when our eyes dilated. Héctor told them of his visit thirty years before, and they replied that all the people he mentioned were gone. As we left, Héctor remarked that they didn't even offer us coffee. I pointed out that Santa Martha was the lesser of two jumping-off points for the cave paintings and that if they served every stranger they'd be running a free cafe, but I could see that the visit left a sour taste. I told Héctor I knew of a ranch that hadn't been spoiled by visitation.

On a pronghorn count we had ventured with a biologist up a strange valley surrounded by enormous free-standing rhyolite domes. We didn't encounter human habitation until we reached a small ranch at the end, where a man in a hand-tooled leather hat explained to us pronghorn experts that the rocks and dense vegetation wouldn't allow speed-dependent animals to get away from their enemies in a valley like this. He had last seen pronghorn where we had, out on the flats. I swore to return without a mission.

Héctor was thrilled by the great formations glittering bronze in the sun, their drainage choked with cactus and datilillo half again their normal size. It had rained the month before and the desert was in riotous bloom. We stopped frequently and Héctor wrapped flowering plants in wet newspapers. As we neared the ranch I glanced in the rearview mirror and saw it filled with a large blue pickup. Another truck preceded us as we pulled in. It turned out that the ranch had been unoccupied and that three vehicles unaware of each other converged as if for a party. "Watch for snakes," called the first man on the porch as we started through the mallow. "This ranch is full of them. The whole valley is full of them." Two men had come to look for lost cattle, two were storing things for a cousin who owned the ranch, and we were the excursionists. The men pulled up chairs, one brewed coffee, and we talked through the midday. One told of a criminal who became teacher of a one-man school because police couldn't enter schoolgrounds without permission, and another recounted a journey so rough that the car came back "bleeding like Cleopatra." This, said Héctor as we left, was what ranches were supposed to be like, and the next morning he showed me his new wildflower garden. Twenty species of plants from the volcanic valley stood in brilliant rows, to bring the desert to people from San Ignacio who were "too old to go to the desert themselves, or too lazy."

As committed birders I thought we should visit Estero Coyote, an anvil-shaped mangrove-encrusted inlet on the Pacific coast that I had never quite reached. We walked along the inlet's mouth with the binoculars and bird book, and gazed across to a concentration of blue herons in the white phase flanked by white seagulls, a far spill of salt. In another direction, hundreds of brown pelicans stood with their toes just short of water. As we scanned the distance, a seagull at our feet rose over our heads, hovered, dropped a small object, then lit on the ground to devour a clam in the shell it had just cracked. Héctor gaped, stupefied. "I saw that on a nature show on TV and thought maybe they made it up. I can't believe the birds are that clever and that I saw it with my own eyes." We returned our gaze to the distance. "What are those birds over there going '*quar quar*'?" asked Héctor excitedly.

I fixed the binoculars on some dark birds with white streaks on their necks. "Those are brants," I said, "a kind of sea-going goose."

"Those are the birds I hear over the house at night!" said Héctor, astonished to have come so far to learn something new about the *huerta*. When we left the estuary I told him it was only a little farther to the town of Punta Abreojos, if he wanted to take a spin. "No," he said, "it's not worth seeing and the people are unpleasant." Abreojos was apparently a miniature Ensenada.

Our most inspired pretext for an excursion came from Héctor's nephew, who had been taken on a school outing to a fumarole spouting sulfur. Héctor had tried a commercial insecticide on his chile plants, found it turned the chiles to mush, and heard that mixing sulfur in the soil made the leaves oily, fending off bugs while sparing the plant. He prepared by fashioning wooden strap-on soles so his shoes wouldn't melt near the vents and beat a sardine can into a scoop. We drove a side road from the highway, hiked a maze of elephant trees and cholla, climbed a ridge and gasped: on the facing slope, framed in a maroon outcrop, was a clay cutaway of fluorescent mustard and lime fissured with hissing steam. As we picked our way to the raw hillside we were assaulted by a wave of putrefied eggs. Steam thickened over the vents, obscuring them and clamming our faces with hot gauze, then dispersed in a breath of wind. Around the vents and in cracks between rocks were small deposits of the sulfur we had come for. I crouched to see one closer, resting my knee against a rock, and nearly singed my jeans. My sneakers were vulnerable but my glasses fogged well before the ground got hot enough to melt rubber. Héctor strapped on his soles and advanced with the scoop, only to find it too large for the tiny piles. "I should have brought a teaspoon," he sighed, scrambled below for a cool rock and beat the sardine can to a blunted point. As I watched, wiping my glasses, he zeroed in on the fumaroles, looking like a prospector in hell, and filled the jar with a soft marigold powder. "A little sulfur goes a long way," he said, and in less than an hour he had a lifetime supply.

So pleasant was it to stay in Oscar Fischer's motel and roam with Héctor that I was shocked, at the beginning of a stay, when Oscar asked me to leave the motel; an incoming group was going whale watching in Laguna San Ignacio, then to the cave paintings, and had booked all six rooms. I asked Héctor where to camp. "In the *huerta*," he replied. Now I was the shy one, with a barrier about intrusion to overcome. More practically, I wondered how to set up my typewriter to write up the latest pronghorn census. He led me through the vineyard, past an abandoned trailer, to a cypress tree with a cleared space beneath it. To my disbelief, a masonite table projected from the cypress trunk as if engineered for a typewriter. Scaly branches drooped shade over the site, and I angled the tent so that from the inside I could see the mission over the vineyard. Héctor opened a gate on the far side of the property, and I pulled in my jeep to a spot hidden by foliage. This tiny move gave me a sense of arrival. San Ignacio itself was situated in the middle of the peninsula, north and south, east and west, and Héctor's property was in the middle of San Ignacio. Under the cypress tree I was at the center of Héctor's property and, in my own mythology, I had reached the heart of the peninsula.

I got out my butane burner, made coffee, set up the typewriter, faced it on a folding chair Héctor had provided, and sat. Beyond me the vines stretched leafily toward the date palms, then the laurels of the plaza and the mission, and white and lavender mallow stood waist-high in a field to one side. A vermilion flycatcher sparked to and from its nest in the cypress, and in a citrus tree behind me, a bulbous nest with a hole near the bottom slurped up a verdin—a small yellow-capped desert bird—like a strand of spaghetti. The trailer was the only discordant note, but I discovered its use when Héctor's father ambled toward me. I thought he was coming. to visit, but he reached a blistered chaise longue in the trailer's shade, knocked off his hat, kicked off his boots, lay on his side, and went to sleep. San Ignacio had the wrong namesake in Ignatius Loyola, the fanatic disciplinarian who founded the Jesuits. Surely here was a perfect patron saint in this vigorous ninety-year-old, surrounded by the bounteous earth, asleep in the blaze of day.

Late afternoon I roused myself to get some beer for the sunset. As I crossed the plaza to Manuel Meza's store, Oscar Fischer hailed me from a park bench. His incoming group had car trouble in Guerrero Negro. They were cutting their trip short, skipping the caves and spending their remaining night camped by the whales. The motel was empty. I could have any room I wanted! "Thanks," I replied, a little maliciously. "I'm content in Héctor's *huerta*."

My new days began before daylight with the silky chitter of the vermilion flycatcher overhead in the cypress. I made coffee inside the tent and gazed at the mission, rose with auburn trim in the first light. As my pulse quickened my eyes played over the inventively balanced pilasters, sawtooth cornices, round windows, diamond-shaped adornments, niches for four saints (one of them headless), a single tower with three bronze bells and two speakers. By the second coffee I progressed to the folding chair and listened to San Ignacio waking up: roosters, dogs, coughing pickups, the mocking laughter of schoolbound teenagers, mourning doves, the chucking of an unseen spade. Hearing and glimpsing, invisible, I was in a blind for observing humanity even as orioles, woodpeckers, cardinals, and kinglets dashed about oblivious of my presence. By the third coffee I made myself type notes. Héctor showed up now and then with things to eat, not meals but treats: manta ray machaca, corn soup, a dessert called *dulce de papaya* to be eaten hot, homemade tortillas, the latest citrus crosses. Occasionally I ventured into town for a full meal at the little restaurant but mostly I stayed by the tent, steeping in where I was. At night, bits of disintegrating cypress cones pelted the tent like fat raindrops. In the words of a La Paz friend, it was so idyllic I was jealous of myself.

At dusk Héctor would come to chat. The first evening he pulled up the blistered chaise longue his father had napped on, insisting I take' it over, and spent his nightfalls on the folding chair. He declined my beer, saying that "cold things are bad for the stomach," and let his thoughts wander over times I hadn't heard about. The Arce family traced itself back to the soldiers who had accompanied the Jesuits, but it was his grandfather Lucas who consolidated the family holdings in the last century. Among Lucas's many children was an unmarried daughter named Anastasia who was credited with prophetic powers. When Héctor was a little boy "still trailing a blanket," Anastasia singled him out as "someone who would spend his life with plants."

Perhaps Anastasia needed only sharp observation to distinguish the young Héctor from the brother who would become an Ensenada-based trader and the one who would become a store manager on the coast. It was the traveling salesman who had deposited the trailer with its useful shade. Héctor's father had preferred ranching to gardening and ran cattle in the desert above town until one year he had to sell off the entire herd, instead of just the calves, because of a drought. Héctor said that the fate of his father's cattle proved the superiority of horticulture, for if you tended plants they never let you down. The others gardened but didn't have a feel for it; they planted, watered, and walked away. Héctor inspected his plants daily, sifted their roots, checked their leaves for parasites and disease, trimmed their dead matter, and kept in touch with them as fellow beings. Reaching for some dirt under the cypress tree, he let it fall through his fingers and spoke a litany so familiar that he must have said it often to himself, if not out loud. "Look what plants are. They're our food, peace, the beauty around us, homes for the birds and animals. They're the very air we breathe. They're the cradles we're born in and the coffins of our graves."

ℋ

From the vantage of Héctor's *huerta*, San Ignacio seemed like an idyllic plant kingdom, but it was clear from talking around town and to Héctor himself that productivity had fallen drastically and the social fabric was shearing. With its tens of thousands of palms, San Ignacio had not gotten rich off its dates. The market was once at the mercy of a single powerful buyer, who paid just enough that Ignacianos sold to him rather than let the fruit rot. Completion of the highway in 1973 allowed traders from Tijuana to arrive by truck and by bus, and a few enterprising Ignacianos even transported dates to Tijuana. But there was still no organized market, nothing so crass as promotion, and most growers were content to let the market find them. The trees, meanwhile, were less and less well tended, and San Ignacio dates were losing their cachet. There were those who whispered the unutterable: that the dates of Ejido Bonfil, a communal farm off the highway where dates were grown on midget clones that could be stripped without ladders, were the firm, succulent sweets that San Ignacio no longer produced.

As with everywhere else on the peninsula where traditional business failed, people looked to tourism. The Hotel El Presidente, built shortly after the highway opened, succumbed so fast that I saw weeds growing through its abandoned concrete three years after it was built; patched and refurbished, it became part of a small motel chain that catered to overnighters off the highway, generally at a fraction of capacity. Day trips from San Ignacio to the whales and cave paintings required so much travel time that people serious about either preferred to camp on site, leaving barely enough business for Oscar Fischer's six-room motel. The unlucrative truth was that tourism, Mexican or foreign, active or passive, was water oriented. People came to Baja California to be on the Gulf, the Cape, or the Pacific, and tourism was profitable only along the coasts. Once visitors had walked around the San Ignacio plaza, inspected the mission, and snapped pictures of the lagoon, they drove on. Said Hercilia, a pharmacist I knew from my first stays at the pension, there was actually more tourism before the highway, when the diehards who fought their way down the old jeep track laid over a few days to lick their wounds and fix their cars.

The chief social problem since the highway was that the young left town as soon as they left high school, to pursue higher education or higher pay. There was little money in the date business and less in tourism. And as Hercilia's husband Carlos, the town's leading doctor, pointed out, because everyone in San Ignacio was related to everyone else, or was a lifetime neighbor, Ignacianos expected free goods and services and little money changed hands. The main destination for San Ignacio's youth was the fishing towns of the Pacific coast, which were primarily founded and replenished by Ignacianos who could not find work at home. "San Ignacio is a kind of incubator," said Carlos, "raising humanity and sending it forth." Ignacianos worked elsewhere, then came home to visit and relax. And here lay the local explanation for San Ignacio's reputation for laziness, the source of the jokes: Ignacianos worked elsewhere seasonally and returned to recuperate in the homes of their parents. Strangers who drove into town and saw working-age people lying around were actually seeing vacationers in reverse, people who traveled to their hard work and came home to relax.

Though San Ignacio was one of the most insular towns on the peninsula, it had—along with visitors and offspring who returned to it from their working lives—television, with its news of disasters. The town, tapping a clean aquifer, with weather that blew fresh from the open Pacific and with a bias against the chemicals of agribusiness, would seem shielded from natural devastations occurring elsewhere, but the one threat Ignacianos took seriously was environmental collapse. Héctor, his father, and others found the palms paler than they had been, thought the deciduous leaves more ashen, and said all the vegetation was looking burned. It wasn't a matter of trees and plants themselves being old, for the same effects afflicted the new ones. Fruit trees were susceptible to parasites and diseases previously unknown, didn't bear as they once did, and those who tended them were getting sunburned more quickly.

Héctor's brother in the coastal village had more alarming news. The abalone had gone soft and weightless. Certain fish now had strange spots on them. Children were coming down with mysterious ailments, including stomachaches that couldn't be diagnosed. The natural support system, even in the seeming isolation of the mid-peninsula, was becoming less dependable, all the more threatening because the danger was so amorphous, so unfocused. It was in the sky and it was on TV. Héctor's brother speculated that the deterioration of marine life resulted from accumulated oil spills along with the mysterious ocean phenomenon known as El Niño and, in a locally flavored touch, that the damage to plants was a combination of ozone depletion and too many eclipses.

The tangible changes in San Ignacio, meanwhile, were slow, subtle, and resembled gestures in a noh play. In the winter of 1992, the main occurrence was construction of a cutoff from the plaza to a few stranded residential blocks. Héctor was conflicted, pleased to gain vehicular access to the farthest corner of the vineyard, dismayed that a cluster of date palms near the mission would be felled. In his mania to document everything, he asked me to take pictures of the palm trees before they went. We stood in the area being cleared, watching ranchers unload a truckful of *palo blanco* trunks to be used for fencing along the new road. Supervising them was a large, dark, smooth-faced man in sunglasses, expressionless among gesturers in the manner of provincial bureaucrats. Héctor identified him as the *delegado*—the nonelected mayor, appointed from the regional seat in Santa Rosalia. As Héctor left the scene, I paused by the *delegado*. He was declaiming to the ranchers about the future of San Ignacio, drawing building lots with his machete in the dust.

In 1993 the road was in and a new structure appeared beside it on Héctor's property—a thatched roof on posts, with obscure objects underneath. Héctor identified it as a small secondhand store put up by his salesman brother from Ensenada. He boasted how it could be left unattended for days and no one ever took anything. As we approached, the contents resolved themselves into old chairs, ironing boards, car parts, stoves, and washing machines, in the middle of which, on a cracked pad, lay Héctor's father, asleep. New shade to conquer. . . .

In 1994, half of Héctor's grapevines had been torn out, leaving pure dirt stretching behind the secondhand store. In what seemed a violation, I was able to drive from a new gate off the new road all the way to the cypress tree. Was this the beginning of development? I asked Héctor. Was this the property the *delegado* had drawn with his machete in the dust? No, he explained, the vines were eighty years old, had stopped producing, and were overdue for tearing out. Even the half that were left, forty years old, were well past their prime, and to prove the point Héctor snapped off a branch that cracked like dead wood. His father thought he should switch to melons and beans, but Héctor intended to plant new vines.

That dusk as I sat by the tent with my jeep next to the trailer, still screened from the outside world but more precariously so, Héctor came and settled on the folding chair. "Are you really happy with these changes?" I asked.

" No," he admitted. "This *huerta* is where I grew up. I'm as much its product as the fruit of these trees. This orchard made me whatever I am. I felt so much at peace when I could go out in the fields and do whatever I wanted and work unseen. Now I feel like I'm on display for everyone. People watch everything I do. I'm not just going to plant more vines. I'm going to plant trees along the fence—pomegranates and bananas so the fence will produce, with thick mulberries in between. I'm going to make this place private again."

A return to privacy, a turning inward, was what might revive San Ignacio as a community, but the town instead seemed to be unraveling. On Sundays families had stopped migrating in groups from one house to another, affirming bonds by exchanging minutiae. People had lost patience, a loss particularly hard on Héctor's father, whose contemporaries were gone and who expected to be sustained by those who followed him. Too few people of intermediate age linked the very young with the very old and all seemed cut loose. For awhile weekend ballgames and picnics were organized near the lagoon so that Ignacianos could socialize, gossip, even get drunk together, but as a replacement tradition it didn't take. Television briefly united people when they gathered to watch the first satellite pickup, but then they communed with their home sets. It seemed inconceivable that only a generation back boys and girls at dances sat in separate rows, with parents and chaperones acting as coaches and each youngster dancing with several partners. Now a dating couple was glued for the evening. The male paid admittance to a metal barn blasted by a bad rock band from Santa

Rosalia or Guerrero Negro, paid again for a table, paid for each drink, paid in a town without money. Because the barn loomed a block from the cypress and made dance nights unbearable, I once ventured as far in as I could without paying. Several dozen youths crowded the door with no thought of entering either. Around two speechless tables pounded the reverberations of amped guitars from sheet metal, surely one of the most desolate sounds of advancing global culture. It was no wonder that instead the kids piled with six-packs into cars and headed to the lagoon, and beyond it onto the highway.

As for the physical surroundings, Ignacianos also saw decline around them. Héctor told me how a *delegado* had introduced a new fish into the lagoon, thinking to provide another food source. No one would eat the fish because it was too spiny, but the fish ate seaweed, algae, and smaller fish that sustained a water snake, a species of frog, and various bird species. My own photographs proved the town less meticulously tended than when I first arrived, the vineyards less extensive. It shamed Ignacianos that a field that had once borne grapes had been taken over by white and lavender mallow. Where I still saw splendor in every direction, they saw an oasis going to seed. But it was difficult to keep perspective when the generations had lost their continuity. It was too much like regretting the pond below the lagoon, where Héctor and his brothers had learned to swim by hanging onto the roots of palms, lost to a flood that was a fact of nature, innocent of decline. Was the vegetation really bleached through the thinning ozone or had color itself lost the intensity that fired one's youth? Was San Ignacio showing signs of a globe in peril or merely human exhaustion and natural succession?

Under the cypress tree, surrounded by birds and flowering weeds, it was hard to think apocalyptically. My own hopes, modest if selfish, were that Héctor would plant his new vines, surround them with trees that bore fruit as they fended off prying stares, and that in the center remained a refuge I could count on. I wanted Héctor to resume tending his plants unseen while I vanished into a nearby quiet, a recording eye or just a cow with sneakers.

from *Almost an Island*

Shishmaref

Carolyn Kremers

I stopped walking the beach and stared. Three black noses pointed north, over the Chukchi Sea, and the ice and snow glowed like a soft pink rose.

Even before I arrived, people had told me about these bears. They said that hunters in Shishmaref get more polar bears than anywhere else in Alaska. I had never seen a polar bear in the wild, only the one in the Denver Zoo. It was blind and swung its head from side to side, as if listening to a distant song. On Sundays, kids tossed popcorn through the spiked iron fence and, on the other side of the moat, the bear caught kernels with its nose.

Twice when I was seven, I dreamed that this blind polar bear escaped from the zoo and pinned my grandmother on the hood of our gray station wagon, a '55 Plymouth, parked on the street in front of our house. Gram was visiting from Wisconsin. I loved her, I think, but I could not tell her that. She was British blooded and not a demonstrative grandmother. The bear ate her alive, arms first, then legs, slowly. She never made a sound. Both times, I woke up before the bear got to her heart or to her soft white hair.

Still, my favorite exhibit at the Denver Museum of Natural History was the one with the polar bears. In a small room, a stuffed white sow and her cub ambled in a display case across ice made of plastic, through the silence of a painted pink dusk. Papier-mâché snowdrifts swept the ice, and a shaded blue bulb cast winter from the ceiling.

I liked to stand in the dark exhibit room after my father and sister had left and pretend I was up in the Arctic with those bears.

Now I was.

Three bearskins and their north-pointing noses hung over long, horizontal drying poles, white fur blown whiter with snow. Their claws reached to rake the frozen beach. All the meat, innards, and rich bones had been passed to ravens, foxes, and dogs. I could see where the eyes had been and the fierce teeth. The three round black noses shone like buttons.

I pulled off my mitten and tried to stroke the fur shoulder of the biggest bear, but it was stiff with ice.

&

I had come to Shishmaref, an Inupiat Eskimo village north of the Bering Strait, to lead a writing workshop for public school teachers and aides. I had never been in a village that hunted polar bears. Such bears are not usually found on Nelson Island. Ginger, the principal's wife, had told me about a polar bear, though, spotted outside Tununak the year before I arrived. That bear had probably been standing on ice, up north, that broke away from the mainland and floated south. Biologists from the Department of Fish and Game in Bethel had said that there was not enough summer food on Nelson Island for a polar bear, so they flew the 125 miles to the island, landed on a small lake, drugged the bear, and flew it back above the Arctic Circle.

People in Tununak are fortunate. They may not have polar bears, but they still speak their Native language. Tununak people have been able to keep their language and traditions alive, because their island was isolated from white influences longer than Shishmaref, and some of the Jesuit missionaries who came to Nelson Island were more respectful of Eskimo languages and culture than the Lutherans in the north. Even the toddlers in Tununak speak Yup'ik. Shishmaref, though, is quickly losing its language, a loss that threatens stories, drumming, dancing, words and concepts for hunting and fishing—all the things that stem from language and from an oral tradition that is not found in books.

When I visited Shishmaref in February 1990, only three drummers were still alive. Each was in his sixties or seventies. The first-grade teacher, a white woman who had married a son of one of the drummers, invited the men to come to the school and perform for her class. All three refused. They did not explain why, but she could guess. What they had to pass on was more than the drumming of a few songs for children who could neither speak nor understand their own language, and the elders knew this, and they were unhappy.

"Being able to speak Inupiaq won't get you a job," a white teacher in Shishmaref had told me, "except in the school as a bilingual teacher's aide. So why learn it?"

Yet this teacher, Tom, was pleased that his three daughters were "taking a class about the culture at school" and that they could "recognize a few words." He had taught in Shishmaref for thirteen years. He said that he could count seventy different teachers and eight principals since he had arrived. Now the faculty was larger than ever: fourteen certified teachers. Two were Natives. The others had moved to Alaska directly from the Lower 48 and, like myself, had known almost nothing about Eskimo culture when they arrived.

Tom's wife, Hazel, a Native woman about my age, understood Inupiaq but only spoke it with her mother. She was a relative of my friend Rebecca, from the fish camp at Port Clarence, where I had worked on the construction crew the previous summer. When I told Rebecca I was flying to Shishmaref to give a workshop, she thought of Hazel. "You should visit her," Rebecca said over the long-distance phone. On my second day in the village, a Sunday, I went to the church, hoping to meet Hazel.

The Lutheran church in Shishmaref was very different from the Catholic church I had attended in Tununak. Shishmaref's was a new church, spotlessly clean, with tall oak-framed windows, white walls, and a white spackled ceiling hung with fifteen fluorescent lights. About sixty people, more than half of them elders, sat in the back rows, leaving the front two-thirds of the church empty. Few small children had come, and the ones who had sat quietly. No little people squirmed or played in the aisles, and there was no shaking of hands or murmuring "Peace."

An organ stood untouched in one corner. The choir, though, all elders, belted out hymns a cappella in a style I recognized, screeching and sliding up and down notes with enthusiasm, even harmonizing. I was surprised when the minister passed around sheets with the words to an anthem and all of the elders appeared able to read.

The short, white-robed minister spoke through a microphone and gave a sermon about not committing adultery, not having murder in our hearts, not thinking bad thoughts, and how we should try to change our ways and be more good. I thought of many Eskimos I knew, how they shared and laughed and lived resourcefully from the land and sea. I couldn't help wondering: how could a people "be more good" than this?

After the service, not many people spoke with the minister nor he with them. I wanted to ask someone to point out Hazel so that I could introduce myself, but people kept coming up to me as I walked down the aisle. I was reminded of my first weeks in Tununak and of every return from a vacation or from a trip some where else in the Delta: how everyone noticed everyone else and how welcome they always made me feel. This was a warmth that I could not have imagined, perhaps had never known, until I moved to the bush.

"Who are you?" a small white-haired woman asked, smile lines crinkling around her eyes as she offered her hand. "What are you doing in Shishmaref?"

Before I could answer, the gray-haired woman who had sat next to me during the service rugged on my elbow and asked, "Where did you come from? Are you from Anchorage?" She showed me the red-paper and silver-glitter valentine her granddaughter had given her that morning. "She made it in school," the woman said proudly.

"My brother has old *uluaq*, very old," said a cheerful woman whom I had met the day before in the Shishmaref Native Store. Loretta. I had heard her tell the man at the cash register to put her purchases on credit. Now she headed for the door, giggling. "You come visit, come see that *uluaq*. Today. Okay? Today?"

I said okay, that I would look for her later. Loretta smiled, then disappeared.

Someone said that Hazel had left with her husband right after the service, but her three daughters were still there. Skipping and holding my hands, they led me in the wind to their house.

&

Inside, Hazel shook my hand gently.

"Sit down," she said, offering a chair at the kitchen table. "Would you like some coffee? We just made some."

Hazel said that her grandmother was my friend Rebecca's grandmother's sister. Soon she had invited me to stay for lunch: reindeer and macaroni soup with pilot crackers and Wonder bread. The family joined hands and bowed their heads, and Tom thanked the Lord for His bounty.

"I hope they find Danny soon," Tom said after grace, ladling the soup into bowls. "He should have come home by now."

Tom said that Danny was the school maintenance man. A few days before, Danny had flown to Nome to pick up a new snowmachine. He was a responsible father and an experienced hunter and fisher. He had left the next morning to drive the snowmachine home and had disappeared, lost somewhere in the hundreds of white square miles between Nome and Shishmaref.

After lunch, Hazel showed me twenty barrettes she had made: flowers, butterflies, geometric designs in all colors. She was known in the village for her beadwork. In the chair next to me, her eleven-year-old daughter, Sasha, carefully threaded a single strand of plastic opal beads.

Hazel pointed to a design of a four-petaled flower on a large hair clip.

"That was a kit," she said. "Usually I make up my own designs, but I sent for this one from that shop in Fairbanks. What do they call it? Beads 'n' Things, that's right. I thought it looked interesting to try. But I can't sew like the Indians. They don't sew like us. I'm not used to sewing beads in circles. I have to practice. Maybe someday I'll get good at it."

I liked Hazel's designs and I didn't think she needed to learn to sew like the Athabascans, but I didn't say so. Could she make me some barrettes?

"Of course," she said. "What colors do you like? What kind of design?" I said blue and purple, with white or maybe pink. "I try to find out what people like," Hazel said, "and then I try to make it for them."

I smelled sulfur and turned to see Sasha holding a lighted match to her wrist. She was melting the ends of a dental floss knot, joining the bracelet. Eleven other brightly colored strands graced her slender arm. Sasha's shiny, straight black hair traded down her back, the way her mother's must have, before a beautician from Nome had come to Shishmaref and given Hazel her first perm.

"I never had my hair cut by a real hairdresser before," Hazel said, pleased. "If she gets promises for eighteen more perms, she'll come back."

We will always decorate ourselves, I thought, thinking of the sealskin and wolverine mukluks that Susan Thomas had made for me in Tununak, and of the black-soled mukluks with big, round beaded designs and long polar bear fur that people in this village wore. I thought, too, of all the times that I had had my own straight hair permed, only to decide perms were too expensive and unhealthy for my hair. Decoration. It's like language, a whisper of all that lies underneath.

Later that afternoon, I sat at another kitchen table.

"Do you have artifacts in your village?" Loretta asked, as she emptied a plastic bag of jade, stone, wood, and ivory onto the gray Formica. I glanced around her house while she returned to her bedroom to get more bags of "artifacts," and I noticed other things besides the Formica table that reminded me of Tununak.

Loretta's was a typical prefab government-built house: impractical white linoleum, a big oil stove in the middle of the living room, a large TV in one corner and a smaller one in the bedroom where the grandkids played, and lots of stuff piled around: cardboard boxes, empty jars, stacks of yellowed copies of the *Nome Nugget*, pieces of fishing net, an open box of Cheez Puffs, a bag of calico scraps, a hammer. A big hole gaped from the foam cushion of the vinyl-covered chair at the kitchen table. I enjoyed knowing that I was sitting on it, covering it up.

Now Loretta showed me the two *uluaqs* her brother had found in the diggings down the beach from the polar bears: two smooth black slate blades set in reindeer antler handles. She said that her brother had found the blades, then attached them to his own handles. A line of clear glue showed where the black slate blade joined the brown antler handle. I smiled at this juxtaposition of old and new.

"I went around to teacher houses yesterday," Loretta explained. "'Only eighty-five dollars,' I said. 'Only eighty-five dollars for this ancient *uluaq*.' But nobody was interested.

"'We already have too many *ulus*,' they said. What about you? Wouldn't you like to buy one?"

I liked the cold smoothness of the slate and the mysteries it hinted at when I brushed my fingers over it. My *ulu* in Fairbanks was handmade, but its blade had been cut from a stainless-steel saw. I did not need another *ulu*, though, especially not one designed for scraping instead of cutting. I was not a hunter.

Loretta poured me more Lipton tea with sugar and opened another can of Carnation milk. She cut two more slices of her homemade white bread and pushed the plate of butter toward me. "This bread is a new recipe, with sugar and salt," she said proudly. "Please, eat."

In Tununak I had never been offered bread baked by an elder, only pilot crackers and Crisco. I did not know any elders there who baked bread. My mother made delicious bread, though, and I liked to think of good bread as a staff of life. I preferred wheat bread to white, but didn't try to explain why. I accepted more of Loretta's "new recipe" and she smiled, as delightful as the elders in Tununak.

Loretta began sorting through the things on the table and handing them to me: pieces of bone tools; more slate blades, chipped and broken; pointed shards of jade and ivory; a wooden bowl, carefully wrapped in brown paper towels; slats of walrus-bone armor pierced with holes for sinew lashings, some holes round, some skinny and rectangular.

Two grandchildren came out of the bedroom to watch, a boy and a girl. Loretta shoved more objects onto the crowded table, all the time giggling and laughing, enjoying the spectacle of her collection as much as I.

There was a fist-sized rock with a thin strip of baleen tied around it. A weapon, a fishing weight? I smelled the blackened bottom of a clay pot and imagined smoky fires, the odor of sizzling meat. Then Loretta unwrapped a peaceful wooden face, palm-sized, with closed eyes and a straight-line mouth.

"This one is not for sale," she said, pausing. "I want to keep this one."

I did not say anything. It was an intriguing face. I wanted to believe that Loretta kept it for its simplicity and magic, not just for the money it might bring.

Loretta wrapped the face carefully in brown paper towels again and rummaged some more in the pile. She pulled out a crumpled page from the Bible. Smoothing it to show me, she said, "Sometimes I take this to the diggings, if I go alone. It helps me feel safe. There are many spirits there, you know."

I nodded, thinking of my own spirit-filled places: the mountains in Colorado, the Pretend People, my flute. The eye of the meadow at Old Chisana. Wolves.

Loretta poured a bag of rocks, shells, and beach bones over the human artifacts already on the table.

"Beachcomb," she said, grinning even more. "I like to look on the beach in fall-time, with my sister. Before the snow covers it."

She handed me three white, fluted spiral shells, graceful as whipping cream, and two clusters of rust-colored rock crystals several inches long.

"'Eagle *anaq,*' our grandmother always told us," Loretta said, fingering more rock crystals, not looking at me now, looking somewhere else.

"Do you know this word, *anaq?*" she asked, coming back.

I laughed. "Yes. It was one of the first words the kids in Tununak taught me."

Not many words are the same in Yup'ik and Inupiaq. Many are similar, though, and can be guessed at, like words in French versus Spanish.

"Keep those," Loretta said, nodding at the shells and crystals. "They're free. I found them free, now I give them to you free. They're free from God." She laughed some more and clapped her hands. "Now, what will you buy? You want to take something home from the ancient village of Shishmaref, don't you?"

I did. I wanted the spirit of Shishmaref in my house, along with the spirits of Tununak, Port Clarence, and other remote Eskimo places I had visited, but the idea of buying artifacts disturbed me. I knew that Natives all over Alaska were digging up ancient sites—not gravesites as much as ancient camping and village sites—and selling the things they found for quick cash. This was understandable to me. Many village Natives needed money for basic living expenses, not just for drugs and alcohol, sugar and snuff. I wasn't sure that I wanted to be part of this process, though.

Still, I knew that if I saw something special I liked and didn't buy it, someone else would. Several white people in Nome had dealt in the buying and selling of Eskimo artifacts for generations, and the town was known as much for its ivory shops and bars as for its gold.

The day before, one of the teachers in the workshop I was leading had told me of the profits that she had heard could be made from an artifact. Karen taught on St. Lawrence Island, known among anthropologists for its ancient Eskimo sites. Like the people of Tununak and Shishmaref, St. Lawrence Islanders depend on the land and sea for food, and they supplement their subsistence lifestyle with cash. Their island is only thirty miles from Siberia, and they speak Siberian Yup'ik rather than Central Yup'ik or Inupiaq. Karen said that one of the St. Lawrence Islanders had sold an artifact—she thought it was an ivory doll—for $18,000. The buyer had sold the doll to an East Coast dealer for $50,000, who had sold it in New York for $108,000.

I bought a reddish-brown spearhead as long as my index finger. Its graceful shape was carved in bone, with a hole in the bottom for insertion on a wooden spear and another hole through the center for a long string of sinew. The spearhead came to a thin point at the end, like a letter opener. It felt powerful in my hand.

I imagined how the spear had been thrown, the barbed point embedding itself in a seal. The spear might have fallen out or been pulled out of the point, but the spearhead would have stayed in the seal, attached to the spear by several feet of sinew, unwinding, unwinding. The seal might have tried to swim away, but the spear would have dragged behind, attached to a float, tiring the seal and helping the hunter to catch it. I was surprised when Loretta asked only ten dollars.

I looked through the other items on the table and picked up a small object: a labret or mouth decoration, from the Latin *labrum*, lip. This labret was carved in the shape of a thick squat nail about an inch long. The ivory was no longer white but rusty red, discolored by time or perhaps by minerals in the wet sand, where the labret must have lain buried for at least a century.

"Do you know these things?" Loretta asked, taking the labret from my hand and holding it under her bottom lip, wrinkling her nose. "They used to wear these a long time ago."

I had seen a few labrets in the university museum in Fairbanks, but I had never held one in my hand. I knew that labrets were worn by indigenous people all over the world, in Africa and South America, as well as in the Arctic.

Later I would read about labrets in Edward Nelson's book *The Eskimo About Bering Strait*. When Nelson lived in the village of St. Michael south of Shishmaref, in the late 1800s, the wearing of labrets had begun to die out. He did not see any young men in St. Michael whose lips had been pierced, and many of the elders had stopped wearing labrets, because white people considered the practice "uncivilized." Nelson noted scars on the old men's lips, however, where holes had been made when the men were boys.

Women wore labrets hung with short strings of beads that dangled when they walked or talked. The labret I bought from Loretta, though, was probably worn by a man. ("You may have it for two dollars—and twenty-five cents," Loretta laughed, making fun of selling things she had found.) When a young man reached puberty and was ready to have his lip pierced, a hole was made below the corner of his mouth and a thin plug of ivory was inserted to keep the hole open. After the young man got used to this, a larger plug was used, like the one Loretta had found, and so on in a series of plugs, until the hole reached the desired size. The hole could be so big that the young man's teeth were visible through it when the labret was not in place.

Sometimes these eight or ten plugs of graduated sizes were pierced at their pointed ends and strung on a piece of sinew. The young man would keep these with his personal belongings or hang them as ornaments on his wife's waist belt or on the strap of her needle case. When the plugs were used as decorations this way, men sometimes etched ornamental lines on them, such as the Raven totem, a three-line sketch of a raven track.

I liked to look in Nelson's book at the black-and-white photographs of labrets he had collected on his explorations by dogsled, kayak, and boat, and on foot.

"While traveling with these people in winter," Nelson wrote, "I found that during cold days the labrets were invariably removed in order to prevent the lip from freezing, as must have occurred had they remained in place. The labrets were removed and carried in a small bag until we approached a village at night, when they were taken out and replaced, that the wearer might present a proper appearance before the people. They are also sometimes removed when eating and before retiring for the night."

After I had counted out twelve dollars and twenty-five cents and Loretta, pleased, had put it in her pocket, I asked if she ever told stories at the school. She shook her head.

"Kids can't understand me when I speak Inupiaq. Some teachers told me I should tape my stories anyway, but I don't want to. I don't want to sit alone and talk to a tape recorder with nobody to listen. Anyway, I can't tell stories with just words. We need hands. We need faces."

I understood. My grandmother had not told me many stories, but at least I remembered her face. And the way her bony hands had moved when she sketched with charcoal or watercolors.

When I stood to leave, Loretta thanked me for visiting, just as Paul Hoover always had. She shook my hand and asked me to come again, but I knew there would not be time. I gave her a hug and stepped into the fading afternoon.

The wind blew and the sun had dipped to the horizon, casting my favorite pink light. I felt in my pocket for the spearhead and small labret, the two shells, and the eagle *anaq* crystals. Not yet cold, they lay in a lump inside my parka.

э

Two days later, I was introduced to Eddy in his family's store. I had heard of his uncle, Herbie Nayokpuk, a musher known in Alaska for his strong finishes in the annual Iditarod sled dog race from Anchorage to Nome. Herbie was in Anchorage, trying to make arrangements to bring visitors to Shishmaref for dogsled tours.

"I know you," Eddy said, when I came into the store. "You're the woman my dog team almost ran over on the ice." He laughed. "Nah, they would never do that. But you were standing pretty close."

The previous Saturday, the Cessna I had flown in from Nome had banked left to approach Shishmaref for landing, and I had glimpsed two long strings of dogs pulling tiny sleds: the start of a thirty-mile race, I learned later. The principal had picked me up at the windy airstrip and had driven me on his snowmachine to the school.

"Minus thirty-seven with a fifteen-knot wind," he had said, shaking his head. "If you don't mind, I'll leave you to make yourself comfortable. I need to get home and finish thawing the pipes."

I left my duffel bag in a classroom and made a quick tour of the building. One teacher was doing laundry and two others were working on lesson plans. As soon as it was politely possible, I headed outside in all my warm clothes.

I walked past a few houses to the edge of the frozen inlet and watched the last of the ten village teams take off. One of those teams had been Eddy's.

Now, in the store, Eddy wanted to visit. And like Loretta, he wanted me to buy something.

"Hey, you're traveling around teaching teachers," Eddy said. "You must be making fifty, sixty thou a year. You need this bracelet and earrings to make you beautiful, now that you're up here in the Far North."

I smiled. I was leading this workshop on almost a volunteer basis, getting paid a hundred dollars plus expenses, but to explain that to Eddy would have been complicated. All white strangers in Shishmaref on school business probably seemed rich to him. I did not have money to buy ivory, but I loved looking at it. I knew that Shishmaref had some of the finest ivory and bone carvers in Alaska.

"Do you know," Eddy said, as he showed me more earrings and an unusual whale-bone dancer, "that the largest Eskimo ivory museum in the world is only a hundred miles from here? It's in Uelen, over on the Siberian coast. Me and my dad are trying to scrape up the bucks and see if they'll let us visit. Imagine that, only a hundred miles from here."

We talked more about ivory, and I asked whether Eddy thought that the school's efforts to try to revive the Inupiaq language in Shishmaref were succeeding. He told me a story.

Eddy had been a representative to the Circumpolar Inuit Conference, held in Greenland the previous summer. "That was the first time I was in a place where everybody spoke Eskimo," he said. "Everybody, even on TV, radio, newspapers. I never felt like that before. It made me realize what we are missing. A Greenland woman asked me why we don't speak Eskimo here and I said I guess it's because, when the first white people came here, they were half missionaries, half teachers, and they didn't want us to speak our own language. They wanted to stamp out our culture, make us be like them. So we lost our language. She said after she heard that, she went home and cried."

I thought about this story as Eddy helped a customer, and I remembered Jenny, the fourth-grade teacher I had met in the school lunchroom. Jenny was a jolly, plump woman, probably in her thirties, with short red pixie hair. She and her husband, the Lutheran minister, had moved to Shishmaref the previous year. She had tried to get release time to attend my workshop but, as in most Alaskan Eskimo villages, only a few people could or would substitute at the school. The principal was willing to find a substitute for only one teacher and one aide, and he had chosen one of the two Native teachers. Jenny said she thought that was unfair, even discriminatory.

As we filed through the lunch line and I passed up the sloppy joes, taking canned, corn, canned apricots, and white bread and margarine,

Jenny told me how hard it was to teach "The Elevated Train." This was a story in the fourth-grade reading book, about a commuter train in a city.

"And it wasn't a subway," Jenny said. "It was an elevated train. The kids don't understand. I just can't get them to understand about this train."

I tried to talk with her about using more culturally relevant reading materials and about leading her fourth-graders gradually to abstract concepts like the elevated train—having them build an elevated train, or draw one, or dance one with their bodies, whistles blowing, wheels clacking—but it was lunchtime. We both needed a break, and I could see that Jenny needed to vent her frustration more than to listen. I remembered feeling frustrated, too, in Tununak. Many times. Not for the same reasons, though.

🚲

"This is the premier polar bear hunter in the village," Eddy said, grinning again, as he rang up a purchase of snuff for another customer, a slight man with long white hair. The man glanced at me with sparkling eyes and chuckled, then looked modestly at the counter and the money he was counting. He tipped his brown fur hat and was gone.

Now a big man came into the store, taking off his beaver hat and store-bought parka, and walked behind the sales counter. Eddy introduced his father, Robert. "I see you must be a new customer," Robert said, grinning. "What are you doing in this village?"

I told him I had come to give a workshop for teachers and aides, and he asked if I had a business card. I didn't, but he produced two.

You must have some power, if you are all the way here from Fairbanks. That is a long way for those people in Juneau to send you. Maybe you can help me get an appointment with somebody out there, so we can try and get our language back."

I glanced at the business cards, then put them in my pocket. There wasn't much I could say, to Eddy's father or to anyone else, that would explain how I felt about this language issue or about other things I had seen and heard, in Shishmaref and in other Eskimo villages. The issues were complex. They would always be that way. But I agreed with this man and his son: things could be done.

"The school is doing it all wrong," Robert said. "They hire people to teach bilingual who are not even bilingual themselves. And anyway, kids must learn by ear, not by reading and books. And they must hear their parents speak Inupiaq, not just at the school. And they must start learning when they are small. Then they can be good at both languages."

Eddy agreed with his father. "Lots of Native high school grads go to college and drop out and then people say Natives are dumb, Natives can't learn, Natives can't succeed in college," he said. "But it's not their fault."

The next morning, I prepared to fly home. I packed the evaluations of the workshop in my navy-blue duffel bag. A Native aide from St. Lawrence Island had scrawled across the manila envelope: *Carolyn! Please, please. Don't you forget us! Your friend, Doreen.*

Just as the principal told me the plane was landing, someone telephoned to say that Danny had been found, alive and safe on Ear Mountain. Everyone cheered.

Although I did not know Danny, I had thought of him every day since having lunch with Hazel and Tom. Throughout my stay in Shishmaref, the thermometer had stuck at minus thirty-seven and the wind had not let up. Weather in the village was clear, but pilots reported ground blizzards over the tundra and mountains, making them difficult to scan for a solitary man and his snowmachine.

At last, three days after Danny was reported missing, a Bering Air pilot had noticed a short stretch of snowmachine tracks not yet erased by the wind and had followed them. He had discovered a cheerful man camped in a snow cave on the north side of Ear Mountain. Danny had lost his sense of direction in the whiteout and knew that the best thing to do was to stop and wait until the weather cleared or until somebody spotted him from the air.

Danny's assistant, Hugo, also a Native, took me to the airstrip on the principal's snowmachine. As Hugo helped load baggage and mail,

I heard the pilot say above the wind, "So, I heard they found Danny alive, and he's fine except for some frostbite. That's amazing."

"Well," said Hugo, grinning, "he's Eskimo, you know."

ɍ

The Twin Otter taxied to the end of the gravel airstrip and prepared for takeoff, but we did not take off. A snowmachine loaded with three people and a covered sled had raced from the village to the airstrip, all three people waving. The pilot cut the engines, taxied back to the loading area, and got out.

Soon he was opening the cabin doors and folding up empty seats. He asked me to sit in the copilot's seat and the other two passengers to move to the seats behind his. Then he helped a young woman and an elderly man lift a stretcher through the door. They suspended it directly behind me, between two seats, and the pilot strapped it into place.

The person in the stretcher lay wrapped in blankets. All I could see were her nose and two thin, veined hands, folded on her chest. A wisp of gray hair stuck out of the hood of her thick calico-covered parka. The hands moved up and down with her breathing, gently. A silent grandmother. Around the hood, cradling her head, was a ruff of polar bear.

We taxied down the airstrip once more, turned around, and took off. Engines roaring, the plane shook the way small planes do. Out the window, I saw the yellow school fall away, and the white church, and two dog teams. I looked for the beach with the drying racks, on the frozen Chukchi, but I had already said goodbye to the bears.

Near midnight, I had walked out on the snow to see them once more, wind blowing, sky studded with stars. Over the arrested sea the northern lights danced, painting a curtain of green, and the three white husks glowed like pearls under the risen, sliver moon.

I had not known my grandmother well. Every few years when I was growing up, my parents had driven to Wisconsin, or my grandparents had come to Colorado to visit. Gram would set up a lawn chair in the backyard or sit at a picnic table and paint with watercolors and oils, or draw with charcoal. Her white hair was always carefully combed, often curled, and she wore bright scarves, red and orange, purple, paisley, around her neck. When she reached eighty, arthritis gnarled her hands and she became allergic to the sun. She could no longer hold a paintbrush, but with an electric mixer she still made the best mashed potatoes I ever ate.

Alzheimer's disease began to take Gram's memory; and she died in a nursing home.

I knew that I might not stand in this place again. The bears seemed intent on the distance. I turned to see what they were pointing to.

from *Place of the Pretend People: Gifts from a Yup'ik Eskimo Village*

Raptors and Flycatchers

Ken Lamberton

At 10:00 p.m. on the eve of *El Día de los Muertos*, the Day of the Dead, a great horned owl materializes at the end of the run. At first I think someone has left a mop leaning against the railing, but then the mop head shifts slightly and a pair of unblinking yellow eyes focuses on me. The bird is huge, out of place. It *should* be a mop head. The yard is on lockdown and the run is dark. Most of the cells I can see from my window are dark, too. The owl perches twenty-five feet away, right outside the last cell on the upper tier.

I wonder about the significance of this oddity. Only once have I seen a great horned owl at the prison. It appeared at the fenceline, a creature of the edges. It was a glimpse at the periphery of my vision; now it's a ghost at the periphery of my mind as I begin to doubt the memory. This one is undoubtedly interested in balancing out our overpopulation of mice, but its presence is still too bizarre, surreal, a wild predator among all this moon-blanched concrete and steel. "An owl of the waste places," as the Psalmist says. Even the human predators don't come out at night here. But I can't doubt my eyes. And there's no mistaking *its* eyes. I wonder if that stare can't see inside me to the awe and pleasure that stirs there.

Manny, one of my Navajo friends, has told me that his people believe owls are something to fear. It's a bad omen to see one. They carry off the spirits of men, and shamans use them for evil." I asked him if it was true that when an owl appears outside your house, it means you'll be dead by morning. He said he didn't want to talk about it anymore. Now I decide not to mention to him that a great horned owl had stood directly above his cell the night before the Day of the Dead.

The owl bobs its head and half unfurls its wings. In an instant it is gone. I'm not sure it flew. It just sort of jumped suddenly and vanished. I blink my eyes and feel cold air leak in from under the door. The owl has restored my faith in things wild, supernatural.

We have other raptors that occasionally visit the prison: red-tailed hawks, Cooper's and sharp-shinned hawks, kestrels, and burrowing owls. Twice I've watched golden eagles spread their huge Pleistocene wings over me. A few years ago a redtail killed a raven as it picked through one of the garbage dumpsters just outside the perimeter fence. Squalid and undignified birds those ravens, ever present, ever numerous (I've counted fifty together in one flock), always prowling the area for handouts or scraps. Some native peoples revere the raven as a mythic figure, a trickster like the coyote. Richard Nelson, writing about the Koyukon of southeastern Alaska, says the raven is seen as "good and evil, sage and fool, benefactor and thief—the embodiment of human paradox." But to me the abundance and vulgarity of the oil-slick birds embody the essence of this place; they are scavengers of landfills, human or otherwise. I felt no pity when the raven, one beakful at a time, joined the food chain.

The scene attracted quite a crowd. A couple dozen men lined up along the fence to study the hawk as it casually pulled breast feathers from its victim, the black plumes parachuting on the air like ashes drifting away from a trash fire. For forty-five minutes we watched the redtail stuff its crop with long, red, elastic ribbons of flesh pulled one after another from the raven's body. When the hawk finally flew off to settle on a light pole, strop its beak, and preen, it left behind an eruption of feathers, some peeled bones, a pair of feet, and a beak. The remnants, splayed and twisted there atop the dumpster, reminded me of those finely detailed fossil impressions of archaeopterix. But archaeopterix may have had more meat on its bones.

The men here still talk about that base act of nature. That redtail made an impact on more than the raven. There are those who believe that "biophilia," the word E. O. Wilson coined to describe our "urge to affiliate with other species," is in our genes, something inherent from our human cultural beginnings. We are a species prone to worship creation rather than the creator. But, 1 think, as is the case of other gifts we are born with, that bond must be nurtured or it withers. It's encouraging for me to see the men stop and take notice of wildness. It demonstrates their humanity, their connection to nature as an integral and essential part of life. This connection to nature may even be more essential than freedom. The worst kind of punishment forbids any form of contact with another living thing: solitary confinement, the "hole," a concrete cell without windows, without crickets and cockroaches. But imprison a man with trees and he will sit under them, with insects and toads and squirrels, and he will make pets of them, with swallows, and he will count them.

A fence is not a barrier to my expressing my innate need to love life. But the mind can be. If I walk laps around our half-mile exercise track with every step clouded with thoughts of what I'm missing being away from my family, I withdraw from life. The walls grow thicker, the fences higher. And, ironically, my family becomes more distant with the years remaining until I again join my wife and children stretching out between us. I won't even see the weeds blooming at my feet.

Lately, a sharp-shinned hawk, the smallest of the bird-hunting clan that also includes Cooper's and goshawks, has been frequenting the prison to dine on bread-fattened songbirds. (It's illegal to feed the birds, but some of us can't help this criminal behavior.) Sharpies are crow-sized with short wings and long tails, the classic accipiter design for speed and maneuverability. Adults show a reddish cross-barring on the breast, but according to the descriptions I'm getting, the one on the yard is a juvenile—brown streaks its breast.

I haven't spotted the sharpshin yet. Two friends told me it had entertained them yesterday during a lockdown by deboning a house sparrow on the lawn outside their cell. Better than television, they said. Biophilia again, and they enjoyed telling me about it, this real-time predator ritual that touched them with the morality of wildness, with the flow of energy from those eaten to those who are the eaters. Primal stuff. We reminisced about the redtail/raven vignette, and I asked them to let me know if they see the hawk again.

A sharp-shinned hawk would be new for me, one more bird to add to my prison "life list." It would definitely be a rare find for this place, in the same category with the immature Cooper's hawk, sighted once several years ago, the twice-seen golden eagles, and that recent, still mystical great horned owl. Seeing a sharpie in prison would, for me, be on the same level as seeing an elegant trogon in the Chiricahua Mountains, or a Mexican gray hawk on the San Pedro River.

For the past week I've been alert for the sharpshin, checking off each pole, fenceline, and housing unit during my exercise walks on the track. Today I'm expectant. It's going to be a fine birding day. Already, before I can get started, I hear the plaintive call of a flycatcher, an uncommon bird at the prison in November. The descending cry penetrates the walls of my cell from a distance. It instantly catches my ear, even above all the distracting and perpetual white noise of televisions, paging systems, heating units, flushing toilets, and chattering voices.

After the noon lockdown and count, the prison yard opens again and I head toward the call. *Pee-ur, pee-ur*, the bird cries in a minor key, delicate as breath. *Pee-ur, pee-ur*. At the first bend in the track I locate the source of the sound. The flycatcher turns out to be a pair of fledgling Say's phoebes, perched side by side on a spring of razor wire. I stop to watch them. *Pee-ur, Pee-ur*, one of the birds whistles. In seconds a parent arrives, cutting a sharp path across the wetland to the begging chicks. Where is the nest? I wonder. And why this time of year? It seems terribly late to be raising a brood.

The parent phoebe strokes back to the wetland and skips for insects in the mangy, yellowing grass. There seems to be no lack of prey. I will encounter this family of flycatchers over the next few weeks, always hearing their wistful and distant song before sighting them. In two days only one chick will call, stationing itself more often than not on a stake in the center of the fallow wetland, and I will think there can be no better metaphor for loneliness.

Later, walking along the fenceline of the visitation park, I hear something unfamiliar in the trees. The sound is a new configuration to my ears, a sharp *cheet, cheet,* and it's disembodied. I can't find the bird, if it is a bird and not some clever insect, among all the gray mottled branches and dark leaves. I wait. When it finally sallies out to crack open a beetle I've dislodged from somewhere, I recognize it as another flycatcher, but I can't guess which one. I make a mental note of its likeness—small, gray on back, white on breast, fleshtone lower beast—so I can look it up after my walk. Of one thing I'm certain—I haven't seen it before now.

Birdwatching in prison gives me reason to leave my cell. There's always the possibility of a new flycatcher to draw my mind away from the heavy aspect of this place and connect me to something untamed by these fences. If not a flycatcher, then a new hawk or owl—or even a new behavior from an everyday bird. While walking my circular course, I may not expect much, but I keep my mouth shut and listen more. I watch more. And whenever I see a flash of wings, an unfamiliar profile, or hear a warble, my senses narrow down to a point. I don't just see or hear but *notice.* When a flycatcher cracks open a beetle I'm involved. It's what I need here. I've decided it's more important, this embrace with nature, than even my freedom. What's freedom without participating in life?

In the evening I complete my daily routine: ten laps, five miles. I don't *notice* the sharp-shinned hawk, but I'm not discouraged. I have time. I have many more miles. (One year I walked more than 1,500, imagining I was unwinding every one of those 3,000-plus laps and hiking cross-country toward Canada. Whenever the wind curled through the needles of the Japanese black pines in the administration area, I could almost transport myself onto a forested spine of the Rocky Mountains.) For now, I'll hold onto whatever grace sends my way: today, if not a sharp- shinned hawk, then a flock of red-breasted house finches strung along the perimeter fence like Christmas lights, or the lonely cry of a young phoebe seemingly as homesick as I am, or something entirely new, like a never-before-seen gray flycatcher, its secretive, half-whispered *cheet* held in my mind.

from *Snowy Egret*

Wild Apples

Barbara Drake

Below our vineyard is a brushy area which when we first moved to the farm I tended to think of as a narrow border or hedge, a small place. It was difficult to get in to look around because some former owner had bulldozed an old prune orchard off the hill and pushed the dirt and brush into a rough line across the property. This line of dirt and stumps had grown up in blackberries, wild rose, and hawthorn, presenting a thorny thicket that defied entry until Bill took the tractor and a machete and alternately mowed and hacked a gateway into the brush. Stepping through the hedge for the first time, I had the elevated, free feeling I get from my recurrent dream about finding a secret room in an old house, the realm of newly discovered possibilities.

Beyond the thicket the brushy area turned out to be large, about four or five acres, not merely a hedgerow at all, and while some parts were impenetrable, much of it consisted of a maze of tiny meadows defined by a variety of trees and bushes. Much of the larger growth turned out to be apple trees. It was spring when I first stepped through to the secret side of the hedge and found myself meandering down alleys of flowering trees, fragrant and electrically alive with the sound of bees.

Spring went by and the apple blossoms turned to little green knobs, then apples. Summer went by and the apples took on various shapes and colors. In late September, I decided to spend a day tasting apples. At first I had thought the apple trees were the remains of an overgrown domestic orchard, but then I realized they were wild seedlings in an amazing variety. Apple trees for domestic and commercial use are produced by grafting the desirable scion onto a suitable root stock, to get predictable results. Thus the fruiting branches are clones of the mother tree.

On the other hand, apples grown from seed, like those in our wild patch, are highly unpredictable. You don't know which ancestors they will resemble. They may be attractive and good tasting, but they also may be runty, warty, hard little objects that pucker the mouth like a dose of alum, dry out the tongue with astringency, and leave a lingering bitterness. The variety in the hidden grove made it clear that these were apples that had been left to their own devices.

Tasting wild apples one begins to realize how many factors play a part in the enjoyment of a good apple. I thought of what I might find. Color: red, yellow, or green; blushing, solid, or streaked. Heft: the weight in the hand that signals the density and juiciness of the apple meat. Character of skin: russet or smooth, tough or fine, waxy or squeaky clean. Taste: sour or sweet or bitter, resonant in the mouth or flat and insipid. Fragrance: suggestive of honey or lemons, strawberries or bananas, willow bark or grape seeds. The way the apple releases or does not release its juice when you bite it. Whether it is pulpy or mushy, or cracks with a satisfying crunch. And beyond the immediate sensation of eating the apple itself are qualities such as whether it's a keeper or not, the time of ripening, whether it bruises easily, and how well it resists pests and disease. Clearly I was in for an adventure.

I took a pack with colored pens and pencils, a small notebook, my camera bag, tripod, and coffee, hollered for the dogs, and set off for my secret orchard. To begin this wild apple adventure, I decided to use my camera. The process of photographing can sharpen observation. As I became engrossed in the process of framing images, changing lenses to move up on the fruit, changing again to get the wide shape and pattern of a tree studded with red or yellow pomes, I began to see how really different the many apples were. Some were pure yellow and small, only a couple of inches across. These tended to be abundant on the tree and bitter tasting. They are the kind you see in hedges in midwinter, still hanging, like ornaments, on a leafless tree. Some were longer and narrower; others were squat and fat, almost wider than they were long from stem to blossom end. Some were green with a purplish cheek and others were heavily russeted. One pretty little apple was such a pale green it looked almost white and had bright red cheeks. Had I been naming it, I would have called it Snow White or Candy Cane. As I looked through my camera at close range, I enjoyed focusing on the ones where the red streaking consisted of distinct stripes, particularly those where the red appeared on a background of deep waxy yellow so that the overall color of the apple seemed dark orange.

Because it was September, the leaves were starting to turn and fall from the trees, and many apples also had fallen. I had seen pheasants going in and out of the thicket and wondered whether they enjoyed the apples. Here and there were the droppings of deer and of squirrels, and I saw a downy woodpecker traveling along one dead branch scattering moss and bark in his excavations. Surely all this fallen fruit could feed a variety of creatures. In spite of all the apples on the ground, the trees still were covered with fruit. I wondered how old the trees actually were. Some of them were good sized but others were small and poorly grown, with only a live branch or two jutting out at a strange angle, holding a clutch of apples. Many of these smaller trees had more dead limbs than live ones, and the whole tree was covered with a heavy growth I supposed was lichen, dry and whitish grey now, but which I knew would gather moisture and flourish in the wet western Oregon winter. Besides the lichen, the trees were draped with brambles and cheek to cheek with hawthorns covered by dark red haws. Great bunches of wild rose briars, with orange and red hips, thrust up and blended with the apple branches, so that the trees looked ancient and hoary and tangled like an illustration from an old book of fairytales.

I used up a couple of rolls of film. The day was hot and I was beginning to feel it as I moved through the protected little meadows, so I decided it was time to begin my taste testing. I picked as wide a variety of apples as I could reach without getting into the poison oak (another element in the tangle of brush), and dropped them—about thirty-five or forty altogether—in a comfortable grassy spot where I could sit in the shade and concentrate. Looking upon the variety they presented, I remembered reading that the ancient Romans described and recognized thirty-seven domestic types of apples. I also had heard that in the original apple forest, in southwest Asia, in the Caucasus region, there were well over three thousand varieties of wild apple. I wondered to what extent the wild genes in my apples had reconstituted those early assortments.

I told Mollie and Jack, our border collies, to sit down and pay attention, and they threw themselves into a shady thicket and stretched out with panting grins as I continued my apple meditations. A small airplane flew over, dipped low, circled around, and came back over my clearing as if to see what I was up to, and then, having taken his glimpse of Eden, the pilot flew on.

I had decided that if I found a wild tree with especially good apples I would tie a rag to one of its branches, to mark it out for future use and observation. There were, after all, at least two hundred wild trees in this little acreage.

One by one I would choose a particular apple, make a quick sketch of it with colored pencil, and then write a description of it in the margins of the drawing. The first apple I chose was a yellow one, not very tasty but not inedible. Its appearance interested me because the lenticels, or pores, on its skin were lighter than the yellow of the skin itself and gave the apple's surface a shimmering, pearlescent appearance that reminded me of boiling sugar. Pretty, but nothing to tie a flag on. The second apple was a wonderful surprise. It was large as wild apples go, the size of a baseball. It was a waxy yellow with a heavy overlay of red striping, like certain varieties of French apples, and had pronounced ribs that gave the whole apple a scalloped appearance. I wondered whether the undulations of its shape were genetic or due to some warping disease. The meat cracked pleasantly when I bit into it and the flesh inside was golden yellow, very juicy, fragrant, and distinctive. I didn't see any worm holes but after I had eaten most of it I broke the core in two to get a look at the seeds and found that some Epicurean critter dining there had reduced the seeds to a fine dust of black droppings. I decided I would definitely tie a flag on this tree to keep track of it, as it was an apple I would find a treat in any company.

The next apple was green with a purplish blush. It had a particularly hard, smooth look. I held it in my hand and stared at it, trying to be alert to its character, and it seemed like a smooth and placid face—a pacific, contained, nun-like apple. I took a bite. It was not fully ripe but its taste and its dense, firm flesh indicated it would be a good keeper, a late, winter apple compared to my delicious scalloped apple which obviously was at the height of its taste and condition. This keeper, my nun-apple, looked evenly spaced on the tree, uniform in size, regular in form and color, almost like a cultivated apple. I gave it a flag.

I tasted many other apples, but most I was happy to cede to the wildlife. I found that I could not predict from the appearance of an apple how it would taste. One tree bore nice red fruit whose appearance made me expect something like a small Jonathan, but the apples were nasty tasting in the extreme. Another tree had apples that were green and hard looking and markedly ovoid in shape, but the meat was wonderfully sweet, pale yellow, with darker yellow honey spots growing even sweeter near the core and no apparent pests or disease.

I almost skipped the tiny crab apples from one small tree that already had lost almost all its leaves because the apples were so tiny and purplish green, their skin matte-looking and covered by a dusty bloom. The apples hung in groups of four at the ends of long, red, wire-like stems and were about the size of large marbles, but I decided to try them while I was at it and was surprised and delighted that they were crunchy and juicy, with clear yellow flesh and a sweet lemony taste with no hint of bitterness at all. The core was small and contained perfect clean little seeds, almost black in color.

It was late in the afternoon when I picked up my bag of pencils and other gear. The restless dogs took off running toward the house as soon as I stood up. Before I stepped through the hedge and back into the order of the vineyard with its vines and trellises, I looked around, and in every direction, gleaming in the yellow sunlight, I saw the temptation of farther apples, more apples. I wanted to taste them all.

Uphill I saw the neat rows of the vineyard serving our human designs. Downhill was the chaotic beauty of wild groves. What a misbehaving, divided mind I have, approving of tidy gardens and fenced pastures, yet feeling such glee that wild apples have their own ineffable plans, if only we leave them alone.

from Peace at Heart

A Wild and Fierce Freedom

David Petersen

We are huffing up Glacier National Park's ungodly steep Loop Trail, a friend and I, bulging packs chafing our sweaty backs. Having launched this little adventure from a scenic pullout along the park's eye-popping Going-to-the-Sun Road, we are headed for a place called Granite Park. Up where the grizzer bears roam.

Back home in Colorado, we have so few grizzlies left (perhaps none) that they seem more like ghosts than bears. So I've come here to Glacier, on the northern border of Montana and these United States of America, in hopes of observing a few of these beautiful monsters where they still exist in relatively healthy, albeit dwindling numbers. To facilitate and enliven the quest, I've enlisted as my guide former park bear manager Neal Wedum, who animates our hike with item after item from his bottomless bag of "Gee whiz!" bear-scare stories.

Like the time he was patrolling a remote park trail and heard a crunching sound somewhere above him. "I looked up," he says, "into the eyes of the biggest bear I've ever seen. The boar grizzly was lying behind a clump of brush on a little bench maybe fifty feet above the trail, its head raised and looking right at me. A big chunk of bloody meat sagged from his jaws and saliva drooled from his muzzle. The adrenaline rush almost knocked me off my feet. My first thought was that the bear was eating a hiker, and having surprised him on his meal, I'd be dessert."

Wedum kept walking, even as he slipped the safety off his canister of OC-10 (i.e., 10 percent oleocapsicum) pepper spray. Not stopping or running was apparently the right move, because the behemoth bear merely watched intently until the interloper had passed on down the trail and out of sight.

When safely beyond the threat, Wedum did what only a seasoned backcountry ranger and grizzly expert should attempt and climbed through a finger of subalpine firs leading up the cliff to a narrow shelf, then worked cautiously across until he was directly above the feeding bear. "I had to know," he says, attempting to explain away such flagrant temerity, "what was being eaten. Or who."

The carnivore's feast turned out to be a full-curl bighorn ram. "The sheep probably died in a fall and the grizzly's nose led him to it. Bears can't catch healthy bighorns, but they can smell a dead one from miles away."

After radioing instructions that the trail be closed a safe distance either side of the danger, Wedum eased back down the slope, keeping to the trees, then inched forward until he was watching the feasting boar from what, in retrospect, was "too damn close." Just as Neal was becoming almost relaxed in the presence of this six hundred (or more) pounds of teeth, claws, and muscle, and with no warning whatsoever, the bear exploded down the hill directly toward him, ending the bluff charge just twenty feet from one badly shaken park ranger.

"That," Wedum recalls, "pretty much got my attention."

The canister of pepper spray had long since been returned to its holster, the safety clip replaced. "No matter," my hiking companion tells me now. "I wouldn't have had time to spray that bear even if I'd had the canister in my hand; he came that fast."

The panting grizzly glared at the interloper for "a real long time," then turned and shuffled back up the slope toward its meat cache . . . only to whirl and charge again, this time getting bad-breath close before abruptly stopping.

"He was so near I could *feel* his breath as well as smell it. The look on his face was clearly saying, 'OK, pal, I've warned you twice. Now move along or you're lunch meat.' I moved along."

And so do we, ever up.

A little farther along, Wedum points to some scuff marks on a slender birch tree. "Right here," says my cheerful tour guide, "is where a down-trail hiker ran into a grizzly sow with two cubs. The man started up this little tree, his boots scuffing the bark as he clamped his feet to the trunk and attempted to climb. He didn't quite make it. That old sow grabbed him by a leg, bit deep into his calf, yanked him down, and slapped him around just enough to get her message across: 'Don't mess with my cubs.' He was lucky—able to walk out."

Yes, *such* luck.

&

Most every summer for God only recalls how many years now, I've wheedled the time and money for a Glacier camping vacation. Because the Northern Continental Divide Ecosystem, of which Glacier is the beating heart, still shelters representative samples of all of its most magnificent native megafauna—grizzlies, wolves, wolverines, moose, wapiti, bighorns, mountain goats, ospreys, eagles, loons—by my lights, it's the most magic-filled place in the Lower 48.

Here Caroline and I come to hike, camp, fish, canoe, graze on bush-ripened berries, make love amongst the ferns and mosquitoes, and lie awake in wonder at the haunting calls of loons and, yes, wolves. And we frequently manage to scare ourselves sleepless conjuring up toothy monsters *out there* in the vast blackness just beyond the gossamer walls of our tent. Thus is generated the spiritual voltage that electrifies the Glacier backcountry experience.

This time, I've come to crank that voltage to the max, and a finer grizzly guide than Neal Wedum I'd be strapped to find: native northwestern Montanan, Glacier backcountry ranger for eighteen years, bear management team leader for six.

At five-foot-nine, 155 pounds, and half a century old, Neal Wedum remains the unlikely champion "human mule" of Glacier Park, having backpacked loads as heavy as 120 pounds into these precipitous old mountains—wearing sport sandals, no less. Once, he and a fellow ranger bet a case of beer with a wrangler that, working in relays, they could backpack a seventy-pound, four-foot-long steel propane tank (full) up the Loop Trail four miles to Granite Park faster than a mule. They won. Even now, Neal's oversized backpack is bulging with such wilderness "necessities" as a 703-page hardbound copy of *Mahatma Gandhi*. Heavy reading.

&

While breaking for lunch on a ledge with a million-dollar view (they're a dime a dozen here), we're passed by a couple of unburdened day hikers whose approach is announced by the annoying tinkle of cheap copper "bear bells."

Local wisdom: How do you tell the difference between grizzly and black bear scats? The grizzly flops are the big ones with the bells in them.

Jangling through the boonies like some amplified Tinkerbell is anathema to my notion of a quality wilderness experience. Yet I understand the park's motivation for encouraging backcountry hikers to engage in singing, whooping, loud talking, and Tinkerbelling: a surprise run-in with a grizzly could spell disaster for all involved. When Neal and I hike Glacier together (this isn't the first time), we talk as the mood strikes us, maybe a little louder than necessary sometimes, but staunchly eschew the hackneyed shouts of "Hey, bear!" that so frequently disturb the otherwise sublime tranquility of this Pleistocene wonderland, trusting our safety instead to Neal's highly cultivated "nose" for pending grizzly danger.

"After a while," he'll tell you, "you get to where you can sense a grizzly presence, like some people can sense an approaching storm or an earthquake." Must be true: my old pal Peacock feels it too, as do an experienced handful of others. As we pass through a small clearing resplendent with glacier lilies, giant cow parsnips, big lacy beargrass plumes, and Indian paintbrush red as lust, Neal says casually, "We call this place Mauling Meadow."

I daren't ask why.

A little farther along, we come to the spot where Glacier's most recent and perplexing grizzly disaster was acted out—the mauling death of John Petranyi, age forty, killed and fed upon by a grizzly sow and her two subadult cubs.

On the morning of October 3, 1992, Petranyi was hiking alone down this selfsame Loop Trail after spending the night at the Granite Park backcountry campground. He apparently surprised the bears at close range on or near the trail. The sow did what grizzly mothers are programmed by natural selection to do in such instances and launched a preemptive assault on this sudden threat to her cubs.

Evidence suggests the sow broke off her attack and retreated after giving Petranyi only a light mauling, which is fairly common. Perhaps, had he played dead until the bears were good and gone, he might have saved himself. But Petranyi apparently attempted to flee—perhaps calling for help as he ran—thus exciting the bears' prey-pursuit instincts and provoking a second attack. This time, for reasons we may never understand, the grizzlies dragged Petranyi to a nearby wooded promontory and . . .

A few days later, following multiagency consultations, the offending bear family was hunted down and killed.

It's hard to keep such horrifying incidents from creeping into your dreams when camping in Glacier, especially in the backcountry. Yet, when you consider the intensity of the overlapping populations of humans (about two million visitors annually) and grizzlies (at least two hundred) here, and when you crank in the unforgivable rudeness and blatant *stupidity* of many park visitors—stashing food and smelly trash in their tents, hiking alone after dark, intentionally approaching and harassing bears, and in countless other ways trolling for trouble— all such things considered, it's a wonder, a gift in fact, that Glacier's grizzlies show the remarkable tolerance they do.

Which is to say: since its creation in 1910, the park has known just nine deaths by grizzly, with six of the nine being attributed to human-habituated "garbage bears," a threat park officials go to great lengths these days to minimize by trucking out trash and enforcing strict backcountry food-handling regulations. "A fed bear is a dead bear," we often hear. A fed bear could also be a dead camper, but that doesn't rhyme.

Maulings and other physical encounters with bears are less uncommon yet still average only two per summer; a visitor's odds of being chomped by a Glacier grizzly are roughly one in a million.

To put all of this in perspective: in a lifetime of hiking the park's backcountry, on trail and off, including many intentional, line-of-duty encounters with known "problem" bears, Neal Wedum has been bluff-charged six times, treed twice, and never even scratched by a grizzly. So far. Across those same years, he's helped to save the lives of several people seriously injured by falls and other park mishaps far more common but far less glamorous or newsworthy than bear attacks.

&

We're nearing Granite Park campground now, finally, and my guide feels moved to assure me of its safety.

"I've spent entire nights sitting on a hill above here, looking down on this ridge with a military starlight scope. Grizzlies come and go along the natural travel corridors on either side all night long, only a few dozen yards below campers and tents, ignoring them completely. So long as folks obey the rules, it's as safe a camp as you can have in intense grizzly country."

Most reassuring.

The original Granite Park campground—a tiny meadow bisected by the Loop Trail and now restored to the grizzly travel corridor and feeding site nature intended it to be—was a different story. It was there, just after midnight on the bad night of August 13, 1967, that park employee Julie Hegelson was dragged from her sleeping bag and fatally mauled by a grizzly. Julie's male companion was also attacked, but survived. The sow identified as the culprit had been hanging around Granite Park for years, attracted by garbage and handouts.

Didn't park officials know that they'd located the campground on a natural bear runway? "No," says Neal. "They didn't worry about such things back then. There had never been a grizzly-caused death in the fifty-seven-year history of the park, and they assumed the bears were benign."

Incredibly, that same night in 1967, at a popular backcountry camp called Trout Lake, another young camper, Michele Koons, was killed by another "garbage bear." This tragic coincidence supplied the meat for Jack Olsen's adrenalizing *Night of the Grizzlies*—a book you may not want to read just before visiting a place like Glacier or Yellowstone.

The new Granite Park campground, where we're now resting, consists of four tent sites staggered along a narrow timbered ridge with spectacular views in every direction, an open-air privy, a food preparation area, and two high, hook-topped poles from which to suspend food bags. No campfires allowed.

"The only animal problems we've had here," says Neal, "are deer brushing against tents at night. Scares hell out of folks."

I can't imagine why.

When my quadriceps have quit burning from the hike in, we head up the mountain to the medieval-looking Granite Park Chalet—a wilderness oxymoron written in native stone. This stately old building was built in 1914 and for decades offered modest but sturdy backcountry shelter and home-cooked meals to hikers. In 1987, the Chalet was designated a National Historic Landmark—only to be closed recently due to water, sewage, maintenance, and political problems. The structure is being renovated even now and the park intends to reopen it as soon as possible.

Which will be none too soon for Neal Wedum, who voices a popular local sentiment when he remarks that "the Chalet is as much a part of the Glacier tradition as the bears and the mountains. And the huckleberry pies they baked here were the best in the world. I had a deal with the baker: I'd bring her fresh huckleberries in exchange for free pie. Once, a friend and I went picking and found a couple of huge fresh grizzly scats loaded with perfect berries—bears have really inefficient guts, and what doesn't get chewed usually doesn't get digested. Feeling ornery, we picked out all the whole berries, washed them thoroughly in a creek, and took them back to the Chalet. The baker made two pies, which the staff ate and raved about."

Did the baker know the history of those berries?

"I may have forgotten to mention it."

Did Neal have a slice of this delicious huckleberry griz-scat pie?

"No way!"

Whether you're for or against the Chalet's presence here, the cloud-piercing promontory upon which it sits offers one of the most sublime mountain vistas in the known universe, was well as frequently lucrative grizzly watching. That's why I've lugged along a spotting scope, which I now train down upon a sprawling subalpine vale south of Granite Park—a mile-square bowlful of grizzly paradise appropriately named Bear Valley.

But in three hours of hard glassing I see nary a single hair of bear. What I do see is enough faulted, folded, upthrust and tilted, glaciated, and splendorous ancient seabed scenery to fuel a lifetime of burning nostalgia, all backdropped by the distant slender veil of Bird Woman Falls. Between her and me, a lone golden eagle, aloof and insouciant, hangs without effort on some invisible thermal. How I envy her.

Losing hope, I make one last perusal of the vallyey before breaking for dinner and—hot damn!—spot a huge dark animal loafing across a big gray slab of granite.

I whoop and Neal joins me, and for the next several minutes we watch the bear as it feeds among the quiltwork of tiny meadows, turns over rocks and rips apart fallen logs looking for insects, digs for roots, melts into then reappears from dense copses of subalpine spruce and fir, and otherwise indulges and enjoys its wild and fierce freedom. The animal is an extremely dark glossy brown with massive muscles that ripple visibly with every step. The late afternoon sun glints on tiny eyes as hard and impenetrable as obsidian.

Here, I reflect, is the flesh-and-fur incarnation of the wildness in which Thoreau advised resides the preservation of the world. The preservation of *my* world, at least.

Suddenly, the big grizzly breaks from feeding, looks back over its left shoulder, then sprints away at racehorse speed, disappearing into the trees. We spend the next hour in a fruitless search for whatever it was that had frightened away a bear so huge you'd think it would run from nothing smaller than a T-Rex. Just another of nature's invigorating mysteries.

🚲

The night is cold and happily uneventful. I rise at dawn and retire to the Chalet to resume my magnified search for grizzlies. Neal soon joins me and we decide to invest the midmorning in hiking the Highline Trail—a major backcountry park byway that traces along just below the Continental Divide—checking out, through our binoculars, pockets of habitat Wedum knows to be frequented by bears.

"What grizzlies like, what they *need*," my friend explains as we walk, calling on his master's education in biology and lifetime of field experience, "is room to move, clean water, dense woods to shelter in, and plenty of high-calorie, easily digestible food."

In Glacier country, the most important bear foods are huckleberries in the fall and glacier lilies (better known as avalanche lilies in the Southern Rockies) spring through summer.

Glacier lilies: grizzlies dig these yellow mountain lovelies by the hundreds for their marble-sized, white-meated, starch-rich root bulbs, while attentive hikers appreciate the little pixies for their cheerful beauty and the sublime surroundings in which they erupt by the thousands—subalpine meadows and alpine tundra.

After an hour or so of speed walking—I can maintain Neal's killer pace for a while, but not forever—we spot a series of bear digs starting just below the trail. We drop down to investigate, finding the open slope pocked with scores of grizzly excavations. Neal explains that shovel-sized clumps of sod flipped over in digs a few inches deep and up to a hundred square feet in area are the spoor of grizzlies grubbing for roots. More impressive but less common are sometimes waist-deep pits with rocks big as basketballs tossed out, where some meat-hungry bear has backhoed after a ground squirrel or marmot.

Obviously, bear digs are important signs to recognize, and to avoid, when selecting a campsite in grizzly country.

Onward, to a place called Ahern Pass, where a lingering snow slide blocks further progress. Just beyond, Neal points out the shelf where, three years before, he met his ram-eating boar.

Good place for a break.

We're sitting and talking and glassing for wildlife when a lone young hiker comes striding up the trail behind us, says "Howdy," sits down, and hauls from his outsized pack climbing boots, crampons, and ice ax. My conviction that, with so much youthful confidence and such fine equipment, he'll breeze painlessly across the slide is given the lie within his first few steps, when the young man slips, goes rocketing down the ice and out across several feet of exposed scree shards before managing a last-second ax-arrest a foot short of plunging over the cliff's edge to certain, absolute, immutable death. Undaunted, the young man stands—his right hand and leg are smeared with blood—grins, shrugs, and continues on, somewhat more carefully now. We hold our collective breath until he makes it safely across.

This incident prompts Neal to comment that when people think of danger in Glacier, they invariably think of grizzlies. Yet bears rank way down the line as killers here, trailing drownings (48), heart attacks (27), car crashes (25), falls while hiking (21) and climbing accidents (18), for a total of 9 deaths by grizzly alongside 138 from other causes since 1913.

"I have friends," says Neal, "who've hiked and camped in Glacier for thirty years and have never even *seen* a grizzly."

Only, I think, because they weren't looking for them.

It's midafternoon by the time we return to our Granite Park digs, where we dally just long enough to raid our food bags for snacks before scrambling down to a secluded promontory on a rocky lip directly above Bear Valley. Any grizzlies seen from here, I reckon, will be plenty close enough.

And the *view*—the aptly named Heaven's Peak dominates the west, the jagged rampart of the Garden Wall saws at the sky along the eastern horizon, Logan Pass (the highest paved point on any park road) lies low in the south, with Oberlin, Reynolds, Clements, Cannon, and other rocky spires jutting up in wild and glorious disarray all around. Purple mountains, majesty, you bet.

We glass intently, but soon grow woozy under the warm July sun; only the incessant pestering of mosquitoes and carnivorous deer flies keeps us awake.

"Once," says my droopy-eyed companion, "on a day just like today, I came down here, right here, and fell asleep. A couple of hours later I was awakened by splashing noises from that little pond over there." Neal gestures to a tiny pool no more than fifty yards away, shallow and lucent and surrounded by an earthly heaven of beargrass, purple gentian, shooting stars, mountain bluebells, and dandelions. "When I opened my eyes, I was looking at a sow and two cubs playing in the water. Didn't have any trouble staying awake after that."

A big black-and-gray Clark's nutcracker dives in and perches atop a perfect little Christmas tree just below us, scolding, it seems, our very existence. Moments later, the resident eagle appears at the far edge of the valley, as if summoned by the Clark's ill-tempered scolds: a six-foot feathered exclamation point written on a flawless firmament.

After two hours of sun, scenery, and bugs, but no bears, we groan to our feet and chug up-mountain to the backcountry ranger quarters, located adjacent to the Chalet and currently occupied by a burly, red-headed ex-Marine named Kim Peach, a mate of Neal's from the bear management team.

And wouldn't you know it, even as we arrive, Ranger Peach spots a grizzly—directly below the promontory we abandoned only minutes ago.

For the next half hour we watch as this big, ruddy bruin with a muzzle the color of parchment and silvery guard hairs across its camel-humped shoulders browses, noses around, and digs.

At one point, having found a particularly dense patch of glacier lilies, the bear settles back onto his ample haunches and uses both front paws—through my scope I can see the ivory claws clearly, as thick and long as a big man's fingers—to roll back a huge wad of turf, which he lifts to his muzzle and nibbles . . . like a squirrel with a pinecone or a fat man eating corn on the cob. We are all saddened when this entertaining beast eventually wanders into the trees and fails to reappear.

After a ho-hum dinner of boil-in-the-pouch turkey and dressing, Neal and I return to our vigil; our time up here is running out. Within ten minutes—I can't believe the luck—Neal has yet another bear under glass.

This one, like the previous two, is big and fat, weighing maybe four hundred pounds. But unlike the others, both of which were dark, this animal has hair the color of autumn grain, the classic grizzly pelage. I'm acutely aware that this lovely blond beast, if properly provoked, could rip my lungs out with a single swipe of clawsome paw. Yet I feel a baffling affection for and desire to get closer to "her." A potentially fatal attraction.

But before that foolish urge can be acted on, the fearsome beauty steps into the long evening shadows and dissolves into the foggy realm of memory.

Just before dark, four sweaty day-hikers straggle in, looking for a privy. When they seem in no hurry to leave, the residual park ranger in Neal suggests that they get the hell on down the trail as fast as possible without running, keeping close together and making *lots* of noise. They shrug, not apparently appreciating the sagacity of this advice, but soon move on. If they knew the history of the Loop Trail, I reflect, they'd sprout wings and fly down. They just might anyhow (as angels).

Come morning, our third and last here at Granite Park, we hike back down to the sunny, soporific promontory of the splashing bears, hoping for one more glimpse of that gorgeous blond grizzly. But the local bruins are sleeping late—or, more likely, have bedded early—and visions of huckleberry milkshakes down at Apgar Village are growing ever more compelling (I'll make damn sure they don't get their berries from Wedum).

After a couple of uneventful hours, we climb back up to Granite Park, pack our packs, and point our sunburnt noses reluctantly down the mountain. Even though he's spent hundreds of nights up here, Neal is overtly sad to leave, explaining that "It gets in your blood."

Does it ever.

We make a fast hike down—past the disquieting Petranyi mauling site, through the erstwhile Night of the Grizzlies campground and the florid Mauling Meadow, past the boot-scuffed grizzly tree.

About a mile from trail's end, Neal, hiking ahead of me as always, stops suddenly and whispers, "Look here." I look, and there amidst the grasses, ferns, and giant cow parsnips just off the trail is a hot-fresh grizzly dig. And another. And a third.

"Those weren't here when we came up the other day," says I.

Neal drops to his knees and examines the dark, damp soil, the torn vegetation. "No," he agrees. "These digs are no more than a few hours old, made last night or early this morning."

I have a good look around, fingering the canister of bear spray holstered on my belt, before stooping for a closer look. In the largest of the excavations, I find a big twisted heap of bear scat, green-white with undigested roots of glacier lily, odorless, and so shockingly fresh it's still warm and oozing moisture.

A quarter-mile farther along, we find a second series of recent digs; clearly, this bear was walking the trail. I think of those four cocky hikers of last night and shiver. By the time they could have gotten this far, down deep in the belly of this forest prime-evil (sic), the night would have been black as death. And this bear must have already been in the immediate neighborhood, as it probably is still.

Had there been an "incident" here last night, to whom would the media and public sentiment attach the blame—blatantly careless hikers or a "killer grizzly"?

Neal Wedum is suffering similar thoughts. "If only people could learn to cut bears as much slack as bears cut us," he says, "grizzlies wouldn't be an endangered species."

I'm reminded of something Doug Peacock said not long ago, as we sat in his Sonoran Desert backyard and sipped Black Jack on ice while half-tame Gambel's quail and mourning doves foraged and peeped and cooed all around us. "If we can't be big enough to set aside a few last-ditch preserves for a species as intelligent, magnificent, and humanlike as the grizzly," Doug mused, "we have little chance of long-term survival as a species; we'll destroy nature, then we'll destroy ourselves."

Doug clearly is a pessimist. And you know what they say about pessimists: they're optimists in possession of the facts.

from *The Nearby Faraway:*
A Personal Journey Through the Heart of the West

Saving Tibet

Natasha Ma (pseudonym)

I awaken with a jolt. I've had another dream, inspired by memory no doubt: a rare snow leopard pelt is hanging on the wall behind the couch where my Chinese boss is sitting. I am back in Lhasa, teaching English at the Tibetan Academy of Social Sciences. I have been called in to be reprimanded by the head of the school. He tells me I must stop asking my students to write essays about how their land has changed since the "Chinese liberation." I tell him that I saw a tiger pelt and horns of the endangered Tibetan antelope in the marketplace yesterday. This is wrong, I say. Your people must stop this before everything is destroyed. In my dream, he appears to be listening. But I always wake up before he tells me I must leave Tibet.

I will never know for sure why I was not allowed to return for another semester of teaching, but I know I cannot forget the people and land I grew to love while I lived among them. I was drawn to teach English in Tibet not only to help an endangered culture but to experience its fragile high-altitude ecosystem. Previously, I had spent four years living among the Chinese in Macau who have no qualms about using rare and endangered species for their herbal cures and aphrodisiacs. I had cried over owls in cages outside of Macau's back-alley restaurants. What a delightful change to live among a people who regard all life as sacred. Even the death of an insect inspires feelings of compassion.

Tibetans traditionally have shown the utmost respect for the environment, refusing to kill even a fly or a mosquito. Nearly five decades of Chinese occupation and influence have brought many changes, and some young Tibetans today might lack the reverence their elders paid to nature and all her creatures. Yet for the most part, Tibetans remain a gentle people, as endangered as their environment.

In 1989 a Nobel citation for the first time specifically referred to the ecological crisis. The recipient of the Peace Prize that year—christened Lhamo Dhondrup, renamed Tenzin Gyatso, better known to the world as the 14th Dalai Lama—has a dream for his illegally occupied homeland. Tibet's exiled spiritual and temporal leader envisions Tibet one day being transformed into a free refuge where humanity and nature can live in peaceful, harmonious balance.

Before the Chinese invasion of 1950, Tibetan Buddhist compassion successfully protected Tibet's environment: all life is sacred and only to be taken when necessary for survival. But the Chinese forced even small children to kill animals and turn over the carcasses to authorities.

One-fourth of the world's population lives downstream from Tibet's impending environmental disaster. The Chinese have built a hydroelectric dam that may dry out one of Tibet's largest lakes within fifty years. Dozens of other dams are being planned for Tibet's rivers, source of all of Asia's major rivers. About one billion Chinese, Indians, and Bangladeshis whose rivers originate in Tibet are in danger.

Clearcutting places the endangered giant panda and golden monkey—and five thousand plant species—-in peril. Gold miners destroy Tibetan herdsmen's rich grazing land. Pastureland is threatened by overdevelopment. Sacred sites are mined for uranium. Tibetan nomads are exposed to radiation from nuclear testing and dumping. Unrestricted Chinese hunting and poaching leaves many species near extinction. Wild yaks and Tibetan antelope are being reduced to tragic remnants, just like the American buffalo was.

When I arrived in Tibet the first time, a hint of springtime hovered in the March air. Prayer flags waved over the dry, brown plains of southern Tibet and over the snow-covered mountain passes. Icicles clung to rocks, and snow blanketed the highlands while the high-altitude sun warmed my chilled body. Purple-tinged, snowcapped mountains reflected in crystal-clear lakes. Yaks dotted the landscape and peaks, as stoic as stone lions guarding ancient Taoist temples in Macau. Yet in three days of traveling overland from Lhasa, the capital city, to the Nepal border, I saw no other wildlife.

In 1981, when nature/adventure photographer Galen Rowell walked for three weeks covering over one hundred miles in the Anye Machin

Mountains of northeastern Tibet, he saw virtually no wildlife. That same year Pema Gyalpo, sister of the Dalai Lama, traveled eight thousand miles overland in three months and saw none of the gazelles, deer, and antelope she'd seen before 1959.

Tibetans have always seen their wild animals as symbolizing freedom. The last words of Milarepa, Tibet's foremost poet-hermit who died in 1123, were

> *Do if you like that which may seem sinful,*
> *But help living beings,*
> *Because that is truly pious work.*

All of Tibet was environmentally protected for thirteen hundred years of Buddhist rule. No need existed for national parks. But unrestricted Chinese hunting now has left wild animals only in remote areas, such as the northern plains of the Changtang, the arid valleys of western Tibet, and the alpine grasslands of uninhabited parts of Amdo and Kham. Yet Tibetans have faith that nearly extinct species can recover if the Buddhist environmental ethic is reordained.

Buddhism, with its fostering of compassion, still does not account entirely for the Tibetans' respect for the environment. The Japanese and the Thai, although devout Buddhists, lack an all-pervading reverence for nature. The Tibetans' unique environment (vast area, low population, and distant neighbors) has strongly influenced them. Their attitude of contentment controls their consumption. They admire simple living. While living among them, I envied their ability to laugh and be happy in oppressive circumstances. Year after year they have watched their land and their wildlife suffer at the hands of their oppressors. Perhaps this environmental abuse has been as hard for them to bear as that inflicted on their own minds and bodies.

No doubt remains that the Chinese are destroying Tibet's ecosystem and culture. Many insist that we must be patient with China, but how long must we wait? How long must Tibet wait? And what if we wait too long and there is nothing—and no one—left to save? Like Black Americans in the sixties, Tibetans give many reasons why they cannot wait any longer for freedom and justice. They have waited too long already. More than one-sixth of their population of 1.5 million have spent their lives, others their youth, waiting.

Ultimately, it is a question of morality. The United States condemned the Soviet action in Afghanistan and responded with sanctions, while not reacting in similar fashion to the no less drastic action taken by China in Tibet. Surely moral principle is not what determines our government's reactions. Yet the question of morality is at the very heart of the matter of environmental abuse. Abuse and destruction of the environment result from ignorance, greed, and a lack of respect for earth's living things. The Chinese may kill rhinos, tigers, seals, and snow leopards because of their selfish desires for herbal cures and aphrodisiacs—but they are not the only ones lacking a sense of universal responsibility. Indeed, there are those on every continent and from every ethnic group who lack a sense of personal and national responsibility. Yet untimately love and compassion are needed if we are to save the environment. Gluttony, waste, and indifference must have no place. We may be forced to sacrifice some of our creature comforts and conveniences. We will be pulled into the political arena, where issues of ecology, economy, and politics overlap. The world grows ever smaller, more interdependent, and now more than ever we need a sense of universal responsibility: nation to nation, human being to fellow human being, human being to other forms of life. Yet if compassion is lacking, is there any hope?

Unfortunately, no international legal instruments exist to expressly protect occupied people's rights to their environment and natural resources. The international community did act in the case of the treatment of the people of Kuwait under Iraqi occupation during the Gulf War. Iraq was required to make contributions to the U.N. Compensation Fund to cover payment of compensation for damage caused by Iraq's invasion. The foremost environmental problems facing Tibetans today include the dumping of toxic and nuclear waste, deforestation, uranium mining, and desertification, pasture degradation. and reduction of biodiversity. Is there nothing the international community can do on their behalf?

If only we could wean the Chinese off traditional medicines and aphrodisiacs, we might be able to save several species from extinction. And if we could convince them to relinquish Tibet before their occupation destroys a culture that once lived in harmony with nature.

On the endangered list are the snow leopard and the giant panda, native of the eastern borderlands of old Tibet (in fact, the Dalai Lama says some of the captive pandas should be named Tashi or Tsering instead of Ling-ling and Mei-mei). But another name should be added to the list: the Tibetan people themselves. Surely we should work to end the slaughter of giant pandas, for whom Chinese poachers get more than $10,000 a pelt—but we must go further to work for Tibet's freedom from forty-nine years of Chinese occupation. And we must work fast. before nothing is left of Tibet's ecosystem. Even if one wanted to shy away from political matters regarding Tibet, how could she turn her back on its environmental crisis?

In considering the roots of the ecological crisis in Tibet, one realizes how much saving Tibet—in fact, saving the entire planet—depends on promoting universal responsibility, transforming economy, and liberating all peoples. Effective environmentalists must be political-social activists and moral agents of society.

First publication

Of Moose and a Moose Hunter

Franklin Burroughs

When I first moved to Maine, I think I must have assumed that moose were pretty well extinct here, like the wolf or the caribou or the Abenaki Indian. But we had scarcely been in our house a week when a neighbor called us over to see one. She had a milk cow, and a yearling moose had developed a sort of fixation on it. The moose would come to the feedlot every afternoon at dusk and lean against the fence, moving along it when the cow did, staying as close to her as possible. Spectators made it skittish, and it would roll its eyes at us nervously and edge away from the lot, but never very far. It was gangly and ungainly, it held its head high, and had a loose, disjointed, herky-jerky trot that made it look like a puppet on a string.

The young moose hung around for a couple of weeks, and it became a small ritual to walk over in the summer evenings and watch it. My neighbor, Virginia Foster, had reported it to the warden, and the warden told her not to worry: the yearling had probably been driven off by its mother when the time had come for her to calve again, and it was just looking for a surrogate. It would soon give up and wander away, he said, and he was right. But until that happened, I felt that Susan and I, at the beginning of our own quasi-rural existence, were seeing something from the absolute beginnings of all rural existence—a wild creature, baffled and intrigued by the dazzling peculiarities of humankind, was tentatively coming forward as a candidate for domestication. Mrs. Foster said that if the moose planned to hang around and mooch hay all winter, he'd damn well better expect to find himself in the traces and pulling a plough come spring.

First encounters mean a lot, and in the years that followed, moose never became for me what they are for many people in Maine: the incarnation and outward projection of that sense of wilderness and wildness that is inside you, like an emotion. As soon as I began going up into the northern part of the state whenever I could, for canoeing and trout fishing, the sight of them came to be familiar and ordinary, hardly worth mentioning. You would see one browsing along the shoulder of a busy highway or standing unconcerned in a roadside bog, while cars stopped and people got out and pointed and shutters clicked. Driving out on a rough logging road at dusk, after a day of trout fishing, you would get behind one, and it would lunge down the road ahead of you. Not wanting to panic it or cause it to hurt itself— a running moose looks out of kilter and all akimbo, like a small boy trying to ride a large bicycle—you'd stop, to allow the moose to get around the next curve, compose itself, and step out of the road. Then you'd go forward, around the curve, and there would be the moose, standing and waiting for the car to catch up to it and scare it out of its wits again. Sometimes you could follow one for half a mile like that, the moose never losing its capacity for undiluted primal horror and amazement each time the car came into sight. Finally it would turn out of the road, stand at the fringe of the woods, and, looking stricken and crestfallen as a lost dog, watch you go past.

Of course you also see them in postcard situations: belly deep in a placid pond, against a backdrop of mountains and sunset, or wading across the upper Kennebec, effortlessly keeping their feet in tumbling water that would knock a man down. Once two of them, a bull and a cow, materialized in a duck marsh as dawn came, and I watched them change from dim, looming silhouettes that looked prehistoric, like something drawn by the flickering illuminations of firelight on the walls of a cave, into things of bulk and substance, the bull wonderfully dark coated and, with his wide sweep of antlers and powerfully humped shoulders, momentarily regal.

But even when enhanced by the vast and powerful landscape they inhabit, moose remained for me animals whose ultimate context was somehow pastoral. An eighteenth- or nineteenth-century English or American landscape painting, showing cattle drinking at dusk from a gleaming river, or standing patiently in the shade of an oak, conveys a serenity that is profound and profoundly fragile. The cattle look sacred, and we know that they are not. To the extent that they epitomize mildness, peace, and contentment, they, and the paintings in which they occur, tacitly remind us that our allegiance to such virtues is qualified and unenduring, existing in the context of our historical violence, our love of excitement, motion, risk, and change. When I would be hunting or fishing, and a moose would present itself, it would not seem to come out of the world of predator and prey, where grim Darwinian rules determine every action. That world and those rules allow the opposite ends of our experience to meet, connecting our conception of the city to our conception of the wilderness. The moose would seem to come from some place altogether different, and that place most resembled the elegiac world of the pastoral painting, an Arcadian daydream of man and nature harmoniously oblivious to the facts of man and nature.

I suppose it would be more accurate to say that the moose came from wherever it came from, but that it seemed to enter the Arcadian region of the imagination. I found it a difficult animal to respond to. It was obviously wild, but it utterly lacked the poised alertness and magical evanescence that wild animals have. If by good fortune you manage to see a deer or fox or coyote before it sees you, and can watch it as it goes about its business unawares, you hold your breath and count the seconds. There is the sensation of penetrating a deep privacy, and there is something of Actaeon and Artemis in it—an illicit, and dangerous joy in this spying. The animal's momentary vulnerability, despite all its watchfulness and wariness, brings your own life very close to the surface. But when you see a moose, it is always unawares. It merely looks peculiar, like something from very far away, a mild, displaced creature that you might more reasonably expect to encounter in a zoo.

In 1980, for the first time in forty-five years, Maine declared an open season on moose. Given the nature of the animal, this was bound to be a controversial decision. People organized, circulated petitions, collected signatures, and forced a special referendum. There were televised debates, bumper stickers, advertising campaigns, and letters to editors.

The major newspapers took sides; judicious politicians commissioned polls. One side proclaimed the moose to be the state's sacred and official animal. The other side proclaimed moose hunting to be an ancient and endangered heritage, threatened by officious interlopers who had no understanding of the state's traditional way of life. Each side accused the other of being lavishly subsidized by alien organizations with sinister agendas: the Sierra Club, the National Rifle Association. The argument assumed ideological overtones: doves vs. hawks; newcomers *vs.* natives; urban Maine *vs.* rural Maine; liberals *vs.* conservatives.

At first this seemed to be just the usual rhetoric and rigmarole of Public controversy. But as the debate continued, the moose seemed to become a test case for something never wholly articulated. It was as though we had to choose between simplified definitions of ourselves as a species. Moose hunters spoke in terms of our biology and our deep past. They maintained that we are predators, carnivores, of the earth earthly; that the killing and the eating of the moose expressed us as we always had been. The other side saw us as creatures compelled by civilization to evolve: to choose enlightenment over atavism, progress over regression, the hope of a gentler world to come over the legacy of instinctual violence. Both sides claimed the sanction of Nature—the moose hunters by embodying it, their opponents by protecting it. Each side dismissed the other's claim as sentimental nonsense.

I knew all along that when it came to moose hunting I was a prohibitionist, an abolitionist, a protectionist, but not a terribly zealous one. When the votes were counted and the attempt to repeal the moose season had been defeated, I doubted that much had been lost, in any practical way. The hunt was to last only a week, and only a thousand hunters, their names selected by lottery, would receive permits each year. It had been alleged that once moose were hunted, they would become as wild and wary as deer, but they have proved to be entirely ineducable. Hunter success ran close to 90 percent in that first year, and has been just as high in the years that followed; and the moose I continue to see each summer are no smarter or shyer than the one that had mooned around Mrs. Foster's feedlot, yearning to be adopted by her cow.

⛖

Late one afternoon, toward the end of September, the telephone rang, and there was a small voice, recognizably Terri Delisle's: "Liz there?" So I went and got Liz. She's old enough to have overcome all but the very last, genetically encoded traces of telephobia—just a momentary look of worry when she hears that it's for her, and a tentativeness in her "Hullo?" as though she were speaking not into the receiver but into a dark and possibly empty room.

Terri is her friend, her crony. The two of them get together—both polite, reticent, and normally quiet little girls—and spontaneously constitute between themselves a manic, exuberant subculture. It possesses them. They are no longer Terri and Liz but something collective: a swarm, a gang, a pack, or a carnival, having its own unruly gusts of volition. They glitter with mischief, laugh at everything, giggle, romp, and frolic, and I believe that, with each other's help, they actually lose for a moment all consciousness of the adult world that watches from within, waiting for children to draw toward it. They aren't destructive or insubordinate—that, after all, would be a backhanded acknowledgment of civilization, maturity, and responsibility. They are simply beyond the reach of reproof, like colts or puppies.

But on the telephone, with distance between them, self-conscious circumspection took over. I heard Liz's guarded and rigorously monosyllabic responses: "Yep." "He did?" "Sure—I'll have to ask Dad." "OK. Bye." And so she told me that Terri's father Henry had killed a moose. Would we like to go over and see it? "Sure," I say, all adult irony. "I'll have to ask Mom."

I knew Henry Delisle in a small and pleasant way. There were a lot of Delisles in town, and Henry, like his brother and most of his male cousins, worked over in Bath, at the shipyard—a welder, I think. But like many other natives of Bowdoinham, he had farming in the blood. The old Delisle farm, up on the Carding Machine Road, had long since been subdivided and sold, and Henry's neat, suburban-looking house sat on a wooded lot of only two or three acres. Even so, he had built himself a barn and a stock pen, and he kept a few pigs, a milk cow, and an old draft horse named Homer. There couldn't have been much economic sense to it, just a feeling that a house wasn't a home without livestock squealing or lowing or whickering out back. He plainly liked the whole life that livestock impose upon their owners—harnessing Homer up for a day of cutting and hauling firewood; making arrangements with local restaurants and grocery stores to get their spoiled and leftover food for pig fodder; getting the cow serviced every so often, and fattening the calf for the freezer. He had an antiquated Allis-Chalmers tractor, with a sickle bar and a tedder and a bailer. There are a lot of untended fields in Bowdoinham, and plenty of people were glad to let Henry have the hay if he would keep them mown.

That was how I had met him for the first time. He had come rattling up to the house in his big dilapidated flatbed truck to ask me if anybody planned to cut my fields that summer. In fact somebody did, and I told him so, but Henry had too much small-town civility, which coexists comfortably with small-town curiosity, simply to turn around and drive off. I appreciated that, and so we chatted for a while—Henry sitting up in his truck, talking with an abrupt and fidgety energy, and I standing down beside it.

He remembered my house from his boyhood: "Used to be a reg'lar old wreck of a place. They didn't have no electricity down here or nothing. Winters, they'd cut ice from the pond. Had a icehouse dug into the bank there; kept ice all through summer. Hard living." He told me a story I'd heard even before we bought the house, how one winter the eldest son had gone out to the barn to milk, as he did every morning, and had found his younger brother there, hanging from a ceiling joist. "Never a word or a note. That was a terrible thing to happen. Unfriendly people, but they didn't deserve that."

He laughed. "But they was *some* unfriendly, I want to tell you. I slipped down to the pond and set muskrat traps one fall. But they musta seen me. They pulled 'em every one out and kept 'em. I was afraid to ask—just a kid, you know. Probably still lying around in your barn somewhere." He looked at me and sized me up: "But I ain't afraid to ask now, and don't you be afraid to turn me down—would you mind me setting a few traps in that pond this fall? It used to be about lousy with muskrats." I hesitated at this—the pond was still full of muskrats, and I enjoyed seeing them sculling across it, pushing little bundles of cut grass ahead of them, or sitting out on a log, grooming themselves with a quick, professional adroitness. But I liked him for the way he had asked it, and there was something else. His country-bred practicality and local knowledge gave him an obscure claim—he was less indigenous than the muskrats, but far more so than I was. "Sure," I told him, "go ahead."

All this had taken place on a bright, airy morning in late July or early August, with the kind of high sky that would make anybody think of haying. Henry said he was glad he'd stopped by, and that I'd see him again once the trapping season opened. I reached up, we shook hands, and he backed the truck down the driveway. His windshield caught the sun for a moment and blinded me and then, as the truck swung up into the yard to turn around, I could see through the glass what I had not been able to see before. He had a passenger—a little girl sitting in the middle of the seat, right at his elbow. She did not look in my direction at all, but stared at the dashboard with that look of vacancy and suspended animation that you see on the faces of children watching Saturday morning cartoons. Henry grinned at me, waved goodbye, and the big truck went lumbering off.

That first meeting with Henry had been the summer before Elizabeth and Terri started school. Later, when they had become classmates and best friends, I learned that the girl I had seen in the truck was Stephanie, whom everybody called Tadpole. She was three years older than Terri, but that was a technicality.

⚬

Bowdoinham is a small, spread-out town. It tries to hold onto the idealized ethos of the New England village, but is in fact well on its way to becoming a bedroom community, a pucker-brush suburb. Like the state as a whole, it is full of outsiders moving in, old-timers dying out, and the uneasy sense of a lost distinctiveness.

The elementary school is the nearest thing to an agora that such a town has. Parents are separated by their backgrounds and expectations, and by the devious anxieties of people who feel that, in appearing to belong to the little unglamorous place they inhabit, they may misrepresent or compromise themselves. But children go to school, and it stands for the world. They make friends and enemies, and suddenly populate your household with unfamiliar names. It is as though you had sent them off as members and worshipers of a stable, self- sufficient Trinity consisting of Mama, Daddy, and themselves, and then had them return as rampant polytheists, blissfully rejoicing or wailing despairingly about the favors and sulks of capricious gods and goddesses named Tommy Blanchard, Vera Sedgely, Joanie Dinsmore, Nikki Toothacre, and Willie Billings. At school functions you would meet the parents of these entities, or, prodded by your child, would nervously call up Joan's or Nikki's mom, and arrange for that child to come over and play. And slowly, with no direct intention of doing so, you would find out about other families in the town—who they were and how they lived, how they regarded themselves and how they were regarded.

So we learned that Tadpole suffered from Down's syndrome. She was the first child of Henry and Debbie Delisle, born to them within a year of their marriage, when they themselves were just out of high school. Perhaps if they had had more education and experience they would have accepted the irremediable fact of their daughter's condition. As it was, they were mistrustful of the state and the school system and all the experts who came to help them and warn them and in some way to deprive them of the right to raise their daughter as they saw fit. Against every recommendation, they were determined to try to give Tadpole all the circumstances of an ordinary childhood.

When time came for Tadpole to go to school, Henry wrangled with the school board and the superintendent and the Department of Mental Health and Retardation. And finally everybody agreed that, for as long as it didn't create any disturbance, Tadpole could go to school with Terri. Word of that sort of thing gets around, and some parents didn't like it, fearing that what Henry had gained for his daughter would diminish the education and attention that their own children would receive. But I believe that most of us admired Henry and wished him well. He was his own man; in his battered old truck with a tottering load of bay on it, or with Homer tethered to the headboard, he implied an old-fashioned resourcefulness and independence, which we could

praise even if we couldn't emulate. It was heartening to see a man like
that acting out of the best and simplest human impulse, and sticking
to his guns, even if, in the long run, the case were hopeless.

And of course the case was hopeless, although at first it didn't appear
to be. Tadpole was docile and affectionate, and in her first year and a
half of school, she enjoyed an almost privileged status among her
classmates. It was as though she were their mascot, like the wheezy old
bulldog or jessed eagle you might find on the sidelines at a college
football game. You would see a crowd of children fussing over her in
the schoolyard, alternately courting her as though she were a potentate
to he appeased, or babying her with bossy solicitude. Liz would report
on all that Tadpole had done or said, as though she were a celebrity, in
whom we should take a communal pride. And we did take a kind of
pride in her. Her being at the school with the other children seemed
proof that humane flexibility, sympathy, and tolerance were still
operative in this overgrown country. Them was something quaint about
it, something from the putative innocence of the past.

But by the end of the second grade, Liz was bringing home bad
news. Tadpole had begun to balk at going to school, and would
misbehave when she was there. She was bigger than her classmates,
and her truculence threatened them. They retaliated as children would,
by teasing and persecution. She regressed, growing more withdrawn
and morose, and would go through days of not speaking, or of only
muttering to herself. Public opinion hardened. I don't think there were
any petitions or formal proceedings to have Tadpole removed; it was
just one of those sad things that had become plain and obvious. Henry
and Debbie had no choice; they had to give in to the fact that confronted
them every day. The next year, Tadpole and Terri were separated, and
Tadpole was sent to school in Topsham, where there was a class for
what the state calls Special Children.

When Terri would come over to play, she seemed untroubled by the
change. She was as quick and inventive as ever. I did not know Henry
well enough or see him often enough to speak to him about the matter,
and hardly knew what I would or could have said. He got himself
transferred to the night shift at the shipyard that fall, and he must have
kept Tadpole out of the special class a good deal. I would regularly see

the two of them together in the truck—usually first thing in the morning, when he'd just gotten off work. But he told me one morning, when he'd come to check the muskrat traps, that he had changed shifts purely to give himself more time for the woodcutting, haying, trapping, icefishing, and hunting that seemed to be his natural vocations.

℮

So on the September afternoon in question, Liz and I got into the car—none of the rest of the household had any interest in a dead moose—and drove over. It was nearly dark when we turned up into Henry's driveway. His garage lights were on. He had set up a worktable of planks and sawhorses along the rear wall, the moose was hanging by the neck squarely in the center of the garage. From the driveway, it looked like a shrine or a crèche—the brightly lit space, clean and spare as an Edward Hopper interior; Henry and four other men standing chatting; and, just behind them, the lynched moose. Terri came running out, excited as on Christmas morning, and took us in to see.

From the outside, the moose's head appeared to go right up through the low ceiling of the garage, but once inside I could see that, when he had built the garage, Henry had left out one four-by-eight ceiling panel, to give him access to the attic. He had put an eye bolt in a collar tie, centered above the opening, so that he could rig a hoist from it. It was a smart arrangement, enabling him to convert an ordinary two-car garage into an abattoir whenever he had a cow or pig or deer to slaughter. The moose he had shot was a cow, and she was a big animal, hanging with her head in the attic, her rump scarcely a foot above the concrete floor. A big animal but not, Henry said, a big moose: "She'll dress out about five-fifty. Just a heifer. She'd have calved next spring."

Henry introduced me to the other men—neighbors who had wandered over out of curiosity, and his cousin Paul, who had been his partner in the hunt.

We were somehow an uncomfortably self-conscious group; it was as though we were all trying to ignore something. Perhaps it was that Paul and Henry were still dressed in their stained and ragged hunting gear, and were grubby and unshaven. The rest of us were in our ordinary street clothes, and only a few minutes ago were watching television or pottering around the house or having a drink and getting ready for supper. We had been in our familiar cocoons of routine and obligation, where the only world that matters is the human one. And now we were talking to men who were in another role, and we were abruptly confronting a large, dead animal, a thing from far beyond our lives.

I think it was more this awkwardness than aggression that made the man next to me, a bank manager new to town, speak the way he did: 'Well, Henry. That's a weird damned animal. You sure it's not a camel?" Everybody laughed, but uneasily.

"Tell us about it," the man said. "How'd you bag the wily moose?"

Henry said there wasn't a whole lot to tell. The man asked him if he'd hired a guide. Henry said he hadn't.

"Well maybe you should have," the bank manager said. "If you had, you might have gotten yourself a bull. Then you'd have something to hang in your den."

Henry didn't answer. He got busy with a knife, whetting it against a butcher's steel. The man walked around the moose, looking at her appraisingly, as though she were an item in a yard sale. Then he said he had to get on back home, and left, and there was a general relaxing. Henry looked up.

Now he was going to tell us how you kill a moose, or how he had killed this one. None of us knew anything about moose hunting. The tradition of it had died out, and hunters—even very experienced ones like Henry and Paul—don't know moose in the way that they know deer. The hunt was limited to the upper third of the state, and a lot of people up there had set themselves up as moose guides, offering what was supposedly their deep-woods wisdom to anybody lucky enough to have a permit.

Henry snorted: "Hire a guide. You know what a moose guide is? He's a guy with a skidder, that's all. You go to his house and he'll take you out and leave you somewhere where he thinks there might be a moose, and charge you so much for that. Then you kill a moose and he'll charge you a arm and a leg to hook it up to the skidder and drag it out to your truck. So I go to this guy that's listed as a guide, and he explains it to me. And I say to him, 'Look. Don't tell me a word about where to find a moose. Now if I get one, what'll you charge to drag him out?' 'Hundred dollars for the first hour, fifty dollars per hour after that,' he says. See, they got you. Law don't let you kill a moose less than fifty yards from the road. So I says to him, 'You prorate that first hour?' 'Fifty dollar minimum,' he says to me. 'Take it or leave it.' Musta thought I was from Massachusetts. 'See you later,' I says. And that fifty dollar, hundred dollar shit ain't from the time he drives his skidder off his trailer into the woods. It's from the time he gets in his truck right there in his front yard."

Paul quietly removed himself from Henry's audience and went into the kitchen. It wasn't his story, and there was a lot of work still to do.

"We had topo maps, and I seen some good bogs. Day before the season opened we drove and scouted all day. I don't know much about moose, but I know a moose'll walk on a log road or a skidder track if he can, instead of bustin' through the bushes. About suppertime we see a cow cross the road ahead of us, and go down a skidder trail. We followed her down on foot. There was a bog in there at the end of the trail, about a quarter mile in off the road, and there she was, feeding. Her and another cow too. That skidder trail was rough, but I figured we might be able to get the truck down it.

"Opening day it was raining. We parked a ways off and walked up to the skidder track and down to the bog. Got there before day. When it come day, one cow was there. I looked at her. She looked good, but not extra good. Animal like a moose got a lot of waste on 'em. Big bones, big body cavity—not as much meat as you'd think. That's what they tell me. And they told me when you see a cow, wait. It's rut, and a big bull might come along any time."

Paul came out from the house with his arms full—wrapping paper, freezer tape, a roll of builder's plastic. He spread the plastic over the table, and he didn't make any effort to be unobtrusive about it. But Henry was occupied by his story. It was like something he wanted to get off his chest or conscience. Maybe he just couldn't get over the strangeness of the moose.

"It ain't like a deer. A cow moose calls a bull. That's what they say and it's the truth. We watched her all day, and ever so often she'd set right down on her butt and beller, like a cow that ain't been milked. So we set there too, and waited, but no bull showed. By dark she'd worked over to the other side of the bog. Shoot her there and you'd have to cut her up and pack her out."

Henry was standing in front of the moose. Her chin was elevated and her long-lashed eyes were closed. All of the things that had so splendidly adapted her to her world of boreal forest, bog, and swamp made her look grotesque here: the great hollow snout, the splayed feet, and over-long, knob-kneed legs. In whatever consciousness she had had, it was still the Ice Age—she was incapable of grasping human purposes or adjusting to human proximity. Her death was almost the first ritual of civilization, yet she was in our present, suspended in the naked light of a suburban garage, and we could only stand, hands in pockets, as though it were something we did every day.

"So we come back the next day, a little earlier even, and I sent Paul around to the far side of the bog. This time I hear her walking in on that skidder track just before day, and she got out in the bog and bellered some more. We was going to give her 'til noon. I figured if a bull showed, he'd come up the track too, and I could get him before he hit the bog.

"By noon she was all the way out in the middle of the bog again, but Paul stepped out of the bushes, easy, so's not to scare her too much. Took her the longest time even to notice him. Then she started trotting toward me, but she'd keep stopping to beller some more. It was almost like she was mad."

One of the men chuckled: "More like she was desperate, if you ask me. If she didn't call herself up a boyfriend pretty quick, she was a dead duck."

"Well. Anyway, Paul had to slog out after her, keep shooing her along. I wanted her to get all the way out on the trail, but she musta smelt me. Stopped about ten foot from the woods and started throwing her head around and acting jumpy, like she might bolt. So I shot her there.

"We had a little work with the chain saw to clear the skidder trail out wide enough for the truck. Then we backed in and put a rope around her and dragged her out to dry ground. Used a comealong to hoist her up on a tree limb and dressed her out right there. Then cranked her up some more, backed the truck under, and lowered her in. On the way out, we stopped by that guy's house. I went in and told him we wouldn't be needing his damn skidder this year."

The whole time Henry talked, Paul kept coming and going, bringing out knives, a cleaver, a meat saw, and a plastic tarp. Elizabeth and Terri had examined the moose and then gone inside. I had been worried about Elizabeth. She was at least as sentimental as the average ten-year-old about animals; at country fairs she would lean against the stalls and gaze with pure yearning at Suffolk sheep or Highland cattle and especially at horses of any description. But she and Terri had looked the moose over as though she were a display in a museum of natural history, something interesting but remote. They had walked around her, rubbed the coarse, stiff hair, and inspected the big cloven feet, and then gone about their business.

Now, as Henry finished his story, they returned, giggling. Terri was carrying a child's chair, and Liz looked from her to me, trying not to laugh. Terri ran up to the moose and slipped the chair under her rump, and then the two of them stood back and waited on our reaction.

It was comic relief or comic desecration. Because the moose's hindquarters were so near the floor, her hind legs were spread stiffly out in front of her. With the addition of the chair, you suddenly saw her in a human posture, or really in two human postures. From the waist down, she looked like a big man sprawled back on a low seat. Above the waist, she had the posture of a well-bred lady of the old school, her back very straight, her head aloof, and her whole figure suggesting a strenuous and anxious rectitude.

In the ready, makeshift way of country people, Henry had taken one of Debbie's old worn-out lace curtains with him, and when he had killed and cleaned the moose, he had pinned the curtain across the body cavity, to keep out debris and insects and to allow the air to circulate and cool the animal while he and Paul drove back home. The curtain was longer than it needed to be, and now Terri picked up one end of it, brought it like a diaper up between the moose's legs, wrapped it around the hips, and tucked it in, so that it would stay up. The effect was funny in a way I don't like to admit I saw—the garment looked like something between a pinafore and a tutu. It was as though the moose had decided, in some moment of splendid delusion, to take up tap dancing or ballet, and was now waiting uncomfortably to go on stage for her first recital.

Terri and Liz admired the moose. "She needs a hat," Terri pronounced, and they ducked into the house. What they came out with was better than a hat—a coronet of plastic flowers, left over from some beauty pageant or costume.

"Daddy, could you put this on her? She's too high for us."

She was too high for Henry too, but he pulled the little chair from beneath the moose, then picked Terri up and set her on his shoulders. He stood on the chair and Terri, leaning out daringly, like a painter on a stepladder, managed to loop the coronet over one of the long ears, so that it hung lopsided. She slid down Henry to the ground, stepped back and dusted her hands together:

"There. That'll just have to do. I think Momma needs to see this. Maybe she'll lend us some mittens and a scarf. Let's go get her and Tadpole to come see."

"Terri, Paul and me got to get to work on that moose right now," Henry called after her, but she was already gone. The other two men who had come over to see the moose said they had to go, and left, one on foot and one in his car. Terri and Liz came back out with Debbie and Tadpole. Debbie looked at the moose and laughed. Terri was pleased.

"Don't you think she looks like a beauty queen, Mom? We could enter her in the Miss Bowdoinham contest."

"Well I guess so." Debbie turned to Tadpole: "Look at Daddy's moose that he brought us, honey." Tadpole looked at it and walked over as though she wanted to touch it, but didn't. Her face had that puffy, numbed look of someone just wakened from a deep sleep, and her movements were slow and labored.

Debbie called over to Terri. "Now your Daddy and Paul have to start, and I've got to run buy some more freezer paper. You and Stephanie come with me, and we can let Liz get home for her supper."

Terri gave the moose a comradely whack on the rump: "Goodbye, moose. You're going in the freezer." Liz patted the moose too, but more tentatively. Then they all trooped out.

I stood talking to Henry for a few minutes longer. He looked at the moose with her cockeyed halo and tried to make a joke of it. "If she'd been dressed that way this morning, maybe I'd have got a bull." But his laughter was awkward, apologetic. His remark about how little useable meat there really was on a moose, for all its great size, had not been lost on me, and yet I felt that it would be right to ask him for something, as a way of restoring to him a vestige of the old role of hunter as public benefactor, bringer home of the bacon. So I asked him if I could have some of the long hair from the nape of her neck, for trout flies.

"Sure thing," he said, all business. "Tell you what. I won't cut it off now—don't want no more loose hair than I can help when we go to skin her. But when she's done, I'll clip some off and drop it by, next time I'm down your way. You can count on it."

I thanked him and left. Liz was subdued as we drove back toward home. You might have asked an older child what she was thinking, but not Liz, not for a few years yet. Besides, I wasn't so certain what *I* was thinking just then: two scenes alternated in my mind. One was a recollection, back from the previous November, a morning when heavy frost had sparkled white as mica on the dead grass, and I had been driving to work. I saw Henry walking across a stubble field, a big fox slung over his shoulder. He held the fox by its hind legs; its tail, curved over and lying along its back, was luxuriant and soft as an ostrich plume, and it stirred lightly in the breeze. I felt some sadness for the dead beauty of the fox, but it was Henry I remembered. He ought to have looked like a mighty hunter before the Lord, holding the bounty of his skill and cunning and knowledge of the ways of wild animals in his hand. But he was walking with a shambling hesitation, to keep pace with the daughter clinging to his other hand and trudging glumly at his side, beyond any idea of triumph or happiness.

The other image was of something that had not happened yet. June would come again, and I would be up north fishing again—this time with a fly that would have, wrapped in tight spirals around the shank of the hook to imitate the segmented body of a nymph or mayfly, one or two strands of mane from Henry's moose. And I would look up from the water, almost dizzy with staring for so long at nothing but the tiny fly drifting in the current, and there they would be—maybe a cow and a calf—standing on the other bank, watching me watch them, trying to fathom it.

from *Billy Watson's Croker Sack*

Heating with Wood

Marybeth Holleman

I sat beside the fire in the recliner. Sinking back into it, I pulled off my wool socks and threw them on the pile of boots, coat, hat, and gloves. I draped my legs over the broad armrest and aimed numb feet at the fire.

My feet had been cold all day. I spent the day in an office whose heat was constant but stingy. After work, I walked to my car through deep snow and spent hour-long minutes warming the engine and scraping ice from windows. Although the car's heater soon blew hot air, it couldn't penetrate my boots. I looked forward to sitting by the woodstove, finding unselfish heat whose intensity increased the closer I moved to it.

When I arrived home, the stove was still warm; I spread the remaining coals from the morning's logs. On top of these glowing remnants I layered crumpled newspaper, a few egg cartons, a bundle of twigs and lumber scraps, and two small split logs. The newspaper ignited as I shut the door and opened the damper.

The new fire crackled in the woodstove, the metal warmed, and the chimney creaked and popped. Birch and spruce logs, some split, some with bark peeling off in rough sheets, lay piled high around the stove on the black slate pad. Warmth from the stove began to envelop me with a heat nearly as perfect as the heat of the sun: radiant and silent.

When the bucket of water on top of the stove sizzled, I pulled off my wool sweater and opened the stove door. The kindling and small logs were now coals, and I stared at their ballet of blue light until my eyes burned from the heat. Donning thick fire gloves, I selected the next log to feed the fire.

I passed up one piece of birch just to admire longer its snowy bark beaded with cedar-red buds and dark lips of ripples. Because the stove was nearly empty, I chose the biggest and oddest shaped log. Its rust bark covered a small burl on one end that would not give in to the maul; on the other end was a thick pink marking several inches long. I remembered this log—it had already warmed me.

I didn't grow up with wood heat, but I've always been mesmerized by fire. As a child I anticipated holidays as the time when a fire burned in our fireplace for days. I would lie on the floor beside it for hours, watching logs licked by flames until they were reduced to embers. My eyes would burn and my face would flush, but my trance was so complete that only the intrusion of a brother or sister, wanting some heat for themselves, would make me move.

In college, I embraced the social benefits of wood heat. I learned how alternative energy sources could keep our energy appetite from consuming the natural world. To use them, though, we needed to scale down the process. Instead of a vast network of wires or pipes supplying energy to hundreds of homes, each home could find its own source: solar, wind, wood.

I joined committees, marched on Washington, listened to speeches, wrote about what seemed the obvious solution. The conversion I experienced, though, was shared by only a few; I became frustrated and disillusioned as our efforts failed to effect change. I lost heart until a friend showed me another way. He built a passive solar home with a woodstove for backup, he quit his commuting job and rode his bicycle, he talked about teaching at least his own children how to live lightly on the land.

So when my new husband and I bought a mobile home to live in— we were saving for a big piece of land instead of a big house—we installed a little woodstove. We bought it for twenty dollars at a junk shop, as much for its quaint looks as for its utility. An ancient wood and coal burner, it sat like a long black log on four ornate iron legs with claw feet.

Only a few small logs or one large log would fit, and we had to get up in the middle of the night to refill it. We quickly learned to wake before the clamor of the oil burner kicked in. It reminded Andy of how his grandfather used to get up and stoke their coal furnace every night. For years after they switched to oil heat, his grandfather still awoke in the middle of the night and paced the house like a mother whose newborn has begun sleeping through a feeding.

Later some friends who were moving gave us a larger stove. It was not pretty—a barrel-shaped Ashley with sheet-metal sides—but it kept us warm all night. We could fit twice as much wood in it and keep the oil burner from starting up at all. Still, for months afterward, Andy awoke in the middle of the night. He paced the house, looked at the thermostat, checked the woodstove. It never needed wood, never needed stoking, and he finally slept through until morning again.

My idea of heating with wood because it was socially responsible melted into my love of the woodstove's radiant, consuming heat. I still appreciated using a renewable source and providing for ourselves, but I became more engrossed in the simple comforts of the home we were creating. I began a ritual of sitting by the stove after dinner, petting my dog and relaxing onto the carpet, my body so heated by the silent stove that I didn't move again until I stumbled to bed. One of my cats used to take my spot after I left, and we'd find her there in the morning, a little black puddle of cat stretched out in the heat.

A year after putting in a woodstove, we bought ten acres and moved out among trees of our own. Before, we cut trees already marked for removal at the golf course where Andy worked or at construction sites around town. Some of the trees were dead; most were not. Even then I knew I didn't like to cut live trees. Besides the fact that dead trees are more seasoned, I simply didn't like to cut short the life of a tree, no matter how misshapen or scrawny or in the way.

When the half-mile of road was carved back into our land, though, trees fell. I watched with agony and awe at the bulldozers and backhoes grinding, digging, and crushing decades of slow growth. White and post oak, red and sugar maple, red cedar, birch, poplar, pine, holly, sycamore—all fell equally in the machines' path.

I tried to spare two maples, by far the largest trees on the entire forty-five-acre tract, but they fell to make the road wider and higher. The land where they stood was low and frequently wet when rain made the creek overflow. The old maples weren't used for firewood, though. Our new neighbor claimed them, saying he wanted to build furniture from their thick trunks. He never did. Instead, honeysuckle and morning glories wound around them, finding footholds in their furrowed bark. For years we watched the once-towering forms slowly sink into soil.

When the bulldozer reached the boundary of our land, I hopped on with the driver, directing him on a circuitous route that spared more than one big tree. We had chosen road builders who would let us participate, if only to watch and ask questions, and this bulldozer driver was particularly accommodating.

"I'm not moving until she smiles," he told Andy more than once.

We kept the backhoe away by digging ditches by hand, and we paid hundreds of dollars for underground electricity and telephone lines, saving the trees that the bulldozer squeezed by. What resulted looked less like a road than a winding path through a forest; it made me smile.

About a year after we bought it, Andy's grandfather came to visit our land. We wandered the woods and showed him the little stream, the grand beech grove, the rare pink ladyslipper, the precious giant oaks.

"Lots of good firewood here," he said.

For years, he had been cutting the sprawling oaks that graced his woods to feed his fireplace. He had lived his life in the surrounding area, growing up amid thousands of acres of wood and farmland. He and his wife inherited several hundred acres from relatives who had owned it since before the Civil War. As years passed, the city grew outward and swallowed the woods, slowly biting into his own land so that when I met him only six acres of woods and farmland were left. Though they had for years heated with oil, I think he just liked the work of felling a tree, cutting, splitting, and stacking it. For much of his life, it was a necessary ritual. On my first visit to his house I admired his long, neat rows of firewood—enough to heat our small home for years.

When they built their house over sixty years ago, they planted a row of six walnut trees in the front yard. The trees were beautiful—tall and spreading and dark. They shaded the front lawn and hid the church, condos, and gas stations that began crowding together across the road. In 1989, the tail end of a hurricane took four of the walnut trees and most of the large oaks behind their house. By then, Andy's grandfather was too old and weak to clean them up himself, so his grandsons gathered and cut and split the trees, carrying them off to sell to others wanting firewood.

Like those walnut trees, many of our bulldozed trees were old, especially the hardwoods that made the best firewood. The dense grains of the oak and walnut take much longer to produce than those of the watery pines or poplars. We extracted as many fallen trees from the bulldozer piles along the road as we could, digging away soil, untangling roots, pulling and dragging parts of trees from the pile. We also retrieved firewood from other parts of our land that had been logged twenty years earlier, where loggers had left behind a tangled mess of bent and broken trees. Harvesting those fallen trees became a routine part of our life in the woods. As I fed the stove, I often recalled where a particular log came from—the birch at the bend in the creek, the lopsided oak at the crest of the hill, the cedar along the ridge. These trees fed me with memory and heat, and I soaked up their gifts gratefully.

A few years after the road was built, age overcame one of our massive oaks. Because it was close to our home, we had to cut it down rather than risk it falling on us in a storm. The dead tree crashed like a giant, trunk indenting the ground nearly a foot deep, and top branches ricochetting into the stream and across the hillside. The thick logs had to be split again and again before we could carry them to the woodpile.

A shelf fungus clung to one limb. I pulled, but it had reached that tenacious age where only a saw could remove it. Its top was smooth brown and tough as a turtle shell; its milky white underside was a network of tiny pores, so small they blurred my vision. I had heard that Indians inscribed pictures into these pores since the plant doesn't shrivel with death. I scratched a line with my nail; the line turned brown within seconds. Later, I cut it and put it on a shelf above my desk. Long after the tree was transformed to heat, I would gaze at the half moon of fungus and imagine its life high in the arms of the oak.

We didn't clean out all the deadwood from our forest, for we knew snags and fallen trunks are essential to a forest community. Down by the stream, running cedar grew thick along a rotted trunk. On the hillside, wild turkeys nested among saplings nourished by another fallen tree. As I spent days and months exploring the land, it began to shrink for me like Andy's grandfather's land had shrunk. It no longer seemed a vast forest; each tree became more precious as I discovered the unique twists of one tree's trunk, angles of another's branches, hollows at another's base.

A dead sycamore stood near the creek in a dark green bed of running cedar. I love sycamores, with their multicolored peeling bark and big hand-shaped leaves. They need wet areas to thrive and don't handle competition from other trees well. Most of the ones on our land were spindly and barely living, with few spreading branches. One day Andy slapped the side of the trunk with his hand as he walked by. Like an echo overhead we heard a great rustling, then saw a giant bird burst from the hole in the top of the sycamore. As clumsy as a chicken, and about the same size, the great horned owl thrashed out of the tree and swooped beyond our view. We saw the owl only twice more, but the snag still stands.

That sycamore reminded me of a snag in our yard in Alaska. I could see it from my office window, a huge dead birch towering above spruce and alder growing beneath it. Andy wanted to cut it but I wouldn't let him. Sometimes a raven sat on its broken limb, a silhouette against a cold sky.

We only had an acre then, so little wood came from it. Then too some of our wood came from others' land and we had to cut down each dead tree we used, carrying it home to our woodpile. This ritual brought me my perfect wood heat.

ॐ

Kneeling in front of the stove, I held up the burled log with the thick pink mark. As I shoved it into the hot stove and watched sparks fly, it brought its own memories swirling back to me.

It came from a large birch we had cut in the fall. It was taller and thicker than most birches I've seen in Alaska, more like the hardwoods I grew up with. Its haphazardly spreading branches reaching for the sky and huge rippled trunk reminded me of the oaks in North Carolina.

The tree was dead and leaned precipitously over the fragile putting green on the golf course where Andy worked. In summer, it had been marked for felling with a fluorescent pink "x".

It had been dying for three years, ever since the golf course was built. Bulldozers and backhoes, reshaping the land to suit the architect's blueprint, had amputated part of its root system. After we cut the tree, I tried to count the rings on its massive stump. I could only guess it was at least three times my thirty-one years.

A sapling growing from its base was alive, and we cut to spare it. Andy angled his cut so the tree fell into the sand trap beside the green. Top branches splintered, broke, and flew up in the air when the great tree landed. I loaded some of these fragments into the truck for kindling. The rest I gathered up and piled into a depression in the woods on the groomed grass's edge, a refuge for small animals and birds against cold and predators.

Hours later, the tree was a pile of logs in the back of our truck. At home we threw the logs off the truck into piles—the smaller ones in the stacking pile, the larger ones in the splitting pile. While Andy split logs, I piled up slivers of wood and peeled-off bark for kindling. I filled the woodbox with the seasoned limbs of the old tree and stacked the rest in the back of the house.

Now the tree danced once more, alive with sparks like twigs tossed out from the center. As I watched orange flames slowly devour the pink stripe, the coals took on familiar shapes, red-hot limbs surrounding the log. The stubborn burl lasted the longest, an oval of coal for hours.

I sat down beside the stove again, my toes warm enough to share the heat. I took off my T-shirt and slid half naked into the chair. The birch warmed me one last time, a warmth made deeper by memory and ritual. It was a heat nearly as perfect as the sun, and I bent like a sapling toward it.

First publication

The Sweet Smell of Pines at Dawn

Jeff Ripple

> *We left the magnificent savanna and its delightful groves,*
> *passing through a level, open, airy pine forest, the stately trees*
> *scatteringly planted by nature, arising straight and erect from*
> *the green carpet, embellished with various grasses and*
> *flowering plants which continued for many miles, never out of*
> *sight of little lakes or ponds.*
>
> —William Bartram, *Travels of William Bartram*

Not far from my home is a forest, an extraordinary forest, that I visit often. I don't consider it extraordinary so much for its heartwrenching beauty—some people might even think it plain—but rather for what it represents. It is a remnant of a landscape that once covered much of the southern United States and now is nearly gone.

Only three hundred years ago, vast forests of longleaf pine reached from the Atlantic Ocean to the Gulf of Mexico, covering 80 million acres, including parts of Virginia, the Carolinas, Georgia, Florida, Alabama, Mississippi, and Texas. Some 70 million of those acres were pure stands in which wire grass and a diverse assemblage of wildflowers and other herbaceous plants tossed and waved like a restless sea beneath the pine canopy. Fires, typically caused by lightning, were frequent and blazed for miles and miles, burning away undergrowth without killing the pines, leaving bare soil from which new longleaf seedlings sprouted and soft, new wiregrass surged forth.

Three hundred years is not such a long time. A longleaf pine may live for three hundred years or more. To think that within the lifetime of a single tree we have changed unalterably the face of the landscape it knew as a seedling. . . .

From the period immediately after the Revolutionary War through the first decade of the twentieth century, longleaf pine—also called Georgia, southern yellow, long needle, and long straw pine—was relentlessly timbered and its gummy resin used for turpentine, tar, pitch, and rosin or "navy stores." Virtually all virgin longleaf had been cut by 1930. Of the original 80 million acres of longleaf, about 3 million acres now remain, most of which is second growth and degraded by grazing, logging, and lack of fire. Only isolated groves of virgin longleaf remain, a thousand acres or so. A few of those rare, old trees, somehow missed by loggers, stand in this woodland I visit so often—Florida's Goethe State Forest.

Goethe would have been insignificant in that once vast Southern forest. Now it represents some of the best pine country left anywhere, covering sixty-six square miles in southeastern Levy County, extending from a point three miles north of the Withlacoochee River to just below the city of Bronson. It stretches a modest six miles at its widest point but runs roughly twenty miles from north to south. Goethe is cloaked predominantly with longleaf and slash pines, interwoven with swatches of hammock, freshwater marsh, and cypress swamp. From its wetlands spring innumerable creeks and the headwaters of the Wekiva River. Longleaf pine and turkey oak sandhill saddle its northern reaches, where the land is slightly higher and much drier and cradles small, sometimes ephemeral, lakes within.

Goethe also harbors several uncommon life forms—Florida black bear, red-cockaded woodpecker, indigo snake, gopher tortoise, kestrel, southern bald eagle, Sherman's fox squirrel, corkwood, pine-wood dainty. Deer, of course. are plentiful, as are bobcats, gray squirrels, wild turkey, and other plants and wildlife no less significant to a woodland than those listed under the heading of Endangered or Threatened Species in Goethe State Forest's Resource Management Plan. It's just that in these days of rapidly diminishing wilderness, what is rare gets attention. The less we have of something—a dainty. a fox squirrel, a longleaf pine forest—the more precious it is to us. Hence. Goethe.

I visit these woods for varied reasons, no one more significant than another. Sometimes I hike or write. Sometimes I sit on a favorite log and watch the morning light play in the trees and clouds. More often, I bring my wooden field camera and photograph. With the camera in my hands I creep along and listen to the forest. I intuit the dance of shadow and light, the pitch and form of trees, the texture of bark and grass and leaves. I wait for the forest to tell me in my gut what I will photograph. When it has spoken, when I settle the camera on the tripod and peer through the ground glass, I feel my body drawn through the lens and swallowed by the landscape before me. I become what I see.

Perhaps that is so with others who enter the forest—hikers, hunters, biologists, birders. I hope so, because it is they-—us—who must speak for this forest, any forest, in the community and in government. Not everyone cares about endangered species or how sweet the pines smell at dawn. The spiritual qualities of a wildland and its inhabitants are often overshadowed by economics, the bottom line: "Tell me how much this forest is worth in dollars and cents." An international corps of economists, ecologists, and policy analysts did so, in terms of the earth's natural systems as a whole and the myriad ways they aid humankind, in the science journal *Nature*. Our whole benefits package, courtesy of Mother Earth, was valued at somewhere around $17 *trillion*. Every year I see figures documenting how much birding, sport fishing, hiking, canoeing, and other recreational activities—and by extrapolation the wild regions in which these activities take place—are worth to local economies. These figures do benefit conservation, and I am grateful for them. But it shouldn't have to be that way. A place, a species, should be held most valuable for what it is—nothing more, nothing less.

Not everyone wanted a Goethe State Forest. I learned this combing through files of newspaper clippings, letters, and memos in the double-wide trailer that serves as forest headquarters. The proposed purchase of nearly forty-four thousand acres by the state from ninety-six-year-old lumberman J. T. Goethe in 1992 was in fact a matter of some contention.

In 1992, the Levy County Forest-Sandhills, as Goethe State Forest was known under its Conservation and Recreation Lands (CARL) designation, was considered the largest privately owned tract of old growth pine remaining in Florida. It was thought to contain the most extensive unbroken expanse of longleaf pine flatwoods in the state. Conservationists deemed the property "a masterpiece of ecology" because of its undisturbed nature, diversity of ecosystems, capacious size, and undeniable attraction to no fewer than sixteen threatened or endangered species—the "best and largest contiguous habitat" for protecting the globally endangered Sherman's fox squirrel, said a spokesperson for the Nature Conservancy. The state agreed to pay Goethe and representatives of his deceased brother $64 million using funds from its Preservation 2000 program, money raised through the sale of bonds each year to buy endangered lands for conservation. It was more money than had ever been spent on a CARL project, but then the Levy County Forest-Sandhills were unlike any other land for sale in Florida. The citizens of Florida could not afford to miss this opportunity to save a unique relic of their natural heritage.

Opponents to the state purchase valued Goethe's land for reasons that had nothing to do with rare wildlife and "contiguous habitat." Levy County commissioners decried the loss of yearly tax revenues from the property. J. T. Goethe's land amounted to 6 percent of the county's total area. His 1992 property tax bill totaled about $130,000. As one commissioner put it, "A person should be able to do what they want to do with their property, but this sale would take much needed revenue from the county"—this despite state law that would require 15 percent of revenues from forest timber sales be paid to the Levy County School Board, money for the county's children that would not exist without the sale. He also proffered his opinion as to the sensitive nature of the property, declaring that the forest was not endangered but "good usable land."

Commercial timber interests worried aloud that ecosystem protection would prevent future cutting in the forest, although J. T. Goethe had not cut timber, with the exception of an area that had burned in 1981, on his property for more than fifty years. Many local folks were uneasy about the state controlling so much land in the county. It smelled of a "land grab," as one writer stated in a letter to the editor of the *Gainesville Sun*. An anonymous ad ran in local papers:

$175,000,000.00

> *This is the amount of money the State of Florida Department of Natural Resources has to spend on special interest real estate purchases. This money is needed badly in the General Revenue Fund.*
>
> *The public school system can't afford adequate facilities or enough teachers; the State can hardly meet its payroll, no pay raises are in sight, and current ones are canceled.*
>
> *The State of Florida is proposing to buy 54,544 acres of pure timberland in Levy County, Florida. This will take $16 million off the Levy County tax rolls. You will make up the difference.*
>
> *If you are opposed to DNR's proposed purchase of the unendangered Levy County timberland, call your State legislators and local Levy County Commissioners and stop the Levy County Forest-Sandhills project.*

I found a copy of the ad stuffed in the file with the other clippings. I was not able to find out who placed it.

Despite the hue and cry over lost tax revenues and state-sponsored land grabs to benefit "special interests"—that is, Florida's citizens—the land was purchased. Goethe State Forest is now open to the public for hiking, biking, hunting, fishing, wildlife observation, and uncontained tree hugging.

One morning in late August, I travel to the forest for a short hike. Near Goethe's western boundary, I turn onto Cow Creek Road, a narrow, two-track dirt path through the woods, drive a few miles, and then get out to walk. The air is thick and wet, customary for this time of year in north-central Florida. Overhead, in the pastel dawn sky, swirls of robin-egg blue infuse clouds as soft and gray as a mockingbird's breast. Thunder mutters sullenly in the distance. The drumming of woodpeckers echoes in the still air.

Fifty yards in front of me, a doe steps onto the road and pauses. We gaze intently at one another for several moments. Then she drifts off the road and vanishes into the brush as suddenly and quietly as she appeared. Sunlight shoots through thunderclouds to the east and the forest warms, the glow climbing the trunks of the pines to blaze fiercely in their crowns.

I glance skyward out of habit, in part to track the progress of the clouds and also to check for raptors. For most of the summer my eyes have been focused on the blade-like silhouettes of swallow-tailed kites. I know that by now the kites have begun their trek back toward South America where they winter, but my summer habit remains. In May, I had been invited by John Arnett and Audrey Washburn, assistants to Dr. Ken Meyer, an international authority on swallow-tailed kite ecology and migration, to join them and Division of Forestry biologists on a trip to check nests in Goethe. The kites typically build their nests in the crowns of tall, sturdy pines. We visited one nest in a stand of pines mixed with cypress. With a little coaching by Audrey and John, I was finally able to pick it out against the dim, overcast sky—a smudge of green lichens, small sticks, and drooping Spanish moss wedged in a fork of branches, nearly obscured by clots of needles near the top of the tree. By moving around to get different angles of view, we were able to distinguish the incubating kite's slender forked tail and wing tips protruding from the side of the nest.

Later that day in a clearcut, John and I watched a kite struggle against the wind with a branch weighted down by a long, thick strand of Spanish moss. The bird flapped vigorously, trying to gain enough altitude to soar, the moss whipping behind. We raced down the trail, trying to keep the kite in sight, finally losing it when a grove of young, twenty-foot-high pines blocked our path. Not more then ten minutes later, as we walked toward a stand of pines where we thought the bird might have landed, five more kites wheeled from behind the treetops, dipped low, and then spiraled quickly upward in tight circles, borne on a great current of air, headed north. By now, the wind had shredded the overcast, and the sun shone brightly as islands of cumulus scudded west. The kites soared higher, their white bodies and black wings etched in sharp relief against the changeling sky. I watched until finally they vanished in the sun.

I have been looking for kites every day since then.

✍

A dense mix of spindly longleaf pines and hardwood shrubs borders both sides of Cow Creek Road. Some of the longleafs are broader, taller, older than others. Many trees wear blue blazes, indicating they have been selected for cutting. I am saddened by this, although I realize the vegetation here is dense, the trees are too close together, that there is no regeneration of pines in the thick tangle of green life on the forest floor. And although I inherently mistrust the Division of Forestry, perhaps because state politics pressureits staff to generate revenue from forests without adequate regard of environmental cost, Goethe's foresters and biologists have patiently explained their plans and shown me what they have already accomplished. Let me briefly recount what I have learned.

The Division of Forestry's Forest Resource Management Plan states the land is designated "multiple use," with "primary emphasis on the restoration and maintenance of native ecosystems, especially the longleaf pine ecosystem." According to Goethe biologist Carol Wooley, the restoration strategy does include logging—occasionally clearcutting planted stands of slash pine that will be replaced by longleaf, but most often selectively removing slash pines from areas where they mingle with longleaf, allowing the longleaf to reseed the cuts naturally.

An area targeted for logging is first burned, then cut, and then burned again. The burning helps prepare the site for longleaf seedlings and encourages the return of native pinewoods understory plants. Nearly all areas of pine will be burned periodically, many during the summer growing season, to replicate the rejuvenating ground fires that once moved slowly across the landscape. Old flat-topped pines and catfaces (trees scarred by turpentining) are spared from cutting and protected from burning because they are potential homes for red-cockaded woodpeckers, perhaps the most endangered of Goethe's wildlife and I imagine one of the more important initial reasons for the state's purchase of the forest.

Wooley spends much of her time studying the woodpeckers—checking nests, identifying active cavities (those cavities the birds regularly use), monitoring the health of the trees they are using, and keeping track of the number of birds. She says right now the forest supports two isolated populations totaling twenty-four clusters, or family groups, of two to five birds each. A mated pair relies on helpers—typically volunteers from previous broods—to help raise new chicks, much like Florida scrub jays and acorn woodpeckers in the western United States.

In spite of this intriguing survival strategy, the population of red-cockaded woodpeckers in Goethe and elsewhere is precarious. These woodpeckers carve their cavities into living pines, typically old trees infected with red heart fungus, which makes the wood softer and easier to excavate. But there is not enough mature pinewoods habitat remaining to support them. Population biologists say five hundred red-cockaded woodpeckers are needed to ensure a stable population in any given area. Each family unit requires 200 to 300 acres of old pine forest. Wooley thinks that only 33,000 acres of Goethe's 44,000 acres are suitable for the woodpeckers—not nearly enough for five hundred birds. And there is another problem looming on the forest's southern horizon—the planned expansion of the Florida turnpike—which could affect how the forest would be burned and, ultimately, the quality and quantity of habitat for red-cockaded woodpeckers and other pinewoods denizens near the road.

The turnpike currently reaches from Florida City, barely twenty miles north of Key Largo, to Wildwood in central Florida. The Florida Department of Transportation wants a forty-nine-mile extension linking Wildwood with U.S. 19 at Lebanon Station because "the upgrading and expansion of existing routes will still not meet the projected needs within this area of the state." The road will provide "a vital link in the state's plan for emergency preparedness" and "high speed access to points north of Orlando." This I learned from the note and accompanying newsletters mailed in response to my request for information from the Turnpike Authority in Tallahassee. In effect, the extension will funnel thousands of cars a day (at high speed) through what are some of the least developed areas in Florida, spawning gas stations, fast-food restaurants, and motels (heaven forbid outlet malls) around four planned interchanges. Where new roads go, rapid development is sure to follow, altering the landscape and way of life of rural people here.

I doubt that building new roads to accommodate Florida's burgeoning human population will solve anything in the long term. Instead, we should be thinking and spending money on innovative ways to move lots of people using the transportation networks we already have. Perhaps, more importantly, we need to think hard about how much of humanity Florida can realistically support. This above all else should dictate "projected needs."

The Department of Transportation's original intent was to run the four-lane extension through the southern end of Goethe, effectively severing nearly 9,000 acres from the rest of the forest. Cost was intrinsic in this decision because the state already owned the land and it would be cheaper to develop than buying private property. Several state agencies, including the Division of Forestry, the Department of Environmental Protection, and the Florida Game and Fresh Water Fish Commission, bitterly opposed the plan because it would, among other things, significantly restrict prescribed burning in the area due to the threat of heavy smoke on the roadway, destroy red-cockaded woodpecker habitat, disrupt the hydrology in nearby wetands, and seriously impede the movement of wildlife through the forest, even with the promise of underpasses and fencing. The governor's office finally appointed a mediator to preside over meetings with the agencies to hammer out an alignment for the road that everyone could agree on. As I write, the exact placement of the road is still uncertain, although it will now entirely miss Goethe, instead falling somewhere between the forest's southern boundary and the Withlacoochee River. Once the alignment is determined, an Environmental Impact Report will be prepared and subjected to review and public comment.

Regardless of where the turnpike passes, its proximity to Goethe will make it more difficult for the Division of Forestry to buy surrounding land to increase woodpecker habitat in the forest. Large mammals, such as black bear, would have to contend with the road in their travels between the forest and wild areas to the south. Foresters could burn certain areas of Goethe only when they were sure no smoke would drift over the highway. And people like me, who appreciate their wilderness experiences free from the sounds of internal combustion engines, will most likely be forced to endure the unrelenting whine of traffic in the distance.

Thunder is louder now, closer, more insistent. The high, broad, cottony summit of the approaching storm has turned dark and ominous. A light rain begins to fall. Suddenly, the storm is on top of me. Gusts of wind tear through the close ranks of pines, showering Cow Creek Road with small branches and pine needles. But the sun is still shining, and the dense green world around me looks as if it is brushed with copper. Then, the light winks out, and it begins to rain in earnest. Thunder cracks. I run for my truck.

I am hard pressed to convey what Goethe State Forest means to me, at least concisely. My feelings dribble out through my photographs, as entries in my journal, in this essay. Alone, they are not particularly notable. But what if every person in Florida took a moment to reflect on their favorite wild place, scribbled an address on an envelope, licked a stamp, and sent a picture, a poem, a letter, a leaf—anything at all— to the governor? Or to a senator or representative or anyone with the power to make decisions about wilderness in Florida? Just to let them know how they feel.

The flow of envelopes might be imperceptible at first, a trickle at best. But over days and weeks, it would increase, individual freshets of envelopes braiding into small creeks, tumbling toward larger streams, until finally they would meld into broad, swollen rivers, like the Suwannee or Apalachicola at flood stage, indomitable torrents of public expression advancing toward Tallahassee and Washington.

How sweet the smell of pines at dawn would be then.

from *Feast of Flowers: Essays on Florida's Wetlands*

Circle of Twine

Susan Marsh

The boulder, cool against my calves, juts into a narrow cascade of Rose Creek. An exhalation from the Absaroka Mountains flows down the canyon like a sigh. I squint under bright sun while dun cliffs still hunker in the gloom of dawn. Rose Creek, tiny tributary of the Lamar River, runs between my feet.

I have enrolled with the Yellowstone Institute, a vacation I would allow myself only by signing up for a class. This morning I have laid a length of twine in a circle roughly twelve feet wide. My assignment: to spend the morning recording whatever I find within.

I start with an inventory. Smoke from the Pelican Valley Fire ten miles away. The talking water, the rasp of grasshoppers in reply. The sun's warmth, the boulder's chill, the breath of autumn at my back. Within my circle are papery seedheads of Mimulus, hanging like tiny Chinese lanterns. Slender panicles of hairgrass, asters and goldenrod still in bloom. Aquatic buttercups with delicate white petals rising from a dark pool.

Across the river, a dozen bison scatter like boulders on the floodplain. Specimen Ridge fades into the distance as columns of smoke spread from Pelican Valley. Rose Creek slaps and clatters between its boulders, murmurs like voices behind closed doors. It splashes my arm. telling me to pay attention. My eye returns to the circle of twine.

A gust rises from the south, bending the grasses backward. Its rush of heated air recalls summer mornings when I was a child. If the day broke stained with yellow light, my mother would predict a "scorcher." Good news: this meant a trip to the beach. There I found smooth pebbles and bits of purple shell, and shore crabs scuttling away from my turned-over stones. I hoped summer would never end. Now in this last week of August, when frost already traces the margins of the sedge, I curl on the boulder, stalling for time. I raise my face to summer and hope it never ends.

Suddenly I laugh out loud, remembering the year I dropped out of college and took a job at a department-store fountain in Seattle.

"What should I do when there are no customers?" I asked my boss.

"Just look busy," he said.

I was good at looking busy. When I lapsed into idleness as a child, the summer day too beautiful for anything but dreams, I would be given laundry to fold, a chore to perform. Even recreation was performance: in my twenties I ran to be in shape for climbing mountains. In my thirties I ran to Drove I could still do it. In my forties, I no longer run. Now I pause on a boulder, like summer fading into fall.

As quickly as it appeared, the south wind ceases. The cold air tiptoes back down Rose Creek. This idleness is luxury; with no need to appear busy, I put down. my notebook, draw up my knees, and watch.

The warm south wind erupts again. My twine billows and gets caught in wands of goldenrod. Summer and winter battle over Rose Creek as I sit in their crossfire. Beyond the Lamar River the meadows have gone straw-brown. As the gust chases the trickle of cold air back up Rose Creek, I cheer it on. Summer stands its ground, though its grasses have turned brittle as parchment. I notice my own dry and wrinkled skin. The difference between the grass and me is that it does not resist.

The cold breeze trickles back down Rose Creek. It carries the snap and buzz of grasshoppers, repeating their urgent chant: "Hurry, get your firewood in. Hurry, time is short."

"Welcome to middle age," my doctor clucked when I complained about my weight and cholestorol creeping upward. I subject myself to mammograms and had what I thought was a hot flash a few months back. Welcome, indeed.

In my twenties, I smoked Winstons, drank too much wine, and got up early the next day to climb a mountain. I marvel that I got away with it. I am relieved that I no longer want to. What I feared then, more than cancer or the dizzying heights, was being in the mountains alone, with nothing to distract me. I hiked all day and walked after dinner until dark. I would have hiked all night to avoid being alone with myself, awake in my sleeping bag staring at the tent seams. I had been purged of idleness.

Another splash from Rose Creek strikes my elbow. The water sounds like laughter overheard.

I always believed the laughter was at me. By climbing mountains I hoped to rise above it, to achieve. Achievement brought the rewards I longed for.

Summer fades to autumn. Where I once found challenge, a chorus of fears now clamors in my head. I fear falling off a mountain. I feel for tumors. I watch for any loose thread that might unravel me. But one fear now subsides, that of being alone. I go to the mountains to hike the easy route and climb the lesser peak, to linger over wildflowers. I sit alone on a boulder in the creek, content to feel the sun on my eyelids or stare across the valley into the August haze.

The wisdom I once hoped for, when I imagined myself an old woman, still looms distant as the horizon. In my twenties, I collected college degrees. In my thirties I collected promotions. In my forties? Sitting on a boulder in a far corner of Yellowstone, I collect myself.

I pick up my twine and sweep it over the nodding grass. It loops across the goldenrod and gentian gone to seed. The morning is almost gone. I want to stay in the space encircled here, made precious by my hours of attention. I realize that my simple act of noticing, alert to this moment with all its beauty and quiet, is more important than whatever I achieve. Just look busy. What I will remember in the end will be mornings rare as this, spent in silent witness as one season changes to the next.

from *Orion*

The Way of a River

John Noland

In this time of rafting fast, clear rivers, I would like to say a few words for a slow muddy river, the prairie river I think of as *my* river, the river that taught me the poetry of the land. It is a murky river, a place of undertows and deep currents where, on an August afternoon, the water is as warm and alive as blood. It is also a wounded river now, a river trapped and fettered by a dam. Still, I go back and check on it every few years. It makes the four-thousand-mile round-trip worthwhile.

"You can't know a place until you can feel it in your blood," my father said, he with the good, strong hands browned by sun to the tint of river water. He also said, though not in words, the river is a prayer, a passage, and a benediction. Perhaps he learned it from my great-grandfather who homesteaded this river valley. Perhaps he learned it from living his life in this place. I was the fourth generation of our family to hear its waters lapping in our veins, and I know now that he might have added that it is a folk song, a reverie, and a meditation.

Before thought, almost before memory, there was knowing. On a late afternoon in a summer filled with light, I was carried to the river by my father to listen in to the voices of little waves seen in sun-flecked surfaces, to hear the deep currents calling, to feel a darkness flowing. "This is our way," he said, though not in words, but in a deeper way, like that dark current pouring through us, an undertow that sucks me back and back, a way I can touch but never hold.

Something there is in us that craves a river. Not even the whole river, just a part of the flow and wildness a river brings with it. For me, just a bend and a couple of long stretches were enough to brand this particular river into my consciousness forever. That, and the river breaks, the no-man's land of ravines, pigweeds, and willows that marked the boundary between "civilized," square-cut farmland and the shaggy chaos and natural flow of "waste" land and the river. This was the place I came to know as a kid. It was a maverick space, a place off-limits to me for years and years because it was "too dangerous." A place, supposedly, of whirlpools, quicksand, undertows, and deep hidden pools.

It was also the place where the Wild gave voice to its feelings. On clear, cold autumn evenings when the stars seemed to flower across the sky like golden poinsettia flowers, the darkness was lit by the yapping of foxes. Later, when the stars became bright, distant points in the winter sky, coyotes chanted mysterious stories burning with dream and possibility, and ancient as the river was deep. Raccoons and possums left their tracks in the river mud after nights of nocturnal ramblings. Bobwhite quail called every evening from the river breaks, and sometimes pheasants exploded from the yellow weeds rimming the cornfields in the fall. And once I watched the delicate steps of a white-tailed doe as she came down to the river to drink, a moment as full of magic as her soft and watchful eyes.

Early memory: wraiths of mist, brought to life by the first light, hang over the water. The primeval odor of river mud rises like the presence of a strong, brown god. Somewhere a bird calls over and over in a high-pitched voice, over and over, insistent, searching. (I can still hear it today.) A light wind rises out of the east, caressing my cheek and shredding the mist. Something emerges like a spirit: white, so white, and soft, like a girl, like the flowing of water. So white it blinds perception. Then it is going away.

Is it a great bird? A ghost? A river spirit? It moves downstream, flowing like fog, a voice, a dream or a memory not quite recalled. The high bird voice that has been calling moves away too, apparently following the figure, insistent, searching, calling and still calling. At the edge of darkness, mosquitoes chant like old women wrapped in black shawls, talking of blood, memory, and the river. It leaves me feeling drowned and hungry.

The river was also the origin place of the honking of Canada geese whose calls always made my mother or father, even in the house, pause for a moment and hum or quote a few lines from an old song: "I Want to Go Where the Wild Goose Goes." Hearing the distant cries, I would feel the restlessness of fall and imagine the geese on a long, clean sandbar, a feathered tribe who knew the ancient, wild ways of the river and told its ballads and stories in the haunting tongue of those who can follow the world around.

My river, like most rivers, was wrapped in story; in fact, that is the way much of the river was given to me. Two old men, my neighbors, would wait until their wives went to town or church and then, with much jolly swearing, would fling fishing gear in the back of an old pickup and roar off, hell-bent, as they said, for the river. They returned with whiskey on their breath, mud on their pants, and stories big enough to wrap a world in.

Which is what one of them did almost every summer evening as he, his wife, and I sat on his screened-in porch. In the gnarled black locust trees, cicadas purred about how deep the dark was as their songs wrapped the ends of day into silver twilight. Occasionally a mourning dove would send its long, haunting voice out over the earth as if looking for its soul. Finally, the call would meld with the swing's slow creaking and the old man's voice going on and on, painting pictures of the river in an evening so rich and warm it almost stopped time. There were stories of giant catfish, quicksand, and big gar. I hardly knew when I passed from those stories into my own night dreams because they were all so tinged with river light.

The river as Folk Way. Evocateur. From the land into mind, into *mythos*. Mythic depth, that which sustains, gives meaning, identifies us. That which inspires stories.

You must grow up inside a myth, hearing the voices yourself. You cannot come to it from beyond and know it in the same way. It must be that which is you, the in-you that informs everything. It makes you see in a certain way, taste in a certain way, feel in a certain way. *Be* in a certain way.

It is structure, pattern, and meaning grown up from the land, risen from the river, like leaves of native plants or hunting patterns of coyotes, the song pattern of a sparrow. It is stenciled into human mind and flesh at a depth beyond understanding. It is folk songs overheard in a mourning dove's call, a cricket's lament. It is the indelible markings of place in the blood; the long, rarely articulated dreams of the land.

Three miles from the city limits and a mile from the river, on a good gravel road that runs through corn and sorghum fields, there is a small unpainted shed. Nailed to the side facing the road are ten huge catfish heads.

These heads are as gnarled and grotesque as tree roots seeking water in a dry time. Patches of bone glare whitely into the summer heat where sun and ants have eaten away the leathery flesh.

But there is nothing pathetic about these heads. In fact, they are not even deathlike. They are, quite simply, creatures from another world. A world as mysterious and known as ancient locust trees that have been shaped by frost, drought, and flood, hail and tornado, and heat so intense that the whole prairie shimmers. A world as powerful as the old, dark river, potent with the life and currents that exist below surfaces.

They glow in the soft evening like roots pulled from the earth. There is a power about them that reminds me of the time lightning struck a steel post only fifty feet from me; a perception so powerful that I could grasp it only in a kind of afterglow within my mind. Big catfish: river roots, ancient river gods, maybe. Guardians and personifications of the deep and dark.

ℝ

The river and the river breaks meant wildness to me and still do. In high school, when I read of Odysseus's travels, I could clearly see him afloat on my own wild river, a dreaming place outside both space and time, a talisman to evoke the magic of creation itself.

But before that, even as a child, I knew with a child's certainty that Indians hovered around the river's edges, that mountain men traipsed the river breaks, and I knew the dangers and hardships the cowboys had pushing the longhorn cattle across my river on their way up from Texas.

My great-grandfather had ridden the Chisholm Trail as a young cowboy and his stories lived on, told by my grandmother and finally my mother. In them the river was always dangerous, a wild and unpredictable place as exotic and powerful as the blue lightning that danced over the long horns of the half-wild cattle. My great-grandfather had been particularly frightened of the quicksand and whirlpools. I knew personally of the dangers of quicksand, having been caught in its sinking on a secret trip a friend and I made to the river while we were still deemed by our parents too young to go there.

Later, in his old age, one of my grandfathers was trapped to the waist in the sucking sand and escaped only after a hard, lucky battle and the use of driftwood to bear his weight. His graphic story, often told, made a deep impression.

In the slow, burnishing darkness, the old man's voice goes on and on like the river, like a deep current below the surface holding all my days together, while outside the screened-in porch the silver twilight turns to darkness soft as cat's fur but tinged with fireflies. And there are just me and the old lady, his wife, to listen.

His old man's eyes watching me, not watching me, staring at me, through me, into the darkness: "In the dark of the moon, we'd go down to the river, the old godalmighty and muddy river. You could smell its breath rising from the mud, and we'd strip there in the river willows and wade out into that water, warm as blood. Wade until we couldn't wade no more, then swim along them steep banks, feeling under them, feeling for a hole, run our hands back slow and easy, feeling for a face, a mouth, gills to sink our fingers into, but like as not never getting a chance. Feeling suddenly something big, powerful, another life beneath the surface. Feeling your wrist, arm, clamped down on, caught suddenly in a mudcat's mouth, a catfish with a head bigger'n yours, I reckon, and maybe a body as long."

And I, the kid, seeing it in the darkness, seeing the head with its spike-sharp barbels, its bulging eyes (I had seen the big catfish heads nailed to osage-orange fence posts, *Like the roots of lightning,* I had thought, the heads nailed there while ants climbed in and out of the eyes, and I wondering, *What could they see in those wild and desolate places?*), and seeing the great shovel mouth that could open up to swallow a hand, an arm, *Why, most of a kid like me,* I thought, and shuddering in the darkness, *It's a monster, a river-monster and one day I am going to catch it, ride it, I am going to ride it clear down into the deep and the dark, down and through the deep and the dark clear to what lies on the other side. . . .*

"You knowed that mudcat had you then, knowed he would try to drown you, to drag you down deep where a man can't go, drag you down and keep you there so that you would not come up for weeks and weeks, your face chewed on by crawfish so you was unrecognizable when you did come up.

"So you would try to pull him out of that river hole to the surface, and he would commence to drag you into that deepness and you fighting back now no longer for sport or even trophy, but fighting back for breath itself, and you thinking, like maybe Jonah did with the whale, 'Have I got him or has he got me?' Just like some fool boy chasing a girl." His and the old lady's laughter pattering soft as rain, but with the half-hush of awe wrapping it, then his voice going on again, "It was like holding onto lightning, that godalmighty blue lighting. . . ."

And I, the kid, seeing my hand filled with the zigzag flash of lightning, then my palm glowing with the blue balls of electricity that rolled across the horizon and exploded into long, blue nets of fire holding the world together; blue balls of lightning like his eyes, the eyes of the Great Mudcat, yes, and maybe the eyes of God, and him pulling me deeper, deeper into a place so far under the surface I could not even name it. . . .

The old man speaking again, the old man of the river who *knew* because he had been there, had put his hand into the mouth, the blue flame, saying, "I could no more breathe, so now I had to fight," saying, "I was deep under the surface seeing things I had only dreamed, so now I commenced to pray."

The boy, me, the kid, feeling my muscles ache, feeling how I was holding my breath, how it throbbed to the beat of my heart, and we fought for the surface, fought through layers of river darkness, fought and gained it, gasped in a breath, were pulled down again. . . .

Into the river darkness flowing out and out like sleep, like the prairie grass running before a high wind, and I caught there, held in that tension, in a place outside of life, bigger than life but informing life with a vision—a moment of such intense possibility that, like a blue ball of lightning, it lit up the world and held it together, seeing things, yes, seeing things that seemed like dream and like forever, and thinking, *I have held the roots of lightning in my hand.*

The story ending with the old man dragging the catfish, the river-monster, out onto a sandbar, pulling his arm from the fish's mouth, then rolling the mudcat back into the water: "I reckon I didn't need to keep that fish because I knowed it, knowed it in the under-surface way of the river, knowed it in the way you know a woman down in the deep and the dark and the dangerous." And the old lady's soft laughter wrapping like a shawl, a blessing, around the mysterious shoulders of evening.

And I, without even thinking this time because I could not think it yet, though I knew because I had seen it in the river, Wherever *the river is, is a beauty and a wildness.* And already caught in the undertow, *Some day I am going to get me a girl like that, a river-girl in the deep and the dark.*

The river created a border to our world, a boundary that even adults obeyed. On its far side was another county that could only be reached by a long drive to cross the river bridge. But the river was also a place where almost all women and many adult males felt ill at ease, even frightened. They acted like children lost in a dark house, as if they expected snakes and whirlpools to rise from the dark water and devour them. Those who, in their houses, seemed to know how the world worked, often seemed out of place here, and impotent. They did not see raccoon tracks in the mud, hear big carp leaping in the river, or notice the strange warbler in the elm tree. They were, for all practical purposes, deaf and dumb to the wonders, the gifts, with which the river enchanted us. It made us think; and we swore that we would never get so old, so blind, that we could not see the life of the river. We would be, we told ourselves, the exceptions: mavericks who did not forget they were men of the river. What my mother called river rats.

To go there toward the end of childhood, to see again the whiteness glowing, like the mist that must have covered the first river, the whiteness like white fire in a dream, light inside the darkness, but without shape yet, without form. To hear that voice calling over and over, over and over, inside the mist, the river, the creation. And to ache to answer, but not knowing how yet.

First, you had to earn that place, to grow big enough spiritually to enter the river, to prove that you had within yourself the dignity and responsibility, the love, to become a river-man.

The first step toward manhood had been a knife, a gift from your grandfather. It glittered there in your palm like a warning and a promise, and it tied you to all those who had gone before. You had seen pictures of stone knives the Indians made, seen the steel knives the mountain men used, and the bowie knife Davy Crockett carried at the Alamo; and now you were one of them. Almost old enough to go to the river and to explore the river breaks.

Then there was the first rifle or the first shotgun. Lethal weapons you could carry that marked you as a man. With them went the hours of practice and training to learn to use them safely and well. The barrels were black and smelled of adventure, and they were dangerous. You never forgot that. They whispered of the river and the river breaks.

The river breaks were a no-man's land, sacred space outside the confines of the workaday world. To go there was to somehow be transported to a different plane of awareness, a place more open, dangerous, where you were responsible for yourself and your own conduct, where you could take a life and therefore where you were responsible not just for yourself but for the world you lived in. It was a place shared by wild creatures with lives alien to your own, and yet apparently so similar, for they too chose to be there; they too must hear and understand the secret, inner voices that called us to the river in a visit of communion and thanksgiving. To enter such a place was to know the necessity of walking responsibly in the world, for to destroy the river-world was to destroy what was deepest in ourselves.

Now you knew you could kill. but you knew you could also reject destruction for the immediacy of entering into the mystery—for watching a great blue heron catch a frog, for glimpsing a coyote, for watching Canada geese on a sandbar. Yes, weapons were the symbol of manhood, the sign that we were old enough to know when *not* to use them. As armed men, we had entered the temple of Great Nature; to dishonor that would be to dishonor all that we wished to be and held sacred.

Ours was a simple code learned through the stories of our grandfathers and the conduct of our fathers, and it was tested in the relative freedom of the river. Such views served us well a few years later when we began going out with girls, for the land, the wild, and the women in our lives were to be wondered at, pursued, and dealt with as nature set them out to be, but always to be honored and cared for; in doing so, we honored ourselves and our creator, for our creator surely understood the way of the river. In fact, maybe *was* the great brown god of the river.

When I fell in love the second time (the first time was with the river), I took her to the river to ask her to go steady. It was the most sacred place I knew, a place of power, a magic place. I wanted her to feel that, and I wanted the river and its magic to help convince her.

I could not say these things then, of course—in fact, could not even think them yet. But I knew them at a deep, intuitive level I had learned from the river. I also knew enough about girls by then to know that all of the mystery, all of the deep and the dark was not contained in the river. The rasp of nylon-clad knees crossed in the night, the flutter of a short skirt, even a girl's secret smile—these things, too, were of the deep and the dark and the mystery. And this girl was the most mysterious of all. Her hair was black as a raven's eye, her eyes green as the deepest pools I had ever seen. She was, in my mind, of the River—a river-woman.

I chose the night of the junior-senior prom to ask her. Because of the prom, I had to wear a suit and tie, both too tight. But it was worth it when she floated down the stairs of her parents' home in a flutter of white, this creature suddenly so feminine and so alien, but with enough bosom showing to call me without words in a way I wanted to hear.

Her smile was dazzling. Like stars breaking through the dusk, I thought. And her eyes were rich with river-light. They called me like a current deep with unknown promises.

The dance was all right as far as dances went. But the drive there had been exotic with her white shoulders glowing in the moonlight, and her perfume flooding over me like the first wild smell of spring. I poured us both some scotch and we toasted like long-lost lovers before we went into the dance.

Afterward, there was a party, a big drunken party in an old stone schoolhouse. It was a warm, late spring night, almost hot, and the road there was redolent with the green odor of young grasses. But I drove past the schoolhouse, winding down secret roads until we reached the river. It lay dark and mysterious in the two a.m. moonlight. The river willows glowed and the sandbars were ghostly as the first creation.

"It's beautiful," she whispered.

I took her hand, felt a current pass between us, then helped her from the car; she pulled a shawl over her shoulders, but left her shoes behind. We were careful not to slam the door on the silence. I helped her down the bank so she would not rip her dress.

On the sandbar, she smiled, and in the smile I heard a calling, a deep, wild calling. Then she lifted the white shawl from her naked shoulders, and suddenly she was a dance of shawl and skirts and breasts and wings, pirouetting like a bird alive with white fire. I watched her dance above that dark water as she touched my oldest hunger. Only one thing I knew so wild. I knelt in the sand, threw back my head and howled a long, wild coyote cry.

Some dark life far out on the river crashed. She came to me and took my hand, then curled against me. Her lips were soft and taught a knowing wild as river water flooding in the spring. What we were rose from the deep and dark in the wild cries of birds. Around us, I was sure, the river-gods danced with dark, indomitable powers while the river went on and on, telling the story of all first things.

&

The river is a path, a no-man's land and a holy place where we can come to know the wild, insistent voices of nature and of the self, where mist rises like ancient fragments of the first morning. It is a folk song where stories sink their roots and grow for generations, enriching us with the knowledge of our own kind: where dark and subterranean lives flow on under the surface as they have for hundreds of years. The river is an altar where life and the land cross and become story, *mythos*; a passage leading us into the long, inarticulate dream of the land. It is a pool which reflects that we become how we remember, a deep current in which to meet the ancient brown river-gods who can still teach us the old ways of knowing that are simple, mysterious, and clear as water.

from *Orion*

All the Powerful Invisible Things

Gretchen Legler

All God's critters got a place in the choir
Some sing low
And some sing higher
Some sing out loud on a telephone wire
And some just clap their hands

Carolyn and I are singing. It is sunny out and we are raking oak and birch and maple leaves into mountainous piles. It is May and the snow has just melted and the leaves are all brown and wet. We are part of the work crew at Camp Van Vac. In exchange for food and lodging for the weekend, Carolyn and I and our friends, along with a handful of others, are helping the owners do all of the work that needs to be done before the resort opens in a week or two for guests. This weekend we will rake paths, reroof cabins, lift the canoes down out of the rafters of the boathouse, sweep the spider webs from the corners of the outhouses, split kindling for the wood stoves, and restock the wood boxes on the cabin hearths.

Carolyn's and my instructions are to clean the resort's winding dirt path of leaves and to rake around the base of each cabin so that the accumulation of wet leaves doesn't rot the logs. Our other friends, Cheryl and Ellen and Wendy, are off doing other chores. This is good labor. It is good to be out in the sun and to be singing. As I work, belting out verses to *The Sound of Music* and *Camelot*, I glance up now and then to watch Carolyn. I harbor a ridiculous hope, despite what happened the night before, that if I sing loud and well enough I will get Carolyn to love me.

"*Yeeow!*" Carolyn screams. I drop my rake and run to her, afraid she has stepped on glass or cut her eye on a twig. But she has raked up a tiny frog. She bends down to pick it up and I touch it in the palm of her hand. It is as still as an ice cube. She puts the frog in the sun by a warm metal barrel and in about a minute it is jumping back into its safe, cool cave of leaves. It amazes me that the frog should be there, invisible and as cold as winter under the leaves.

I ask Carolyn what kind of frog it is. She says she doesn't know. I expect her to know all the names of the animals in the woods, and the names of plants too, and of stars. She is getting a degree in conservation biology. I think of her as an expert.

If she had said anything else at all the night before, I would have dropped it, this wanting her. I would have realized that singing wouldn't help at all, that nothing would make her my lover. But the night before, she took my hand and held it in hers and said, "I am so lucky." As we rake and sing I am still clinging to those words, having not listened at all to the rest of what she said. I make those four specific words mean exactly what I want them to mean—that she will come to me some day. Those four words hold my hope, like cupped hands holding water.

The previous night the five of us had driven up from Minneapolis, completing the six-hour drive at around midnight. Along the way I dozed in the back of the van, with my head in Ellen's lap, feeling her gently touch my hair, listening to her and Wendy quietly reminisce about their travels in the Southwest. Carolyn's and Cheryl's soft women's voices traveled back to me from the front seat, reminding me of when I was a child and the sound of my parents' voices in conversation filled our car in exactly the same way, anchoring me.

We all pressed our faces to the windows of the van when Carolyn said that there were northern lights. The sky was full of them: full of dancing lights, full of pale green sheets. I imagined them then as the flowing skirts of goddesses, moving among the stars like fabric in the wind.

The northern lights were still out, still moving, when we pulled down the narrow drive into Camp Van Vac. After putting our bags away in the big cabin the five of us were to share, Carolyn and I walked out onto the point. The point is a jumble of greenstone jutting out into the lake, where you can sit and catch the wind, or listen to the ice go out, or feel night sounds—a late-calling loon and water against rock.

Across the lake, the green and yellow and cream-colored lights of the aurora still danced. As I watched, in my imagination I too danced and twisted and loomed among the veils. I too was some spirit dancing around a fire, my body lit from the inside by flame.

We were sitting on the rock, close enough so that our knees and shoulders touched. Caroyln pointed out stars to me—the Northern Cross, the Sickle, and the Archer. I pointed out the ones I knew: the North Star, the Big and Little Dippers. I sipped port from a styrofoam cup and munched on a ginger snap.

Port and ginger snaps and sitting out on the point at camp Van Vac at night were a part of a ritual I had worked up. It was a relatively new ritual, only in its second year. Not a tradition yet, but something that seemed important that I repeat, on this night especially. I told Carolyn how happy I was to be here, how I used to come here with Craig when we were married, and how it had been two years now since I had left him and how I had come back both of those years—first with Cate and now with her and the others, my friends—and I couldn't be happier *and, and, and. . . .*

Soon enough, because Carolyn was so quiet and because when I looked at her she was staring at her feet, I realized that my voice had become annoying. My urgent need to mark this time, to make this time something monumental for me, was too much for her.

"Sometimes it's good to just be," she said. "Sometimes being so self-conscious takes us away from where we are." All of a sudden I was ashamed. I would have blushed if it had not been so cold out.

For a while we sat without talking, then she began, in the low, smooth voice that I hve always thought matched the darkness of her hair and eyes, the broadness of her shoulders, to tell me a story that came from the time she worked with Wilderness Inquiry and was out with a handful of kids on a canoe trip.

One of the boys on the trip had mild mental retardation. Another of the boys had autism. As is common with people who have autism, this boy organized his life by a series of rituals: to bed every night at the same time; breakfast every morning just so. The boy's routine was sometimes maddening; he needed absolute regularity, Carolyn said, and he was always checking his watch to see that he was doing the right thing at the right time. He had received tremendous love and care, she said, and could report in writing whether he was happy or mad or sad, but, as is also common in people with autism, could go no further in explaining or examining his feelings.

One night the northern lights came up brilliantly, Carolyn said. She and the kids lay back on their sleeping bags on their flat rock point, a point like the one she and I sat on as she told me this story, and gazed unbelievingly at the sky. All except the boy with autism, who, as the lights were coming on, folded his clothes, combed his hair, brushed his teeth, and climbed into his bag.

After they had watched the lights for some time, the boy who had mild mental retardation asked Carolyn if she could write something for him. He wanted to tell his mother about the lights, he said. He wanted to tell her how powerful, marvelous, and unbelievable the lights were. Carolyn took out a pad of paper and a pencil and took it all down:

> *Dear Mother, we are on West Bearskin Lake watching northern lights. They are green and red and blue and yellow. The lights are all over the sky, moving. I wish you could see them. I love you.*

After a while, Carolyn said, she and the boy and the rest of them became bored, confused. What do you do after you have looked at such an awesome thing for so long? You must, at some point, stop and get into your sleeping bag and close your eyes. What else is there? There isn't any way, is there, to go to the lights? You always must go back to your own particular life with a vague ache in your heart, an ache that suggests to you there is another place you should be, although you don't know where it is.

As Carolyn finished her story, she tilted her head back to look up at the sky and I saw a silver strand of tear snake its way over her sharp cheekbone and down the side of her neck, into the hollow of her shoulder. Suddenly, I thought that I had to tell Carolyn that I loved her. I had to seize the moment and tell her something. Anything.

Our knees and hands had become stiff from the cold. We rose, helping each other up, and we made our way back toward our cabin along a dirt trail crisscrossed with the shadows of thin birch. We rounded a corner and from a distance through the trees I saw the light from the window of the cabin, yellow and safe. Our friends were there sitting around the woodstove, talking. Before we got to that light, before the light broke the bond that the night had created between us, I had to tell her.

I turned around suddenly so that Carolyn stopped short of running right into me. I touched her face and said, stuttering and halting, "I've been attracted to you." I felt ridiculous, light-headed, kicking myself already for the banality of what had just come out of my mouth. "And I've been struggling with what to do about it," I said. "And I decided a long time ago that the most important thing to me was to be your friend." This had been true, but at that moment was not true at all. I wanted her as my lover. I was lying even as I was trying to tell the truth.

Carolyn took my hand and said to me, "I am so lucky," and we hugged each other. Then I held her as she turned toward the lake, so that my body pressed into her back, and I could feel the heat of her through her jacket and wool shirt and she started to cry and we stood like that looking out at the water. Soon we were both shivering, and we walked back to the cabin.

Ellen was still up and we sat with her in the hot orange light that made the cabin walls glow gold. Carolyn talked, nervously, I thought, about her work, about seed patents and genetically engineered plants. I was afraid that I had scared her and that what she was doing was trying to put words between us: hard-edged words and ideas.

Finally, she lay down to sleep on the floor beside the cot I was lying on, in front of the fire, and I asked her if I could lie next to her for awhile. She said yes. I asked her if I could touch her. She said yes. I ran my hands through her thick hair, again and again. Her face showed up against the firelight, ruddy, sharp, and full. I touched her cheeks, ran my fingers across from bone to bone, pausing, fingers trembling, at her lips. I touched her collarbone, my fingers like feathers, brushing the length of it.

I asked her if she had ever kissed a woman. No, she said. I asked her if she had ever loved me. How? she said. As a lover, I said. No, she said. I told her I had known her for long enough to know that she was one woman I could be with forever. She asked me, in a sleepy voice, what exactly these qualities were that I thought she possessed and I told her to never mind what I said, it was all right, and I ran my hand through her hair again. I asked her how this felt. How what feels? she said. When I touch you, I said. It feels friendly, she said. I told her it didn't feel that way to me and I stopped. It was wrong to touch her like that if we weren't both in it together. I told her I loved her and she smiled and then I said goodnight and went back to my cot.

> *Swing low, sweet chariot*
> *Coming for to carry me home*
> *Swing low, sweet chariot*
> *Coming for to carry me home.*
>
> *I looked over Jordan and what did I see*
> *Coming for to carry me home?*
> *A band of angels coming after me*
> *Coming for to carry me home.*

Carolyn sings these verses out loud and deep in her clear voice. I join in later, softly, almost under my breath. I apologize all morning, until I know I don't need to do it anymore, until I know that she forgives me and that it is all right. We rake and sing songs from Broadway musicals—from *Fiddler on the Roof,* from *The Music Man,* every musical tune and every bad campfire song we can remember. We sing spirituals, even Christmas carols, any song we can think of that sounds happy, and we see the frog and we make big piles of leaves and sit in the leaves together and talk and I know that everything will be fine between us.

Even as I am still in love with her, as I hang on to the hope of having her as a lover, I feel as if I have been saved by her. Anything could have happened the night before. Instead, I was saved by her. It was as if I had jumped out of a canoe on a windy day, on purpose, just to see what she'd do, and she didn't pull me back in but instead threw me a life jacket. She didn't foolishly come in after me, to get wet and cold too, and maybe even drown with me, but she threw me the life jacket and told me, "Put it on."

All morning long as we rake and sing, I feel as if Carolyn has pointed out to me the shape of an idea—the ghostliest outlines of a concept—the idea of the difference between a friend and a lover. I squint hard when I think about it, staring into the bushes, or at the mortar between the stones of the foundation of the cabin I am raking around. I stand there, on the shady side of the cabin, raking at a clump of leaves still embedded in ice, smelling the rich mildew coming up from the leafy earth, squinting, trying to focus on the idea, so that next time I will recognize it all on my own. All day I feel like I am walking around something, something that has mass and weight, something that has shape, that has color, but that I can't see yet. When I do see it don't even know what it will be.

The five of us take the afternoon off from raking and chopping and stacking and hauling to go into Ely to visit the International Wolf Center. At the center, I follow the curving walls of an elaborately laid-out display, pushing buttons to hear wolves howl, flipping through plastic-sheathed pages of thick books about werewolves and wolf-men and wolves who ate children and wolves who lovingly raised children. I read about St. Francis and the wolf, about wolves in sheep's clothing, about the Lamb of God. I look at pictures of wolves fornicating with maidens, wolves with their dreadful, lustful tongues hanging out.

I am particularly taken with a display of pictures and stories elaborateing pre-Christian myths about wolves. I stand, my work-blistered hands clasped behind my back, my dusty, booted feet apart, reading from an illustrated panel on the wall all about the Scandinavian story of Fenris.

Fenris, the wolf, offspring of the gods, must be bound by a magical cord to restrain his destructive impulses. The cord that binds him seems as light as gossamer, but in truth it is unbreakable. The cord is made from the powerful invisible things of the world, such as the breath of fish, the roots of mountains, the noises of cats when they move, the beards of women, the anguish of bears, the yearning of glaciers, the voices of red leaves as they fall. When the world is about to end, according to the myth, Fenris will break loose and devour the world and the gods. And then a new and better world will begin.

I marvel at this and the other ancient stories that I go on to read, making my way slowly through the display. These are stories so powerful that for different people in a different time they made perfect sense of an entire world. The stories remind me of how a simple thing, a wolf, is made complex by humans. The stories remind me of how an ordinary thing is made sacred or profane, how it becomes so much larger than itself. And the stories remind me of the power of the word. The stories we tell about each other, about our own lives, about wolves and the world around us, join together to form some kind of invisible narrative net that is thrown over us, binding us all.

At dinner back at the resort, all of us at the work weekend share stories of our accomplishments: a new roof is up on cabin eleven, the wood crew split two cords of birch, the sauna and shower floor has a new layer of blue paint, the paths up to cabin twenty are leaf-free.

After dinner, Carolyn and I walk around the point and look at birds. She has the bird book and is looking up into the birches and pines, which I see now, looking through binoculars, are full of birds, so many small yellow and brown birds, as dense as Christmas lights. I want to know what they are. Carolyn tells me she thinks there are at least two different kinds of warblers—a male Cape May Warbler and Palm Warblers whose sex she can't determine.

Finally, we sit down on the rocks of the point in the windy evening sunshine. Around us the warm rock gives off a dusty, flinty smell. A bird zings past me at eye level, fifty yards out into the lake, and I ask Carolyn, pointing, my outstretched arm and finger following the bird around to my right, "What is that?" She doesn't know. "Is it in your book?" I ask. "I don't know," she says, then she is quiet for awhile and I hear the wind in the tall pines behind us. There is that smell again, dusty and sweet: the smell of the drying surface of the earth and thin, warm yellow-white sun.

She is sitting back holding up her strong torso with her arms propped behind her. Her bluejean-covered legs are crossed. Her brow is creased just a little bit, and her mouth is set in a straight line. I ask her what she is thinking. She says this: "Sometimes I think we observe and name not to find out what is there where we are, but to try to figure out whether we are in the right place." She is talking about herself as much as me. It is the most frenzied observers of the surface who miss the most in the depths. I know what she means. It is those who are most meticulous at recording observable phenomena who miss the faces of the dead when they visit, the importance of dreams, the sweetness of water. It is those who name the most and the hardest who are at least aware of where they are.

Early the next morning, before the others are awake, I walk outside and pee, squatting in the bushes beside the cabin. I look out at the lake and it is gray and frothing. I walk around to the front of the cabin and wake Carolyn, who is bundled in her sleeping bag on the ground. She wanted to sleep outside, she said, to be out there when the sun came up.

She and I hurriedly dress and paddle out into the lake in a canoe. We are headed toward an island where I had hidden two small deer-hide-wrapped packages the previous spring. I had asked Carolyn earlier, on our way up to Camp Van Cac, if she would go to the island with me. There was something special I had to do there, I told her, and I needed her help. Even on a still day I wouldn't want to paddle it alone, and today with the wind and waves there would be no way I could make it out and back by myself.

The spring I put the packages on the island, shielding them with a piece of birch bark, nestling them in the deep moss under some blueberry bushes, I had tried to motor out to the island. I had a new metal Grumman canoe with a square stern and a 2.5-horsepower motor. The motor stopped halfway across the lake and I couldn't get it started again. Every time I primed it, gas pooled out into the lake and Cate, who was with me, got angry and then sad and told me to just stop trying because I was getting gas in the lake.

So the two of us paddled and Cate waited in the canoe for me while I got out on the island and lit a candle and put the bundles under the blueberry bushes and said a prayer. The prayer was a hope that, sometime, what was hurting me so much then would hurt less, and that in the meantime this place was safe and sacred and a good place to lay these parcels.

Back at the dock at Camp Van Vac Cate and I were unloading the canoe when I fell in. I was lifting the tiny motor off of the back of the canoe, and the canoe tipped and I went sideways, my whole body, parka, hat, boots, and motor, into the five-foot-deep icy water. I came up spluttering, gasping, and afraid, water dribbling off my hat brim. Cate told me to run, run to the cabin and get out of my wet clothes. I was standing naked in front of the woodstove when Cate came in finally, laughing, to rub me warm with a soft towel.

The deer-hide-wrapped bundles were all about a woman named Anna, who showed me what it was like, for the first time in my life, to love myself. In them I put small sacred things—a love poem, a picture, chocolate, a vial of water from the Ganges, silk scarves, silk panties, a small red piece of iron ore, a spring of sage—ordinary things dense with meaning only for me.

It is hard paddling and Carolyn is having a difficult time keeping the canoe straight in the wind. Waves are breaking over the bow. My shoes are already wet and my arms ache. The idea in going out to the island this time is that everything is over between Anna and me, and I will bury the bundles deep because this door on her has been shut.

At first when I put them there and I told Anna about it, she cried and said she didn't want to be buried, and I said no, no, I didn't bury you, that wasn't it, I had only put them under a piece of bark, for safekeeping, until I knew what to do. Now I am going to bury them.

Carolyn and I pull the canoe up on the rocks at the island and I walk directly to where I left the bundles a year earlier and I find them under the bark beneath the blueberry bush. They've been chewed on by a mouse or squirrel, and tiny bits of red thread and white paper are scattered about on the moss, but the bundles are still mostly intact. Carolyn helps me look for a big rock. We wander around the island until we find one, and together we roll it back and I begin to dig beneath it, making a hollow for these bundles.

I did and dig and dig, my fingernails filling with dirt. The whole time I am digging, Carolyn is sitting beside me and I tell her about Anna. I tell her how the last time I talked to Anna she said that she didn't love me. I asked her if she loved me and this is what she said: "You might as well ask someone else that. Ask them, does Anna love Gretchen?" I asked her, didn't she care about me any more? What about the tie between us, that powerful tether that would bind us together forever, and she said this: "What tie? I don't want that anymore. I only remember bad things when I think of you."

&b

Of course it had started out differently. We had had good times in the short time we were together, like the ski trip we took to northern Minnesota. One night on that trip snow fell in flakes the size of cotton balls, and the woods were dark and sweet and little red lanterns set out by the owner of the resort we stayed at lit our way along the trails.

The lanterns made me feel as if I were inside the stories about Narnia that I'd read as a teenager, or inside the stories about Shangri-la, inside those stories about a secret safe place away from everything that could ever hurt me, or Anna, or anyone.

She and I stopped and leaned forward on our ski poles, breathing hard, our breath coming out in tiny puffs of steam. There was something in the woods then. And we didn't know whether to be afraid of it or to be happy, but mostly we were happy, and I kissed her and said, "It feels like anything is possible here, doesn't it?"

Later, at the cabin, I told Anna that I needed to do something to mark this time. It was a special anniversary. It was spring and it had been a year already since I had left Craig and moved into a new life. Only a year. A whole year. A yawning, spreading year and also the shortest year of my life so far. "What do you want to do?" she asked me. And I said I didn't know, but after dinner I dragged two sleeping bags and a candle out the cabin door and through the deep snow past the woodpile to the hard-packed ski trail. I spread the sleeping bags out and asked Anna to lie with me.

The candle would not stay lit. There were stars. She whispered to me, "What are we waiting for?" I told her I didn't know. I began to feel as if things were coming out of the woods and looking at us, that I could hear movement, breathing. I thought I heard footfalls. I tried to reason that I was hearing the blood in my veins, coursing, moving the hairs in my ears. "Maybe it's just this," she said. "What?" I asked. "Maybe it's nothing, maybe it's just being here." She reached out and stroked my hand.

After we came in from the night and were standing brushing our teeth, she locked the door. We were in the middle of a northern Minnesota forest. No one was around except maybe a few people in the other resort cabins and the old couple who owned the lodge. But she was afraid. When we climbed into bed and snuggled into our sleeping bags, I asked her, "Are you afraid?" I didn't tell her that if she had not locked the door I would have. Whatever I sensed in the woods she had too, and we both felt, vaguely, that it meant us harm.

She thought I was mocking her and she turned away from me and started to cry. A part of me saw her then only as pathetic. Her back shook with sobs. Curled up in the sleeping bag, she looked like some thin baby bird. I felt helpless. I had never felt so mean. I had never wanted to hold someone so much. I had never felt love like that before.

I broke it off between us because, for one reason, she was married. But long after we left one another I kept writing letters to her. I was insistent. Even bothersome. I wanted something from her even though I wouldn't give her a thing.

In one letter I wrote:

> *I am looking out my apartment window to the yellow light coming from the stained glass across the way where workmen are plastering some new walls. It all looks orderly and hopeful.*

*A friend asked me the other day if I grieved over Craig. "Yes,"
I said. "But not necessarily for him?" she asked. I thought for a
moment and said, "Right. Not necessarily for him, but for what
we had that was perfect and wonderful. For what I'll never
have with someone else. For what is irreplaceable."*

*With you I felt enormous and beautiful. I didn't believe you
when you said you loved me because you were so beautiful and
perfect and complete. When I gave you flowers, you received
them so gracefully that you made everyone around you feel they
had gotten them instead of you.*

*My friend says that now I have my work and that is good
labor, as hard or harder than any love with another person. But
I tell her, with Anna I became the person I want to be. I leapt
into myself. It is not as if my relationship to my self can be
separated from my love for her.*

*Being with you was being in a state of grace. I have called
you an angel. My friend says this stuff, this magic, is in us and
we don't always need another person to bring it out of us. She
talks of certain religious practices through which you can also
come to this place of grace. She tells me about practicing yoga—
about the time when the Swami comes and touches you on the
head, and when he touches you you experience enlightenment.
The touch is meant to give you hope and focus and purpose, to
show you where it is you are supposed to be going, to show you
what grace feels like, so you will know what you are moving
toward. But then the Swami leaves you and you do the rest
yourself.*

*My friend says that maybe other people in our lives are like
this, they awaken hopefulness in us, this focus and sense of
purpose. They awaken us with love, and then the rest is labor,
our labor. Eventually we come to the same state of grace
ourselves, through our own persistence.*

&

"She said she didn't love me," I tell Carolyn, and tears drip down into the muddy earth I am digging in. I feel Carolyn's hand in the center of my back. In that clear moment when I feel her hand, I also hear the words I just uttered repeated. I realize, as if I have been shocked with electricity, that this is not what Anna said at all. She didn't say, "I don't love you." In fact, she never answered me. She turned the question back on me. In this crystalline second I see beyond everything, down into the roots of my life, her life, all of our lives. and I understand that I might as well have asked her, "Do you think I love myself?" And if I had asked her that. she would have said, "I don't know that. Only *you* know that."

The hole finally dug, I take each parcel and place it gently in the dirt, pushing hard to make sure it is in place. I tell Carolyn that the last time I spoke with Anna I asked her if I could be sure that she would carry me in her heart. I asked her if she would do me just one favor— keep the memory of me safe. She said no.

"She said no," I tell Carolyn. I didn't say it to Anna then, but I thought this: if Anna wouldn't do it, keep me safe, hold me close, even the memory of me, then who would? And again, I hear her voice echoing in the chamber in my head. and it is saying over and over again, "Do you love yourself? *Do* you? *Do* you? *Do* you?"

Carolyn helps me roll the rock back on top and I pack the sides with moss, so it looks as if nothing unusual has happened here. We heave the canoe off the rocks and paddle back to camp, paddling hard against the waves, trying to stay as much as possible in the lee of islands so that we don't get swept back out into the lake.

> *'Tis a gift to be simple,*
> *'Tis a gift to be free.*
> *'Tis a gift to come down*
> *Where you ought to be . . .*

I am humming now, humming bits and pieces of all the songs that Carolyn and I have been singing all weekend. It is evening and our last night at Camp Van Vac. The five of us sit around the woodstove and tell stories. There are long moments of silence when we sit comfortably, with our legs stretched out, or bending forward with our arms resting on our knees, looking at the woodstove, at the cracks along the side of the door and at the small triangles in the grate in front where the fire shows through. There is nothing tangible that binds me to these women: no blood line, for instance, nothing visible. Only friendship. I am at home with them.

After what seems like hours, during which the air in the cabin grows so hot my face feels on fire and my head begins to spin just a little from sipping the last of the port, I go outside to get some air. I stand on the concrete steps of the cabin, listening, and off in the distance I hear a wolf howl. First the low notes rise, then they trail off into the night.

The cabin door opens and light comes flooding over my back, illuminating me from behind. It is Carolyn and I hold up my hand for her to stand still. She hears the wolf howl too. Then I point to the woods in front of us, where I hear faint skitterings and branches breaking. I ask her what that is, that soft sound. She looks at me with her most beautiful smile and she says, 'The wind in the leaves," and then she smiles again and says. "The footsteps of mice," and then I say, "The breath of fish, the roots of mountains, the noise of cats as they move, the beards of women, the anguish of bears . . ."

Then the door opens again and everyone comes out and goes into the woods to empty their bladders before bed. There is laughing and the sounds of zippers being undone and done up again and then footsteps on the wooden stairs leading up to the bedrooms and someone raking the coals in the woodstove and then shutting the cast-iron door and the scrape of the damper being closed and then we call to each other, "Good night."

from *All the Powerful Invisible Things: A Sportswoman's Notebook*

Beyond City Limits

Glen Vanstrum

If we didn't die, we would not appreciate life as we do.
—Jacques-Yves Cousteau

One by one, two by two, we gather in near silence on the La Jolla sandstone bluff this bright February afternoon. Old friends murmur greetings, nothing more. A small knot of wet-suit-clad divers attends to a wreath of flowers down on the beach, only feet from the harbor seal haul-out. A few of the pinnipeds watch them with one eye, but most just stretch out, luxurious on the sun-warmed sand. The ocean breeze carries up to us the salty tang of kelp and the dank, gym-socks odor of seals.

Only 10 feet from where I stand, a bagpipe player splits the clear day with the sharp, sudden force of an ax blade, blowing an "Amazing Grace" so startling, so piercing, that every one of the seals stares up at us and starts barking in dismay. Slowly now, as if careful not to harm a single blossom, the divers slip the wreath into the chill Eastern Pacific and start swimming for the open sea. In one step they leave the civilized megalopolis behind and enter the territory of the kelp forest and the opal squid.

The megalopolis, the greater San Diego-Tijuana border complex of some four million human souls, is my home. A Minnesota boy with a strong addiction to the wilderness, there is only one reason I've been able to stay here—the big wild that borders the city, 64 million square miles of wild, one-third of the earth's surface. The Pacific.

For many years after moving to California, I was content to explore only the surface of the ecotone zone where ocean meets land, the surf.

Wrapped around a board waiting for a set, dangling my feet in the drink, I often wondered, what was down there? At times a garibaldi would swirl in an orange flash, or a dolphin would crease the surface with a knife-edged dorsal fin, but it seemed to me there was only one way to get to know the real Pacific: put on a tank and drop in.

Snorkeling and free diving, I gleaned brief glimpses of the blue-green undersea world: startled schools of barracuda, a scuttling crab, the gentle sway of kelp. Air hunger, the constant need to clear my ears with each dive, and the difficulty in making photographs made these excursions less than satisfying.

Unfortunately, an experience in medical school delayed my scuba career some years. We admitted a young, formerly fearless Navy SEAL to out internal medicine ward for hyperbaric treatment. He'd been diving mornings with his unit and then moonlighting in the late afternoons working underwater salvage. All this bottom time got the poor guy bent, and he ended up with rotary nystagmus—his pupils spun around and around in his head, putting him on perpetual bed rest. He couldn't walk and could barely talk. He just lay there, gripping the mattress, trying to get things to stop spinning. My rotation on that ward was twelve weeks long; when I left, he was still there, white-knuckled, hanging on to his bed for dear life.

Then came that fateful trip to Hawaii when my surfing buddy, Joe Gifford, talked me into going down with a scuba tank. Joe has a receding hairline and a mischievous smile. He looks and acts a lot like the actor Jack Nicholson.

"Just remember," he said, "clear your ears when ya go down, and come up real slow. Don't hold your breath comin' up, 'cause the air will expand in your lungs and kill ya."

"What about the bends?" I asked, wimpering.

"Don't worry," said Joe, "we ain't goin' deep enough."

On that first dive we swam, weightless, past some whitetip sharks into a cave. I followed Joe through a long tunnel into a small lava cavern. There was an air pocket there where we took off our masks and felt the atmospheric pressure rise and fall with the swell. On the way back, amid abstract sculptures of rainbow-hued hard corals, we saw a trumpetfish, a moray eel, and a vast school of blue and yellow surgeonfish that darkened the water. Astronauts in inner space, free from gravity and civilization, we were visitors in an alien world. I was hooked.

After getting certified I started diving back on the mainland, although with some reluctance. California diving was a different animal from Hawaii diving. The water was bitter cold. The visibility was less clear. The wildlife, though, was just as fantastic. Sea lions, leopard sharks, moray eels—they were all there. The city planners, showing rare foresight and wisdom, established a biologic preserve in 1970 along the La Jolla coast and prohibited the taking or harming of sea life there in any form, ensuring my local coastal waters would remain pristine, if frigid.

One day, checking out the visibility at a spot within the reserve called Second Reef, trying to screw up courage, I saw a kelp-draped figure crawl out of the sea, a man who looked like Neptune himself. Squinting up at me through weathered, sparkling eyes, handlebar mustache dripping saltwater, strands of sea grass stuck to his wet suit, he broke into a Pacific-sized smile.

"How was it?" I asked.

"Un-be-lievable," he answered in a voice rough as beach sand. "I'm down there at about 60 feet, 60 feet, you understand, and I feel this pecking at my shoulder. I turn, and do you know what it is?

"A kelp bass?" I ventured.

"A cormorant! Un-der-water!" he said. "Can you believe it? A bird! And he's pecking away at my mask, peck, peck, peck, like he's trying to figure out what I'm doing down there. Can you be-lieve it!"

This was Ron Starkey, soon to be a good friend, a dive instructor still full of amazement and joy at the discoveries to be made under the sea. If it wasn't a cormorant at 60 feet, it was a pair of tame moray eels wrapped around his neck, or an inflamed garibaldi defending its nest. It was Ron who spurred me to forget the cold and poor visibility of the Eastern Pacific and just go diving.

For starters, Ron hauled me out on my first night dive. After all the hype and talk about sharks, I wasn't too sure about restricting my view to a small light. On a moonless night we waded out into the wilderness from the warm glow of a seaside restaurant. The incongruity of it struck me—inside the restaurant, elegantly coiffured ladies and well-heeled gentlemen were sitting down to five-course meals, while, a few feet away, we were slipping into the cool black ink of the unknown.

Ron had a powerful flashlight, and my fears washed off with the incoming tide. In quick order, he showed me a cusk eel burrowing into the sand, a he-man-sized lobster dancing over the bottom with ballet legs, and a round stingray. He scooped the ray up and held the stinger and tail, letting me touch the sandpaperlike skin, then gently released it. We turned off our lights, and an iridescent violet and yellow jellyfish wafted by, all but invisible, shimmering ghostlike amid trails of glowing plankton.

There is something both peaceful and exhilarating about swimming along 30 feet deep in the quiet Pacific at night. The warm glow of the flashlight limits one's visual field and focuses attention. Daytime fish like garibaldi and bass disappear, and a new shift of characters—octopi, crabs, and eels—comes out to explore and feed. To me it was sheer wilderness joy, the same feeling found, say, hiking in Alaska's Brooks Range—only this joy was just a few feet from my urban home.

As I got to know Ron, it became clear he was obsessed with getting wet. Recovering from a bitter divorce, he seemed blind to topside life, ignoring culture and events not related to diving, smoking too many cigarettes as if uncomfortable inhaling noncompressed air. An old injury from the construction trade left him with pinched nerves in his neck, a painful condition relieved only while he was weightless underwater. The classic surfer adage fit him well: "At sea, one leaves the problems of land far behind." He made maybe five or six dives a day, taught hundreds of students, and lived, talked, ate, and breathed scuba. Maniacal? Maybe. In love with the ocean? Definitely.

Another dive with Ron did not go so well. It was my first trip below in serious kelp forest. The ocean off San Diego, like much of the West Coast, is blessed with the world's fastest growing plant, really a brown algae, *Macrocystis pyrifera*. Able to grow 2 feet in a day, kelp produces dense forests in water from 20 to 130 feet deep, where rootlike holdfasts grip the bottom. In and around these "trees" live, or used to live, marine mammals, fish of every description, and invertebrates from holocanth to cephalopod.

Researchers at the University of California have shown that the local kelp forest thrives on nitrogen from treated urban sewage and wastewater discharged miles from shore. This contrasts with the Palos Verdes Peninsula bed, once thirty miles long and now gone for thirty years, a victim of untreated pollution from Los Angeles. In San Diego kelp ships run in reverse as huge circular mowing devices on their sterns cut and haul aboard the oil-excreting seaweed, harvesting only the surface fronds. The resulting product, algin, is used in making products like ice cream, pie, pudding, and beer, which, in an odd twist to the circle of life, find their way back to feed the forest once again.

Although the kelp in San Diego is still doing well, the animal life that makes the beds unique has been decimated. Abalone used to carpet the bottom between holdfasts; today the tasty molluscs are so depleted that four of the five species are in danger of local extinction. Sea otters, who eat the urchins that eat the kelp, no longer exist in Southern California, most probably hunted to extinction by Native Americans thousands of years ago. Recent overfishing and use of gill nets, now outlawed, have destroyed local populations of sheepshead, rockfish, and bass. San Diego divers in the forties and fifties commonly found monster-sized black sea bass in the forest, some weighing up to 500 pounds. Mia Tegner, a Scripps Institute of Oceanography researcher, reports, "Our group (at Scripps) has made about twenty thousand dives (in the kelp) in the last twenty-seven years and never seen one."

On this clear October 13 Friday, hoping to view at least some wildlife, we hopped onto a boat, got a dive briefing from the skipper, and dropped in. Assuming my years of surfing had taught me everything I needed to know about kelp, I plummeted with the coruscating sunbeams into a murky, blue-green world 95 feet deep, at four atmospheres of pressure. In spite of the sun the visibility was only 5 feet, and the kelp was dense as Amazon rainforest. Since Ron was my dive buddy, I tried to follow him but fell behind, hung up in shiny green leaves and branches. An improvised 360-degree roll not only failed to free me but got me stuck even worse. I whipped out a dive knife and started whacking kelp fronds, using up a lot of air, trying not to panic, trying not to cut my regulator hose.

Suddenly free from the kelp, I started rising, overbuoyant. I tried to dump air. My buoyancy vest overexpanded. Couldn't find air release valves. Rocketing for the surface. . . rush of bubbles . . . open mouth scream . . . terror . . . AAHHHHHHHHH!

A champagne cork released at 16 fathoms, I bobbed up to my waist in the bright sunlight in a wad of bubbles and fear. The skipper looked over from the boat in surprise, saw that air embolus and the bends had spared me, and shook his head at my idiocy.

Ron came up fifteen minutes later, angry, sputtering, going off.

"Where did you go? I mean, you disappeared! Some buddy! All I could think was 'Friday the 13th, Friday the 13th,' and man, you are gone."

After a lot of discussion and debate, we reviewed the lessons learned from this uncontrolled ascent. Never roll in the kelp. Never let yourself get grossly overbuoyant while worrying about some task. And never approach any dive without realizing that dropping into the ocean is no different from unaided mountaineering—one slip, or series of slips, and you are history.

After that I started to doubt the wisdom of buddy diving. A buddy, I realized, could drag you into trouble that you might have avoided. A buddy might want to go deeper, or be braver in exploring wrecks, or be less patient when photographing. A buddy could give you false assurance when you needed to rely on your own skills and equipment, and anyway, things could go sour too fast for a buddy to help. And so, upon learning of the great squid run, I ventured out solo.

Each January a spectacle occurs in the ocean wilderness off La Jolla Canyon, a spectacle with everything Hollywood could want and more—sex, violence, death, and rebirth. Millions, maybe billions, of opal squid, *Loligo opalescens,* swim inshore to gather and spawn. These cephalopods form one of the bulwarks of the ocean food web, taking up a huge position somewhere in the chain above the zooplankton and below the tertiary predators. Just about every big fish, marine mammal, or seabird loves to eat them; by the same token, these voracious animals gobble up anything they can wrap their beaks around: crustaceans, bait fish, smaller squid. For years fishers neglected them. Now, as fishery after fishery is depleted, as markets in the Far East are developed, and as

Americans get used to the idea of calamari as a food (it's rarely called squid on the menu), human predatory pressure is increasing. In fact, opals could go the way of the abalone and the black sea bass.

David Au, from the National Marine Fisheries Service, told me that until recently there was no regulation of the industry. California boats hauled in a record 78,825 tons of squid worth $30 million in 1996; the harvest in 1997 dropped to 70,791 tons. Because of El Niño-induced ocean warming, the 1998 catch will be a small fraction of these previous two years. Although fishers must now buy a permit, there are no limits on catch size, and year-round fishing is allowed.

Squid are fascinating creatures; they use water jet propulsion to move, they release ink clouds to protect themselves, and they have remarkable nervous systems. Chromophores in their skin change color with kaleidoscopic speed. Although not as brainy as their cousins the octopi, squid have neurons similar enough to our own that they have been used for decades in medical research.

It was not only a general fascination with cephalopods, though, that led me out one evening to photograph the great January spawning run. Opal squid have this odd method of reproduction. They don't just have sex and smoke a cigarette. There is more involved; the stakes are higher. Once a male deposits his spermatophore packet with a special tentacle in the female, and once she safely plants the fertilized egg packet into the sandy bottom, they both die. Like salmon, they perform one final, heroic act, and it's over.

There are nuances to this coital parade, I learned, that illustrate how odd and crafty these creatures are. Offshore, where there is room to manuever, pick, and choose, females find the male of their choice, mate head to head, and retain the sperm packet in their mouths where they carry it for months. Inshore, where eggs are deposited, sexual mayhem and orgy are the norm. Squid cloud the seas. Large bully males fight for mates, grab the female they desire, and deposit sperm under the female's mantle near her egg chamber. With all the pushing and shoving there is no time for offshore-style squid fellatio.

Near the sandy bottom, where she can release from her mouth the stored sperm of her choice, early mate, a female withdraws her egg packet and holds two hundred gelatinous eggs in her tentacles. But with her arms occupied, she can no longer fight off the ever-present and pesky small males, who dart in and deposit sperm directly on the eggs.

While this is going on, predators knife through the water to devour distracted, love-struck squid. Birds, sharks, rays, marine mammals, all take advantage of the mass of bio-protein. When the orgy is over, exhausted males and females die, their bodies, if missed by predators, littering the ocean floor among the egg sacks.

In hopes of seeing this display of sex and violence, then, came one novice solo diver, yours truly, loaded with a new, heavy photo strobe, a camera, and the sparest of information.

"Just swim out to where the seabirds are the thickest, and drop in there," was my thin advice. I'd dived the canyon before, during the daytime with Ron, and was confident the terrain would hold no surprises. The setup: a gentle sand drop-off, punctuated by vertical cliffs. The walls were pockmarked with holes favored as home by the ubiquitous red and blue goby, a beautiful fish the size of a toothpick.

As the sun settled on the horizon, I punched through some small surf and kicked due west out to sea, toward a raucous gathering of hundreds of gulls, cormorants, and pelicans. The long swim took me much farther out than my recollection of where the dive spot should be. At last, there were as many birds inshore as to the west; diving, resting, and conversing avians surrounded me. An unseen bird bomber splashed the back of my head, a little too close for comfort, and got my teeth chattering—a gift, no doubt, from the late Alfred Hitchcock. The sun by now was long gone, and the reds and oranges on the horizon were fading fast into a deep indigo-violet. Resting on the surface after the long swim to slow my heart rate and calm down, I checked my gear once again: plenty of air, no weird leaks, camera OK.

Weighed by the new strobe, I left the surface without effort. At 90 feet, my flash showed a brief vision of twirling mini-submarines, jetting every which way in pairs. My descent was so rapid, though, that the scene appeared but for a moment, then down, down, down I dropped.

Not wanting to overcompensate and rocket to the surface again, I cautiously added air to my vest. My ears kept requiring clearing, telling me I was still sinking, and the water turned blacker than the night sky of Neptune. After taking his bathysphere to a record depth, William Beebe wrote of this place, the abyss, a world so dark, "it seemed as if all future nights in the upper world must be considered twilight."

I was flying totally on instruments; there was no bottom, no point of orientation. And no bathysphere. My heart pounded at hummingbird tempo. La Jolla Canyon dropped here to a depth of 900 feet. Once again panic seized me. I added air to my vest—"Pssst, pssst"—then shone a light at my depth gauge. Uh-oh. 144 feet. Recreational divers are not supposed to go over 130 feet.

At last my ginger efforts at neutralizing buoyancy paid off. I rose back to 90 feet, saw the squid once again, but now shot up past them. My heart whirring, my ears popping, my drive to be a squid voyeur withered and vanished. Finally neutral at 30 feet, I checked my body. Everything seemed normal, all limbs wiggled; my brain, though pulsing with adrenaline, functioned. It was time to turn east for shore. The squid would have to wait another day.

Twenty-four hours later I returned with a new strategy—dive in 30 feet of water, follow the sand bottom down, and never mind the birds. The scheme worked perfectly. At 60 feet squid surrounded me by the thousands upon thousands. Opal-eyed, mantles flashing red with passion, oblivious to the big, clumsy mammal that spouted bubbles and was so easy to avoid, they rocketed about in a furious, intricate mating dance.

Each creature was 6 to 8 inches long and festooned with ten tentacles. Some were clearly engaged in that final, heroic act of reproduction, the males wrapped around the females, their tentacles probing, their delicious quivering a universal sign of *amore*. There were times, though, when a third squid joined the party. Later, at a Scripps Institute of Oceanography lecture, I learned this was just what it appeared to be: a *ménage à trois*.

"The females clearly have certain males they prefer," said the researcher in sterile science-speak. "If you are a male that is eschewed, you still have a chance at reproduction. These males manage to insert a sperm packet into a female that is otherwise preoccupied by a desirable male."

There were other strange goings-on as well. The females planted egg cases in the sand by the millions, giving a snowy appearance to the bottom. Kneeling to photograph them, I concentrated on timing images to give the best combination of natural history and design. An eerie feeling came over me while I worked, disrupting my concentration— something was watching me. When I looked up, my flash revealed a huge bat ray, holding motionless above, wings barely quivering, a living, inner spaceship studying an odd, bubbling intruder.

How did this silent, cartilaginous fish make me aware of its presence? Since it made no sound hovering motionless in the black water, could I have sensed some kind of electric life charge? Sharks have a lateral line—perhaps submersion in the ocean activates ancient, vestigial sensory organs in the human body. More likely, compressed air expanded my cerebrum through nitrogen narcosis, the rapture of the deep.

This concentration of life—birds, fish, cephalopods—made it clear that the squid formed a vital cable in the ocean food web. Bright lights offshore told of commercial fishers luring the spawning creatures into their nets. Most fisheries take apex predators, such as shark or tuna. In years past blue sharks gathered in great numbers off San Diego to feed on the squid—now these sleek hunters are gone, fished out for their fins. What will happen to the oceans if species that support the base of the food chain, such as the opals, are overharvested? Like the crucial stone holding an arch together, a keystone species binds entire ecosystems. Could overfishing of squid cause the whole oceanic life web to falter and collapse?

Pondering these and other things, I found myself driven to dive with the oversexed multitudes many times. Although no further diving misadventures befell me, more questions came. Why must the mating couples die? Do their bodies provide nutrients for the voracious young? Does their death remove competition for food? If squid nervous systems are like ours, does sex feel good? Does dying hurt?

On some nights dozens of divers were in the water, photographers diving solo, mostly, each carrying a torch that punctuated the 90-foot black depth with an eerie halo of light. Ron was among them, but he always brought a buddy. With each exposed image, strobe lights flashed like silent grenades, adding a surreal element to an already bizarre spectacle.

Ron appeared at the dive shop one February afternoon; we talked story, shared photographs, and dreamed of the South Seas.

"Why don't you travel to Fiji or New Guinea on a dive trip someday, Ron?" I asked.

"Hell," he answered, in his sharkskin voice, "I've already made plans. I'm heading to the South Pacific, and soon." He shifted to a conspiratorial tone, a wild light shining in his eyes. "But I'm using a one-way ticket, man. Once I get there, I'm not coming back."

He asked me to join him for a squid dive that afternoon, and I thought about it long and hard.

"Come on," he said. "It's just about time for the egg sacks to hatch. Let's go watch life begin!"

Exhausted from working the night before, I passed, wistful about missing something great.

I did miss something, but it wasn't great. That night, on the evening news, viewers watched rescuers pull a diver through the surf at La Jolla Canyon. Paramedics pumped on his chest as lifeguards loaded him into an ambulance. I stared in horror at the diver's face, pale, squid-white, endotracheal tube protruding. It was Ron.

Why my friend died never became clear. His buddy said the dive was uneventful, a 95-footer, and that, after surfacing, Ron started waving his arms around, reaching for her wildly. Then he went limp and sank. In 15 feet of water, his dive partner was unable to inflate his vest or release his weight belt; by the time lifeguards brought him up, it was too late. Most probably he suffered a heart attack or cardiac dysrhythmia and just happened to be diving. Perhaps an errant nitrogen bubble fizzed into a crucial artery in his heart or brain. Only Ron could tell us for sure, and Ron wasn't talking. One thing was certain. He died doing the thing he loved.

So here we are on the bluff, a crowd of people touched by a diver, a keystone species sort of dive instructor, someone who managed to interest hundreds of people in the magical, dangerous wilderness so close, and yet so far, from the city limits. Would our fascination for the sea collapse now that Ron was dead? No. In death there is rebirth. We'd learned that much, at least, from the squid.

The seals have gotten used to the bagpipes. They return to their sunbathing, although they do not seem as relaxed as before. The swim is starting to get tough now; the divers round the breakwater with the floating wreath and hit the surf. Kicking hard with their fins, they break through the waves and stroke out into calmer, deep water.

A Forster's tern, its elegant black cap molted to winter white, plunge-dives for baitfish near the group of wet-suit-skinned humans. As we watch the swimmers' progress, a fleet of ten brown pelicans cruises southward in single file, updraft windsurfing on an obsidian-edged wave. Gliding motionless as long as they can, the pterodactyl-like pelicans flap their wings at the last instant to pull up as the wave hammers into the breakwater. The males are dressed in their best winter mating plumage, their gullets a bright crimson, their crests a golden wheat color.

At last the divers are far enough out and, with a small prayer, they set free the wreath. It drifts in the current toward the kelp beds, dwindling to a tiny speck. Only when it is out of sight does the bagpipe player cease, releasing the day to the wind and sea.

First publication

Looking Up

Kathryn Wilder

I tracked water into Margaret's house for at least ten minutes before I met her. I had become acquainted with her husband earlier that day as he and I carried bales of hay through standing water to a barn. We had joked about being lucky because they were two-wire bales, not the heavy threes.

This was shortly after the neighbors rescued the horses—seven horses cornered on a hundred square feet of rain-soaked land, the river that had become lake rising visibly, crowding them toward the barbed-wire fence. I had already called the sheriff and asked what could be done, the image of horse limbs getting twisted in wire, the sound of horse screams as they tried to flee fence and flood, haunting me. "Nothing," the dispatcher said. I could not get free of the picture any easier than those horses could have gotten free of the wire, so my partner and I left the house on a mission, his bolt cutters in his raincoat pocket.

Just as we reached the end of our gravel driveway I heard a nervous whinny and the hollow slapping of unshod hooves on wet pavement. A muddy white pickup rounded the corner in low gear, and a man sat on the open tailgate with a flake of alfalfa in his lap. A woman led a fat pinto mare, another led an old swaybacked mare, and five loose horses followed, their heads high and wide-eyed as they blew steam into the rain, or low and snaky as they searched for escape.

Several other neighbors walked behind and a second pickup rode sweep. Up and over the hill they went toward someone's well-fenced, dry-land pasture, and my image was freed.

The man who sat on the tailgate holding the hay was Jerry. He and some others had organized this rescue. When my partner and I walked through the rain that night to see if anyone could use our help, it was

Jerry's house that had the flurry of people and pickups crowding the street out front, the floodwaters lapping at the threshold of his home.

We joined those carrying furniture, boxes, and loaded garbage bags to the waiting trucks, which transported them to garages on higher ground. As I reached for a box in a back room, Margaret looked up at me over a stack of books. She asked who I was. "A new neighbor," I said, "from up the road." She smiled and said, "Thank you." Later, I found myself in Jerry and Margaret's bedroom, stripping their bed. I felt intrusive, like I was sorting a stranger's laundry, yet they just kept thanking me as I worked.

☘

The "window" is open from six to eight in the morning and five to seven at night. During those times we are allowed to drive this broken road, which winds through the canyon alongside water, connecting one small mountain town to another. It has become routine to wait for the opening, to share a sense of closure to the day, or impatient beginnings, with strangers.

I sit in the pickup and write, leaving the engine to idle till we're warm, then shutting it off. Quiet envelops us, followed by the soft voices of people standing outside their cars, visiting with one another in the altered darkness. Backup warning sounds from D-8s, monster dump trucks, and motor graders drift along the canyon. Rock and metal scrape asphalt far away. Beneath it all flows the river.

Tyler, my son, draws while I write. We exchange few words. Sometimes I close my eyes and ask him to tell me if the car in front of me moves, though I still listen for the start-up of one engine followed domino-style by another.

Tonight we're stopped on the bridge over the mouth of Indian Creek. Here Indian Creek joins Spanish Creek, and that confluence is the beginning of the East Branch of the North Fork of the Feather River. Two highways meet here as well, and the floodlights stationed at the "Y," to help the workers as they rebuild the road, cast light like moonglow over the water, capturing the white of the rapids. I see ghosts moving eerily downstream, floating beneath the bridge and on, downcanyon, toward other ruins of roads and railroad tracks, of homes and dreams, the house we were buying down there among them.

Tyler spent the winter break in dry country with his father. I tell him, as we watch the water ghosts floating forty feet below us, that two weeks ago waves crested at highway height in some places, crashed down on blacktop in others. He has seen the logjam lying atop the rocks—whole ponderosas, their needles still green, crisscrossing the tallest boulders. I showed him the gouges in the bark of the giant trees, pockmarks made by other trees, rocks, maybe a guardrail or a chunk of road, some of the gouges worn smooth from the passage of so much debris, so much water.

Standing alone under that tangle of ponderosas one day, looking up, I envisioned the amount of water that filled this canyon, involuntarily holding my breath while doing so. I have spent time close to a river's bed in a Class V rapid, but there the river ran clear, I saw bubbles and recognized up, and I scrambled toward the surface like a maniacal water dog. Here, fifteen feet under these pines, the bottom of the river another fifteen feet down, I know I would only have seen the dark muddy water, would only have felt the hydraulics and the rocks and the branches, pulling me apart.

I have moments in which I am glad my son missed the flood, like now, as he quietly studies the ghostly whitewater below. He has seen the damage up- and downcanyon. And the pictures. But he doesn't see that churning chocolate water thrashing about in his dreams, as I do.

Another week has passed. We missed a day and a half of school. On Tuesday I got to the window at Dog Rock seven minutes late and they turned me back. No amount of pleading would make the flagger change the rules. We went home and called a friend in the town where my son's school is, twenty miles away, and he agreed to meet us. We parked the truck on our side of the window and hiked the rain-soaked mile-and-a-quarter-long trail to the other side. Nobody awaited us. We searched for another wet half mile before planting ourselves under a large ponderosa. I suggested we hitchhike; my partner pointed out that there were no cars on the road. We stood under the tree, under the rain dripping through pine needles, waiting for a solution. Eventually a woman who had crossed the trail behind us, and had her spare car parked on this side, drove along. She couldn't resist our hang-dog, wet-dog appearance.

I got Tyler to school at 1:00 p.m. When we found our friend, he informed us that the flaggers had turned him back at the "Y," miles away. The next day traffic still moved over the muddy one-lane passageway at Dog Rock at 8: 15. I wanted to scream. And yet, I know these road workers are wetter and more miserable than I could possibly get, working their butts off to fix our lives.

Rain turned to snow on Wednesday. When we got home—after dark—we had no electricity. The three of us ate a kerosene-lamp-and-candlelight dinner under the covers in our bedroom—my partner had built up the fire in the wood-burning stove earlier to take the chill off the bedroom. The power came on long enough for us to indulge in a movie, warm up the house, reset the clocks, and go to bed. When I awoke in early light I saw the blank face of the clock. Over a foot of fresh snow coated the ground, and large clumps of it weighted down the trees. I went back to sleep.

And woke up a while later. I called the school to affirm my prediction that it would be a snow day. A cheery voice answered—I was wrong. I asked what time it was. Eight o'clock. I had missed the window again.

Later, still no electricity—which means no water because we're on a well. We packed a change of clothes and loaded everything, including the dogs, into the truck. We wanted showers, and I wanted Tyler in school the next day no matter what. When we reached the window, we found that it had been open all day due to the snow. I could have taken Tyler across at any time.

Power returned Saturday afternoon. They left the window open all weekend. Snow has turned into rain, melted into lake water. Again, the river rises.

ℝ

I get random phone calls from my parents, who live in other parts of California. I'm in the middle of the Sierra, where the flooding begins. My father lives on the other side of the valley, my mother near the bay, at the flood's end.

I report the facts. Valleys turned to lakes. The downhill neighbor's Volkswagen floating until the water filling it became an anchor. A van, a telephone booth, a tavern buried in sand and stone. A huge boulder stuck on a bridge, other bridges washing away. Sections of road disappearing downriver, train tracks clinging to mountainsides by their rails. Muddy canyon walls sliding onto the highway, into the river, still. Three feet of sand around the house we were buying, walls caved in, silt on windowsills, doors and windows downriver, the inside high-water mark near my collarbone. Six days in three weeks without electricity, without running water, except for the skies. Roads closed. The window.

My parents' unspoken concern travels through the line each time one of them calls, They had both expressed their doubts about me moving here. My words underline their fears. I say to them, "Despite all the obstacles, I'm just so glad I'm here to witness this." Silence returns. I don't tell the rest.

Though there was a heaviness in the damp air outside our ruined river house when I went to visit it, and the inside smelled of decay, though tears moved through me when I stepped from room to room on floors thick with mud, I felt something else move through me as well. Something like pride. Outside again, I walked across the three-foot-thick sand carpet with which the river had covered the yard, and noticed the patterns of currents frozen in folds around cedar trees and ponderosas, across the flats and around the corners of the house. The carpet reached a good hundred yards up into the woods.

The power of the river running wild lay carved there in her banks, on the widened riverbed, in the debris caught high in the pines at river's edge. Nothing engineered by humans could stop her. The sculpture she made will change as roads are rebuilt, debris cleared away. But what she has carved in my heart is there to stay.

&

Margaret and Jerry's home didn't receive much damage, the flood peaking two hours after we left—it turns out Jerry was lucky after all. The horses were returned to their field when the ground had dried out enough for firm footing.

The snow that shut off the power melted slowly—the river rose, but not enough to burst her banks again. Tyler made it to school every day this week. I heard that the road at Dog Rock will be open tonight, one month after the flood. Two lanes of dirt until late spring, when they pave it, but who cares—no more windows. I like the scars anyway, the reminders of wild rivers.

I have found another house—not on the river this time, but close. After all, here, in this country, lives are made by water.

from *Sierra*

Grabbing the Bull by the Antlers

Peter A. Christian

It is late September on the Kobuk River in northwest Alaska and my season as a ranger with the National Park Service is winding down for another year. Already shelf ice is starting to form along the edges of the creeks and sloughs which feed the Kobuk as it winds like a snake down to the Bering Sea. I've just returned to the Onion Portage ranger station, having spent the last grueling month working the river during the always frenzied caribou hunting season. September is usually the time when the massive Western Arctic caribou herd migrates across the Brooks Range on the way to its wintering grounds on the Seward Peninsula. The terrain funnels the caribou to a few spots where they cross the river every year. Onion Portage is probably the best known of these, and on any given day during the month you can see hundreds of caribou making their way over the tundra and down to the riverbanks.

Onion Portage is also the place where, for thousands of years, Eskimos have waited stealthily for the opportunity to hunt the caribou as they swim across the Kobuk. The place has an aura about it, as if it has absorbed and now radiates back the desperate energy of life-and-death survival. There is a silent watchfulness that hangs in the air and seems to permeate the willow, birch, and spruce that line the river, as if the vegetation itself has absorbed ten thousand years of blood and fear. When the caribou cross, stepping noisily into the cold water, it is as if the whole river is holding its breath at the first breaking of the silence since the world began.

So the caribou have lived and died here from the beginning, feeding Eskimos and other carnivores with an endless banquet of fresh meat. But the Kobuk shares its bounty with more than hunters and scavenging bears, wolves, and ravens. Also hiding in the willows is a team of biologists who make a different type of annual trek to Onion Portage—to capture live caribou, draw their blood, and place radio tracking collars around their powerful necks—all for the sake of holy science. This year I happen to be free during the week they have gathered opposite my station for the commencement of this strange rite of their strange profession.

I get to talking with Jim, the leader of this year's expedition. Jim is a big man, and seems less a scientist and more a Viking with his red hair and blue eyes, but his manner is easy. "We're a bit shorthanded this year," Jim mentions offhandedly. "If you're not too busy, we could use some extra help." It just so happens the hunting season had recently ended and I am free for the next couple of days. Soon an agreement is made that, in exchange for a good steak dinner, I will help the team catch and collar caribou as they cross the river. At the time I think the bargain is a good one. After all, how hard can it be to tag a few oversized deer? I shake Jim's hand and, although it's warm, his poker face seems to suggest there's more in store for me than I know.

I soon learn that catching live caribou is as much an art form as a science. Part of the job is to catch the calf of whatever mother is being sampled and hold it until she is released. This is a particularly enlightened approach since it keeps the young calves near their protective mothers. But when soaking wet, a caribou calf is more slippery than a greased pig, which provides more than a few moments of hilarity during the long days.

The real business, however, is capturing the big bulls. Here is how it's done. Like ancient Eskimo hunters, we hide in a blind of logs and sand on the south bank of the Kobuk, hunched over against the wind that blows ceaselessly now from the north, and wait for a group of caribou to enter the river. They emerge tentatively out of the willows on the north side and look around as if checking for traffic. Caribou are wily and difficult to predict and they seem. reluctant to break the silence that somehow acts as their protective cloak. They are a hardy lot by now, having survived the spring calving ordeal, swarms of famished mosquitoes, hungry wolf packs, and not a few two-legged predators. They have forged countless rivers and crossed the Brooks Range twice in only a few short months. Once they're in the river, they swim with purposeful intensity because they are in the open and vulnerable. The bulls and cows form a swimming wedge of bodies, followed by their tiny cargo of calves who are sucked along in their wake. When the caribou reach midstream, Jim gives the signal for action. We burst from cover like an ambush party and run madly toward the waiting boats. Like some ridiculous circus of ducks, a gaggle of madly huffing scientists waddles across the sand, swathed in rubber raingear and oversized boots. Holding hypodermic needles like spears, they chug along in the sand and tumble pell mell into the two boats. Jim gives the engine full throttle toward the caribou while the rest of the crew clings desperately to the bow. Skillfully cutting a bull out of the herd, the boats form a wedge, bows together. The bull is corralled and two biologists in either boat, now in their element and suddenly looking competent, grab the bull by the horns, so to speak, while two others draw blood and apply the collar.

It sounds smooth and simple. It isn't. A bull caribou weighs about three hundred pounds. He has hooves the size of buckets and antlers four feet high. He is strong and terrified. As we grab for him, he lashes out furiously with his front legs, thrashing and beating the water like a living blender. Humans and boats are new to him and his ancient instincts compel him to *Run! Fight! Escape!* Sometimes his hooves slash the side of the aluminum boat with dangerous force and it appears as if he is trying to climb into the boat with us. The men holding the twisting antlers struggle to maintain their grip. Imagine trying to draw blood with a hypodermic needle from the neck of a thrashing hurricane of horn and hoof. It ain't fun. It's a lot of fun! It's fun, maybe the first five times. After ten times, I start wondering what I've gotten myself into.

By late September, the sky is often cloudy and and on this day a cold, arctic wind whistles endlessly across the nearly freezing water, dousing us with icy spray. Soon my arms feel heavy as lead and my feet are numb lumps of ice. But as promised, Jim has fed me well, and over the course of three days we repeat this procedure seventy-five times, lending new meaning to the word "exhaustion." Despite the difficulty of the work, after weeks of poking at the moldering carcasses of poached animals,* it feels great to actually touch a live caribou, to feel its warm and breathing sides.

On the last day, we capture a bull that is blind in one eye where a milky cataract formed. This caribou is calm, almost quiet, maybe because his blind eye is facing me and he can't see what is going on. Suddenly, I have an unquenchable desire to touch his face and so, very gently, I reach out and stroke the soft fur of his muzzle. At first he jerks wildly and tosses his head, but after awhile he seems to accept the intrusion, submitting to my touch. He is treading water and soaking wet, but I am able to warm my frozen hands in his thick, hollow fir. What a pleasure and a privilege it is to feel this wild and vibrant life force! Every muscle in the animal's body is taut with energy. Through the pads of my fingers I feel I am brushing against a high-tension electrical wire, touching the raw and quivering tip of wilderness. I stare into that single deep brown eye and detect there an unfathomable question, somehow sensing that, in a one-eyed caribou, I am confronting the mystery of life itself. I am aware of being observed, not simply by a caribou, but by the eye of the Earth—and it has consciousness, knows I am there, and is staring back at me. But the boats, drifting in the current, pull apart and nearly pitch me into the frigid waters.

I yank my eyes from the caribou's gaze and steady myself on an antler. As I look up, I catch Jim's bright blue eyes regarding me with interest. At first, I feel a wave of embarrassment, like I've been caught reading a secret diary or forbidden book. But a smile erupts from his red-bearded face as if he completely understands my purpose, as if he remembers his own devotion to wild things, and the reason why he has gotten involved in the search for answers to unanswerable questions. Staring at each other over the tangled antlers, we share an unspoken moment of perfect understanding.

---

* The author's regular job as ranger involves documenting the carcasses of animals that have been illegally killed, primarily by wealthy non-native hunters who take only the heads.

Then, suddenly, it is over. The blood has been drawn and the collar has been slapped into place. The bull is released and we dive out of the way. The bull surges forward like a racehorse out of its gate and swims hell-bent for the bank. Once on shore he frantically shakes the water from his pelt, lunges into the willows, and disappears with a crash. The whole episode lasts maybe sixty seconds, but it's one minute I'll remember for a lifetime. I have been blessed with the opportunity to touch a piece of the living wilderness as few people ever do, and besides, it's not often you get the chance to grab the bull by the horns.

First publication

White Poplar, Black Locust

Louise Wagenknecht

Then

The valley is still there, of course, in the lee of Mount Ashland, lambent with shadows in the early morning sun, an unearthly Christmas card under the winter moons. You pass it quickly, looking down to the west, as you cross over the California-Oregon line on the grey ribbon that splits the mountains asunder. But Hilt always existed where things break apart, on a knife edge balancing a single object or a whole world for decades, only to lose it in a single breath, and forever. Hilt was dying even as I first knew it, and for its sake I mourned all things gone, and hated change, without for a long time knowing why.

At Hilt the pointed timber-clad slopes of the Siskiyous become rounded brown hills, capped by remnants of ancient seabeds. On them grow oak and juniper and sagebrush. Here the large mule deer of the high deserts meet the small Pacific blacktails, creating hybrid bucks with tremendous antlers. Here the remnants of the ancient coastal salmon culture come to terms with a drier, poorer country. And in this little valley logging, mining, and ranching met on Cottonwood Creek, and Hilt was born with a railroad meeting a sawmill when the century was young.

Hilt disappeared almost twenty-five years ago, with words spoken around a boardroom table nine hundred miles away. All the people who had lived in Hilt had planted some trees and rearranged some rocks. The thing that I had seen approaching, before I could have said its name, was accomplished, and then all the rest was gone, torn down, sold. The mountains remembered us no less than the prehistoric animals whose bones were sometimes found nearby, but no more.

Hilt's valley was sheltered by a circle of peaks, which we saw on one plane, since we lived, after all, in the center of this world. We could name them all, right around the compass: Mount Ashland, Pilot Rock, Skunk's Peak, Sheldon Butte, Black Mountain, Mount Shasta, Bailey Hill, Cottonwood Peak, Bullion Mountain, Shaft Rock, the long rolling gap into the Beaver Creek country, where the logging was, then Hungry Creek Lookout with its lone tree against the horizon, and Mount Ashland again.

Closer still were more personal landmarks: Watertank Hill, Little Italy on the rise across the railroad tracks, Adobe Street at the north end of town, and the little juniper-topped ridge behind the old ballpark, where yellowbells bloomed at the start of the dry season.

Closest of all, and the first places we explored in life, were the neatly fenced yards around the company houses, with their two-by-four fence tops just made for walking on and their hog-wire mesh for easy climbing. Bordered with irises and Shasta daisies and tulips, the yards were little kingdoms of green, none older than the 1920s, but as grown and settled in thirty years as anything in the hundred-year-old county seat.

In the middle of each front yard, a board sidewalk ran down from the bottom of the porch steps to a gate and out to join the wider boardwalk beside the dirt street. Our own front porch was draped with Virginia creeper, cool and breezy in the summer. The north side of the front yard was dominated by an enormous white poplar tree.

Four feet across at the base, with craggy wrinkled gray bark, its lower branches were as thick as a pony's barrel and almost as low to the ground. We could dig our toes into crevices in the bark and scramble astride. Above our heads, the corrugated gray skin of the old tree smoothed out; the younger branches were mottled white. The leaves, bright green on the upper side, fuzzy white beneath, shook and spoke in the wind that spilled down Bear Canyon on hot afternoons.

The old tree cast deep, dark shade, under which hundreds of sprouts sprung from the hidden, knobby ankles. White poplar, like aspen, likes to live in a grove of family, of clones really. My grandfather mowed them all down, unsympathetic to such ambitions.

In spring, long tendrils of catkins, oozing white cotton, drooped from the tree, falling in a litter, blowing into fence corners. In autumn, the tree dropped layers of leaves, six inches deep, until my aunt led us, armed with rakes, in an assault. We scraped the leaves into huge crackling piles, shoveled them onto tarps, and dragged them across the road to a strip of weeds beside the railroad tracks where they were burned to gray ashes under Grandfather's vigilant eye.

We called our tree a cottonwood, ignorant of its proper common name, but there were many of them in Hilt. Squat, weedy, wide-branching, virtually unkillable, they were brought to the dry lands of the West by white settlers. They mark old towns and homestead sites from Montana to California and beyond, surviving and sprouting through heat and drought and cracking cold.

Utterly useless for fenceposts or lumber, barely adequate as firewood, white poplars are solely and staunchly shade trees. I think the women spread them, by giving little sprouts in cans of mud to friends and relations. Genetic studies of white poplars in the West might show some interesting connections between families, once connected, who were destined to lose each other once they entered the vastness beyond the wide Missouri. Perhaps all white poplars, like so many Westerners, are ultimately related, lost members of a single clone, scattered over the far dry lands.

Our own tree's base was built up with a ring of pale water-washed rocks, filled with soil. The rocks came from a bar on the Klamath River, ten miles away. The ring was supposed to grow flowers, but between the shade and my sister and me stomping on it, no flowers grew. We hid behind its trunk, or lay on our backs beneath it in the summer heat, ants crawling under our shirts as we watched the sky behind the rippling leaves.

To me, the tree was a live presence, aware of us but preoccupied by the past. When the high-tumbled clouds turned fiery in the sunset, evolving majestic shapes, when the nighthawks wheeled in the summer dusk, I felt that the tree saw these things, and remembered many others, still part of the valley and the old, old hills, but just out of reach, just behind the mountains.

The West was full of small company towns once. They existed for the benefit of the extractive industries—primarily lumbering—but they differed from the cut-and-get-out logging camps that were their parents and siblings. The investment made in a real company town presupposed a resource that was going to take a good long time to extract, and a company willing to make life fairly comfortable for a stable workforce.

Railroad logging had been going on for some years in the woods west of Hilt when Fruit Growers Supply Company, a subsidiary of Sunkist, the giant California orange growers' cooperative, bought the town and the mill in 1910. It built small frame houses for the workers, a hotel, a boardinghouse, a store. The town survived a couple of massive fires, always a danger where wood-burning stoves, uninsulated flues, and wood roof shingles coexisted. The rows of burnt houses were replaced willy-nilly, entire streets being realigned in a matter of a few weeks. When I see photos of Hilt from the early 1920s, I have to look at the hills behind to figure out precisely where those houses were. In the alley behind our house, the rains brought teardrop-shaped pieces of black glass to the surface, where buildings had burned to the ground.

Hilt boasted eighty-five houses when I knew it, not counting those in Little Italy across the railroad tracks. A store/post office/company office building, a carpenter shop, a hospital and doctor's residence, the Southern Pacific's railroad station and stationmaster's house, a community meeting place universally referred to as "The Clubhouse," a school, a gas station, a small firehouse, a boardinghouse, a moribund hotel (used only for dances in my memory), and the great mill complex across the railroad tracks completed the architectural part of our world. The latter was a world in itself, with its sawmill, box factory, planing mill, millponds, and the mighty log decks: rows upon rows of logs stacked thirty feet high, waiting to be sawn into lumber and bathed in a perpetual mist with sprinklers to keep the wood from checking.

The mill and its logs *were* Hilt; without them there would have been no work and no town. Our days were ordered by the mill whistles that called the men to work, signaled coffee breaks and lunch, and sent them home at five o'clock. The whistles ran on the steam generated by burning bark and wood scraps in the huge tepee burners, steam that made the electricity for the entire manufacturing operation. The wail of those whistles in siren mode meant a fire in town or mill, and the combinations of short and long notes told us where to look for the smoke. Beside the crank telephone in every house was a list of these signals.

Hilt never reported a murder, although less than a mile from our front door, Black Bart once robbed the Oregon-bound stagecoach. During the early years of the century, when Oregon was dry, trainloads of loggers and railroaders came across the state line on Saturday night to drink at Frank Warren's saloon on the edge of town. The Warren's Building still stands, and in my childhood men still drank while leaning against its mahogany bar, but they went home to their families, and Tony Marin, the town constable, had little to do besides capture stray dogs.

The chief deterrent to misbehavior in Hilt was the impossibility of hiding much from the neighbors. Everyone worked for "the Company," so unemployment and homelessness were unknown to us. Hoboes off the railroad tracks might, indeed, camp for a night or two at a jungle beside the tracks a mile below town, but we rarely saw them. Grandmother told us that during the Depression wandering jobless men sometimes appeared on the front porch and asked for something to eat. She made them sandwiches, and they thanked her and kept walking up the tracks. We locked our doors at night, but in summer they stood open with only the screen doors hooked. I cannot remember so much as a minor burglary on our street.

In the night passing trains rattled the windows and woke us. We fell asleep again almost immediately, as the comforting whistles dopplered away. On winter nights, as the fire in the big living room stove died down, the house creaked and popped alarmingly, settling onto its foundations, competing with Grandfather's snores and the edge-of-town wails of coyotes. In college I slept serenely through rock concerts and earthquakes, my mind lulled by the old memories of those reassuringly loud childhood nights.

Now and then I dream that I am on the streets of Hilt, alone, set down in a black, black night on the street in front of the company store. I run down Front Street, where all the houses are dark, and empty, and deserted, like the street. At Grandmother's house, midway down the row, the big front-room window gapes black and dead. Worst of all, the old white poplar doesn't know me. It thrashes in a cold wind, leaves rattling, a stranger. The pale undersides of the leaves are leprous under the dim streetlight.

I run through town, searching the other streets, but everywhere doors are locked against me, windows are dark. Desperate, I run back to Grandmother's house and find the lights on and the big white front door open, and Grandmother standing in the doorway, holding the screen door open for me. Inside, the white wainscoting is glaring and stark because the living room is stripped of furniture and drapes. Nothing remains except the big mirror, still hanging on the southern wall.

Grandmother is unsurprised by my sudden appearance, and I know, without her saying it, that she herself has just returned to this place where she raised two daughters and two granddaughters. She speaks to me while I walk through the house, through every empty room. No one else appears, but Grandmother talks quietly and cheerfully, not minding the barren space. Somewhere around my third circuit through the kitchen, I wake up, with her voice in my mind but her words gone from memory, in the way of dreams. For the space of a whole day the certainty of her continued existence stays with me, even as I remember that that valley on the border now holds, for me, only the wings of nighthawks, brushing the evening air, silhouetted against a falling sun.

And There

When I was two years and four months old, my mother bundled my two-month-old sister and me into a taxi, left a note for her husband, and boarded an airplane that carried us from Boise, Idaho, to Medford, Oregon. Her parents met her at the airport and they drove in grim silence over the backbone of the Siskiyou Range and down into Hilt. It was October, and the dogwoods and bigleaf maples must have flamed on the mountainsides above the old highway, and perhaps I glimpsed, for the first time, the long sweep of the drainages leading down into Cottonwood Creek and the country that would claim my soul.

If the weather was clear, I may even have seen the pale bulk of Mount Shasta floating serenely just above the southern horizon. I don't remember. Yet nothing in all our lives would so affect my mother, my sister, and me as this single journey.

Our mother, Barbara Roush Johnson, was less than five feet tall and weighed exactly one hundred pounds. Dark of hair and eye, she inherited the proud, straight nose of her father's family and the expressive mouth and firm jaw of her mother, a Danish woman raised in Iowa. Neat, trim, and ladylike, she has all her life had to grit her teeth against people who think that she is sweet and gentle and unworldly, and so try to run roughshod over her, recognizing too late the toughness and a tendency to settle her mind into the firmness of reinforced concrete.

Our father, Richard Johnson, found this out. A few weeks after that flight from Boise, he followed, bringing with him his older brother, our Uncle David.

"He wanted me to come back to him," Mother told us many years later, "but I wouldn't. I just couldn't respect him." That was as close as she ever came to explaining the rift between them, in so many words. He gave up and sued for divorce on grounds of desertion. Mother received sole custody of her children.

Our father came to visit us just once more in the next ten years, when I was five. He had remarried, and I recall sitting on his lap chattering happily, perfectly conscious that I was showing off, and not feeling that I had missed him at all.

Our mother was frankly relieved when he left, having made no demands for our company at any time in the future. "Dick just wanted to show off his new wife," she said, her lips hard and tight, as she stood with her back to the stove, a cup of coffee in her hands. Her mother and sister stood to her left and right, a ring of women, closing in to protect their own.

Did Mother know how hard it would be to pick up her life again in Hilt after leaving it in a blaze of glory four years before? A formal wedding in the small white community church was a hard thing to renounce in those days. Did she know how hard it would be to be the only divorced woman in a town of four hundred people? Although she was never an optimist, the discouraging surprises must have depressed even her practical mind. On the day that two of her former schoolmates swept their calf-length New Look skirts aside as they passed her on the sidewalk, she may have realized finally and forever just how hard her life would be. After that, she said once, she had no illusions left, and no hope at all. Her family became her world, and through all the years to come in Hilt, despite attendance at church and Eastern Star and the PTA, she never had a close friend.

A big part of that world was Grandfather, whom our father had called "The Voice." Although only five feet eight inches tall, he was nevertheless the tallest person in the house, and his bass voice seemed to emanate from someone much larger. To children, of course, he was quite large enough. My sister Elizabeth and I always thought of the house on Front Street where our mother had grown up as Grandmother's, but Grandfather certainly regarded it as his. He never spoke when he could shout, never used one word where a hundred would do. Grandmother sometimes said that he should have been a preacher.

Like most men who had worked for thirty years in sawmills, he was deaf in the upper registers, and that was all to the good, for much of what was said in the house by its women and girls was not meant for his ears. This probably contributed to a sense of paranoia on his part. He was right: we *were* plotting against him. Young and old, we formed a conspiracy of silence, of hiding, of evasion and omission. He disliked cats, too, for they saw through him, just as we did. They were sneaky, as we were sneaky, and he hated it.

The pride of his middle age was his ability to support his family, for his own father had been an ineffectual little man who failed at farming and shopkeeping and was finally bullied by a stubborn, desperate wife into the purchase of a small candy store in Rainier, Oregon. She ran the business and made the decisions; he just worked there. In photographs he looks sheepish and slightly lost; she stands dressed in black, as solid and as wide as a refrigerator, clearly the boss.

Grandfather was the seventh child born to a couple whose Nebraska farm was failing under the weight of drought, grasshoppers, and the Cross of Gold. In evident desperation, he was named William Jennings Bryan Roush, but not even the Great Populist could prevent the inevitable hegira to the cool timberlands of Oregon, where Permenias Roush left Lena and the children in a rented house in Canyonville and joined thousands of other men in the logging camps.

In old age Lena told stories of trying to feed seven children on a single sack of white flour for a week. Bryan, as his siblings called him, left school at thirteen and went south to work in a lumber mill in Sisson, as the town of Mount Shasta in northern California was then called. He boarded with his married sister Fanny. His older brother Grover had preceded him and was already spending too much of his time in saloons.

Bryan was a smart boy, but the insecurities of his childhood made him cautious about overstepping himself, and a steady job was worth more to him than the risks of advancement and possible failure. He accepted the prejudices of race and sex and class without question, moving beyond them only rarely and late in life, as when one of Grover's grandchildren married a black National Guard officer. He once shared a hospital room for a few days with a black man of about the same age and found to his astonishment a similarity of political and cultural opinion that made us laugh when he told us about it.

He identified, however, with authority and with the bosses so easily that during his stint in the army during World War I he quickly rose to corporal. He ended his career in lumber as the foreman of the box factory in Hilt, literate but unintellectual, having gone about as far as he could go on an eighth-grade education in industry. The Company trusted him, and so when his eldest daughter returned to her hometown, they trusted her, too, and quickly hired her into the typing pool. In a year's time she was the general manager's private secretary, her life seemingly set in stone, her children secure.

For our first few years in Hilt, we three immigrants shared the back bedroom off the kitchen with Aunt Jo and her upright piano. Mother, Aunt Jo, and I shared the big double bed, while Elizabeth's crib stood across the room, next to the bathroom door.

The bathroom was an old-fashioned one, meaning large. It contained a claw-legged tub, a big built-in towel cabinet, and about a mile of the coldest linoleum in the world. Grandmother preheated the room for our winter baths with a dangerous-looking portable electric heater that glowed red and smelled ominously of burning dust.

Little as she must have liked it, Mother needed her parents and their house. Most of all she needed her mother, for she had no alternative child care. She paid for our room and board, and our absent father in turn paid her seventy dollars per month in child support. Every weekday morning at ten minutes to eight, she walked down the sidewalk to the Company's office, a few minutes after Grandfather had put on his old fedora, the silk hatband stained with sweat, and walked across the tracks to the box factory, half a mile away.

Aunt Jo, still in high school, had already left to catch the school bus to Yreka, twenty-two miles away. Elizabeth and I were left alone with Grandmother.

My most vivid early memories are of winter, of Grandmother rising early in the dark, lighting a fire in the trash-burner stove in the kitchen, then another in the big brown enameled stove in the living room. When the second fire was glowing hot, she allowed me to creep out and get dressed behind it. I remember great fernlike traceries of frost on the inside of the panes of the living room windows, gradually melting with the heat.

I remember Elizabeth standing and screeching delightedly in her crib to an admiring audience of two, evidently the first time she had succeeded in this, or we would not have been so impressed. I remember crawling beneath the big dining table, while the warm light shone through the open kitchen door and cooking noises came out.

As we grew from infants to creatures more nearly approaching humanity, Grandmother became the most important person in our lives. We knew her moods and stories and discipline much better than Mother's. Grandmother comforted and praised and punished us, rocked us to sleep late at night when we were sick, smacked us with switches tom from the cottonwood tree, got us ready for school, sewed our costumes for Halloween and dance recitals.

On evenings and weekends, Mother taught us the Episcopal catechism and heard our nightly prayers, and we loved to watch while she painted her nails or curled her hair in little damp ringlets around her finger, then stabbed them with crisscrossed bobby pins or ironed a blouse for the next day. As time went on she seemed less and less a parent and more and more an older, more sedate version of our talented, fascinating aunt, who banged out "Heart and Soul" on the piano and taught us a dance routine to the sound of Fats Domino belting out "Blueberry Hill" on the big cabinet radio/phonograph. Mother and Aunt Jo were our friends; Grandmother was our parent. In keeping her children, Mother had also lost them, and to the person she loved best in the world.

Martha Kristiane Vilhelmina Dittmar had been just another immigrant girl in Clinton, Iowa, a Dane who started work in a bakery at thirteen, hoisting hundred-pound sacks of flour onto the shoulders of her five-foot frame. Her eyes were a very light blue, her thick long hair a pale brown, darkened from a childhood blonde. Narrow-hipped, with wide shoulders and magnificent biceps, she was awe-inspiring to a four-year-old as she pounded tough round steak with a mallet in a hot kitchen, a sheen of sweat on her high pale forehead.

While she pounded and chopped and kneaded food for us, she told stories. She was born on the island of Sjaelland, in a tiny village called Ronnebaek near the port city of Naestved, on the other side of the island from Copenhagen. Her mother, Anna, endured a succession of stepmothers and, as a small barefoot child, was sent out to work as a goosegirl, before marrying Niels Dittmar, a twenty-eight-year-old fisherman, at twenty-three and giving birth to our grandmother the following year. Another girl, Sophie, and a boy named Andrew were born after the family emigrated to the United States.

The name Dittmar is said to be a common one among people whose ancestors hailed from the marshes at the foot of the Jutland peninsula, deep in the disputed statelets of Schleswig and Holstein. But Niels Dittmar was born in Stillinge, on the island of Sjaelland, and his diminutive bride in the nearby hamlet of Lininge. He endured the misspelling of his last name during the ordeal at Ellis Island sufficiently well to accept being called Dithmart for the rest of his life. It was a small enough price to pay. He stood five feet four inches tall, towering over Anna's four feet eleven. He was a veteran of the Danish army, which had been pretty thoroughly whipped by the Prussians in 1868, the year of his birth. Nevertheless, Denmark was still conscripting young men for two years of national service twenty years later.

By the time Grandmother's memories came alive in the family's new home in Iowa, the Danish fisherman had worked his way through a series of labor-intensive jobs to become a builder and bricklayer. He laughed at the Iowa winters after the icy North Sea storms, but he had not come alone and penniless to the new land. He followed several brothers and sisters.

None of these great-uncles attained a place in family legend except for Uncle Chris, the only brother with a sense of humor and a reasonably good temper. His brothers ascribed his good nature to insanity and let the matter drop. The other brothers had more limited concepts of wit and, by taking themselves seriously, made an easy mark for practical jokes. Niels, proud of the handlebar mustache he first cultivated in the Danish war machine, once horsewhipped a barber who shaved it off while he was asleep in the chair. Anna and the children noticed the loss but held their peace, fearing the fate of those who bring bad news.

Grandmother learned early the art of telling men only what they wanted to hear. She would need it later.

Niels had a horsewhip because he bought, trained, and resold buggy horses in his spare time. Sometimes he bought a mare and raised a foal from her. Once, Grandmother said, she harnessed one of her father's horses and drove herself and her brother and sister into town without her father's permission. She wanted the horse to step out as he did when her father drove him, but the wise animal refused to go at more than a walk.

When Grandmother told stories about these relatives, I could walk into her bedroom and see their faces, hung on the wall: five small photographs taken in Denmark and set in a wooden frame carved by her father from the cedar pieces of cigar boxes. It sits beside me today as I write this, still jointed together so cleverly that the seams are almost invisible.

On top is a photograph of a dark, jowly middle-aged woman in a black dress, her mouth turning down at the corners. This was one of Anna's stepmothers. When I said that the woman in the photograph looked mean, Grandmother would say, "She was good to Mother, though," and our eyes would travel to the two photos in the second row of the frame, Niels on the right, Anna on the left. Niels wears a derby and the full regalia of coat, jacket, vest, and white shirt. His eyes are merry and his well-shaped mouth under the famous mustache turns up slightly at the corners. Anna's arched brows frame her hooded blue eyes. Her hair is pulled back into a bun, and her poignant expression is made more so by an unfortunate attempt at bangs that leaves the top of her head looking as if it had been attacked by an eggbeater. She has delicate bones and a cleft in her firm chin.

Below these two ancestors stands a row of Norns: the three Dittmar sisters, Marie, Anna, and Sophia. Marie, in the center, is a Valkyrie, her wavy blonde hair pulled back, her beaky nose proud, her eyes self-confident. She lived to be more than ninety. Anna and Sophia are brunettes, with smaller features. Anna's hands are at odds with her wide-set eyes and fashionably bow-shaped little mouth; they are large, with big knuckles—the hands of a peasant. Sophia holds one arm behind her back, akimbo, and shields the other behind a potted plant, so that the most noticeable features above the stiff, high collar of her black dress are the high forehead below the swept-back hair, and her gentle, slightly open mouth.

First publication

Autumn of Failing Leaves

John A. Murray

September 19th is a day I never forget. I always hunt round and find some of the old boys who were there. I look around for a musket and a tree and listen for the rebel yell; I hear it in my mind; visions of that day come to my eyes; no apple brandy delusion, mind you, but there comes the rebel line of battle, a part of Hood's division from Virginia, at quick step.
—Charles W. Evers, writing of the Battle of Chickamauga
(September 19-20, 1863) in his newspaper,
The Bowling Green Sentinel, 1886

i.

Some of my fondest memories are of listening—a six- or seven-year-old boy—as my grandfather told stories of his grandfather, of faroff places then new and strange to my ears: Shiloh, Corinth, Perryville, Stone River, Cripple Creek, Lookout Mountain, Missionary Ridge, Chickamauga. Gradually this long-dead relative named Charles Evers, who had worn the uniform of the federal army and fought in every battle from Shiloh to Chickamauga, assumed a recognizable shape, came alive in spirit if not in form, and sat on the sunny back porch in southern Ohio with my grandfather and me. On such days, with a voice that has been shaped by the story it tells, the fog of time rolls back and the distant past comes vibrantly alive. Captains cup their hands and shout commands, sons and uncles and brothers and husbands and fathers advance to the line and take their positions and the long dark rifles rattle as the autumn leaves fall brightly to their doom. From

197

such stories, I now realize, more is learned than history. No man, no boy, should live without having heard a grandfather recite a story that was old when he was young.

He spoke of whistling balls and bursting canisters, of staggered columns crossing open fields, the thunder of artillery behind, the muskets going off in unison ahead. He spoke of an ambiguous order misunderstood, and a line opening and a terrible force descending upon the center of an army like a tornado. He spoke of courage and cowardice, brilliance and stupidity, amazing luck and deadly misfortune. He spoke of men holding their ground and men running for their lives, of men badly wounded and still fighting as if they were not hurt and men superficially grazed and falling to the ground in shock. He spoke of the barely controlled chaos that is battle, and of the train wreck that is defeat. He spoke of many things surrounding the Battle of Chickamauga, but none of them were as interesting as the tales of that sergeant from Ohio named Charles Evers. My grandfather, who had worn a gas mask for entire nights in the trenches of France, related the stories that had been bestowed upon him by their original owner, and asked that I always remember them. He said that a family was like a tree, and that its roots were made of stories, and that so long as those roots ran deep into the past the family could withstand anything that might happen. It has often occurred to me that a nation, which is also a family, is no less different, and that our national battlefield parks and national historic sites have been set aside for the same essential purpose.

When Grandfather Murray passed away in 1986 at the age of nintey-two I inherited his legacy of hundred-year-old maps, letters, books, unpublished typescripts, newspaper clippings, faded tin plates, and parlor-room daguerrotypes. These artifacts are held in the same esteem by our family as any of those documents exhibited under glass at the Library of Congress are by the larger family of America. Even as a boy I understood that one day this would occur, that my grandfather had intended me to be the custodian of the archives. He had reminded me in our last conversation to visit Chickamauga one day, and to see the place where his grandfather, my great-great-grandfather, had left his blood on the earth defending the flag. It was, he said, a place that I would already know, that would be familiar to me, that would feel to me as though I had been there before.

One day, after many years and nearly halfway through the journey of life, I visited Chickamauga National Battlefield Park, with a briefcase full of antique maps and letters and a five-year-old son at my side, and the knowledge that I had honored a promise first made on a sunny back porch long ago, when the Civil War was not yet a century old, and the grandsons of the dead still lived.

ii.

The story of the Battle of Chickamauga is quite simple. It is a tale of retaliation and it begins with Gettysburg. The South had too much pride to let the defeat go unanswered, and so, several months later, a trap was prepared in northwestern Georgia. Chickamauga, like many battlefields, is itself a nowhere place, located in a rural area at a distance from any major cities, an unlikely minor valley for two large armies to dash in pitched struggle. To the north a few miles is Chattanooga, then as now an important rail hub, and to the south one hundred miles is Atlanta, the cultural and political heart of the region. But it was here, in the foothills of the Appalachian Mountains, that they found themselves, the federal and the rebel forces, in September of 1863, three months after Gettysburg and two years into the war. To destroy its ultimate target—Atlanta—the Northern army had to pass through the swamps and forests south of the Tennessee River. And here, along the banks of Chickamauga Creek, the sons of the South, on familiar terrain and with all the advantages of cover, were waiting for them.

It was that simple.

Who was this Charles Evers?

He was the father of the woman who bore my grandfather. He was a person of my height and stature, which is to say he had straight brown hair and a high forehead and gray eyes and the physical build of a tradesman. His grandfather had come over from Germany as a foot soldier to fight for King George Ill, who as a member of the House of Hanover was himself German. After the issue of the revolution was settled, the original Evers decided it might be prudent, with his accent, to remove himself from Virginia as quickly as possible. Obtaining passage to the old country proved impossible, and so he set out on foot with his musket up the Potomac River and over the mountains into the Ohio valley, where he had beard people didn't care where you came from and there was land that could be cleared for farming. Eventually he built a cabin and married and had a son named John Evers, who grew up and became a carpenter and married a woman named Celinda Fuller White. Celinda had lived among the Shawnee Indians from the time of her abduction at thirteen to the time of her escape at eighteen. She would become the mother of Charles Evers (born July 22,1837), and her home would remain one of the last gathering places for the Shawnee.

Charles Evers had an ordinary childhood for that time. At an early age he loved books, and read widely, from Shakespeare to Daniel Defoe to Byron. His second passion was the outdoors. In his late teens, feeling restless, Evers roamed west and got as far as Sioux country. Back home in Ohio, he worked with his father for a time as a carpenter, studied at Oberlin College, taught school in the village, and then enlisted in the 2nd Kentucky Regiment in 1861 when President Lincoln called for volunteers. He was older than most of the others and soon found himself a sergeant. At Shiloh he took a bullet through the jacket but was not wounded. In a war in which 20 percent of the combatants regularly became casualties, Evers must have known that such a favorable state of affairs could not continue indefinitely. He had survived a dozen battles and skirmishes, and seen the many sudden entrances to death, and had long ago ceased to harbor any youthful illusions of immortality.

iii.

Crows overhead. Southern white oaks and black gum trees bent across meandering creeks, studying their reflections. A pileated woodpecker thumping for bark beetles. I turn and turn. Everywhere trees. Gray days of winter, but still a June green scattered through the Big Woods of northern Georgia. Frost is uncommon in these valleys, a school-closing snow as rare as an honest politician. Live bracken ferns and

Virginia creepers adorn the sides of ten-story shagbark hickories. Grapevines dangle temptingly from the heights, perfect for the arms of truant twelve-year-olds. Early violets and dandelions herald spring from beneath hurricane-felled loblolly pines. Leopard frogs chant. Deer listen. Bereft of their leaves, the hardwood trees appear to have recently received a jolt of electricity, extending their branches upward like an unfolding nervous system, each twig reaching for the clarity of sky. Hornet nests and honeybee hives, once hidden in the canopy, are now visible, as well as dozens of summer bird nests.

My grandfather was right. There is an unusual quality about Chickamauga.

One hundred and thirty years ago, this peaceful sanctuary, this blessed national park, was the scene of a violent battle right out of Homer, Herodotus, or *Henry V*: 37,129 men fell, killed or wounded, during the span of two solar days, among them Sergeant Charles White Evers. The combatants represented twenty-nine states, from Maine to Minnesota, Texas to Florida, Maryland to Kansas. They served in units as varied as the Chicago Board of Trade Artillery Battery and the 125th Ohio "Tiger Regiment," Slocomb's Louisiana Battery, and Longstreet's Corps from Gettysburg. There were two future presidents at Chickamauga—James Garfield and William McKinley—and who knows how many others who had might have gone on to notable careers, had they lived. Some of the dead are buried nearby at the national cemetery. Others were lost in the forest and reach now for the light as crested wood fern and green dub moss, wild spearmint and honeysuckle, sweet magnolia and red azalea, transformed through that strangely beautiful metamorphosis we, the living, call, for lack of a better word, death.

These woods are, if not haunted, then hallowed beyond what words can express.

My five-year-old son Naoki and I return to the car and drive down Lafayette Road a mile farther to the Chickamauga National Battlefield Park Visitors' Center, a large, solid government building guarded by two vintage pieces of field artillery. The park rangers behind the front counter see us coming—the briefcase full of memorabilia, the earnest look on my face, the excited little boy keeping pace—and the older one makes a break for the back offices. The other, trapped by the duty roster, smiles patiently. He has seen this variety of park visitor before. After a brief and somewhat incoherent explanation of the Evers connection, the name, unit, and date are entered into a computer, and I am shortly provided, as if by magic, with a detailed itinerary providing hour-by-hour information on the whereabouts of Sergeant Charles White Evers and his unit, the 2nd Kentucky Infantry, for September 19, 1863.

I am amazed that such a priceless document is so readily available.

And I am once again profoundly grateful for such an institution as the National Park Service.

My son is relieved that he will not have to stumble around an 8,000-acre national park with his father and a century-old map.

iv.

First historical stop, after the preliminary scout in the wild woods, is Crayfish Springs. Here Grandfather Evers's day began on September 19, 1863. Back home in Denver, poring over the family maps, I had pictured Crayfish Springs as a bathtub-sized basin of the sort that has replenished my empty water containers in the deserts and mountains of the West. Not so in the Old South. Crayfish Springs is the size of an Olympic swimming pool. You could play a game of water polo at one end, hold a class in canoeing at the other, and still have room for a diving competition in the middle. The smooth, immaculate bottom is lovely, with green aquatic plants distributed like an underwater Japanese garden. Look closely and you see that the clean white sands percolate continuously from the powerful upwellings of the subterranean river, a nice effect, conjuring up images of William Bartram's celebrated spring in Florida, the lyric description of which so inspired Coleridge in his narcotic reverie "Kubla Khan." Huge red oaks and osage orange trees loom around the spring on all sides. Along these brimming banks dusty bison and elk once bent to drink, and bands of Cherokee Indians camped, and purple-winged passenger piegeons roosted. Civil War-era pictures show the spring surrounded by thick forest. Today it sits incongruously, a city park, in the center of "Old Chickamauga," a quaint, slightly run-down historical district. My son gathers acorns—each the size of the .69-caliber Confederate mini-ball that shattered Grandfather Evers's leg—and I help him. There are enough to reseed an entire forest.

Here Charles Evers and the four hundred soliders of the 2nd Kentucky Infantry fell in behind Colonel Thomas D. Sedgewick that fateful morning, so many wars ago.

"A soldier dislikes to go into battle with an empty canteen," wrote Charles Evers in 1886, returning to Crayfish Springs as a tourist. As a combat veteran, he knew that shock and death quickly follow hemorrhaging and dehydration. So he and his unit gathered at the spring that morning, each man wondering if he would see Jesus Christ, Dante's Inferno, Hamlet's oblivion, the surgeon's bloody saw, or a friendly bivouac by nightfall. No one contemplated disappearing. Company officers summarily hung or shot deserters to ensure proper military discipline (Evers witnessed two such executions in his unit during his period of service).

On the hill above Crayfish Springs, at the top of a long U-shaped drive, is Lee Mansion, where General Rosecrans, the Union commander, maintained his headquarters. It is today by all appearances a prosperous bed and breakfast, with license plates from states all over the East Coast, Midwest, and Deep South.

Back on Lafayette Road now, en route to Lee and Gordon's Mill, where a portion of the Union army assembled itself for battle, the Allman Brothers Blues Band is on the radio, strumming the major seventh and minor sixth chords of "Midnight Rider" on their Fender Stratocasters, a warm melodic tune as natural to rural Georgia as fried chicken and corn on the cob, a Southern-born music I never fully appreciated until right now. Fertile farmland abounds: peach orchards, wandering spring-fed streams, quarterhorse pastures, blue-gill ponds, chicken coops, gray squirrel woodlots, gigantic oak trees, pig yards, vegetable patches, satellite dishes and solar panels, pecan groves, dairy-cow barns, cultivated soybean fields, clean honest homes. Poor folk in the country always live among riches.

Shortly the mill comes into view. Here, where Chickamauga Creek runs as brown as the back of a water moccasin, a Union division (roughly fifteen thousand men) prepared for battle. As they gathered, the first artillery shell of the day screamed overhead and the men glanced nervously in the direction from which it was fired. Less than a mile to the north and east were the 43,000 soldiers of Confederate General Braxton Bragg, laid up in the swamps along Chickamauga Creek. Although the entire Union force totaled 60,000, it was facing an adversary that was well dug in.

Word soon spread through the army, in the instantaneous fashion of a rumor anchored in fact, that General Rosecrans had decided to make a frontal assault on these fortified, well-defended positions.

The men were not happy.

A different commander might have pursued a less suicidal strategy. Grant, who had leveled Vicksburg with artillery rather than risk his people in street fighting, might very well have sent an officer under a white flag with the following ultimatum: surrender or we will set fire to the tinder-dry September woods around you. Sherman might have opted for a feint down the road to Atlanta, pretending to ignore the Confederate army in an attempt to draw it out into the open where it could be destroyed between the hammer and the concealed anvil.

Rosecrans's tragic flaw as a military commander was that he had no imagination.

The history of warfare teaches, time after time, that victory goes to the clever as well as to the strong, and that deception is no vice on the battlefield. Those who are innovative and unpredictable nearly always prevail: With his daring strategem of the wooden horse, Ulysses broke into the impregnable fortress of Troy and enabled Agamemnon and the rest of the Achaians to lay waste to the army within. During the Revolutionary War, Francis "The Swamp Fox" Marion, adopting the guerilla tactics of the Native Americans, successfully wreaked havoc on much larger British forces. More recently, U.S. commanders during the Persian Gulf War in 1992 were able to hold down an entire enemy division by making it appear as though an amphibious force would invade Kuwait City. In contrast, the inflexible and orthodox nearly always go down to defeat. In 430 B.C., Persian King Xerxes sacrificed his "Immortal Ten Thousand" at the Pass of Thermopylae because he could not comprehend that five hundred determined Spartans could easily hold off an entire elite force, given the tactical advantage of geography. Similarly, the rigid thinking of King Harold at the Battle of Hastings in 1066 led to a crushing defeat that brought French rule to England for the next three centuries. In our own time, the doomed fire-base strategy in Vietnam, pursued without change for a decade in the face of continued failure, led to the first significant defeat in history for U.S. forces.

My son and I leave the car behind and walk the rolling hills in the vicinity of Lee and Gordon's Mill. The original stone mill is gone, and a more recent one, vintage the Great Depression, crumbles now like something from a Wordsworth poem. It is a quiet, pastoral scene, milk cows and spreading oaks and pasture grass, and it requires a considerable effort to conjure images of war. My son runs off a distance, stretching his legs with the boundless energy of childhood, and I picture it as I once heard it described: it was late morning then, a warm September day with not a cloud in the blue, windless sky. There was a stillness in the air, and the mood was autumnal, a mixture of summer's passing and seasonal fruition and spent fertility. Horsedrawn supply wagons were pulling up in front of the regiments and quartermaster corporals were issuing each soldier—the waiting men were sun-darkened, lean, hard—enough ammunition and food rations for three days. Serpentine columns were marching in over the hills as more troops poured into the staging area. Guidons fluttered in the breeze. Crows gathered. Freckle-faced recruits nervously asked advice from taciturn veterans. Brown-bar lieutenants, always the first to die, sadly sharpened sabres that flashed in the sun. West Point captains and brevet majors hopefully studied hopeless maps. Long-bladed Bowie knives were stashed away in boot tops. Belt-budde derringers were loaded and concealed. Steady hands, shaking hands, fixed bayonets to loaded rifles.

An out-of-breath courier galloped in on a fine-looking Morgan horse white with sweat. General Palmer, the division commander, read the dispatch and immediately began shouting orders to colonels and majors. Somewhere a trumpet sounded and a bull-chested master sergeant from County Cork, Ireland, bellowed out for the troops of the 2nd Kentucky, "Fall in by company on this mark."

Across the assembly area the same order was heard.

Units formed up around the guides, each flag bearer, usually the short man of the outfit, holding the bright unit colors erect.

There they stood, the men of the 2nd Kentucky, standing at ease in staggered ranks, telling dirty jokes, arguing politics, farting and belching and complaining about the chow, talking sports, running off for the third time, reading a worn copy of Francis Parkman's *Oregon Trail,* silently praying, remembering loved ones back home, superstitiously fondling good luck charms (a little coin purse with locks of the children's hair, a fossil from the favorite fishing hole, a photograph of the fiancée bravely smiling at Fate). Although it was not cold, some men could not keep their teeth from chattering, but most stood calmly, resigned with appalling ease to their impending death or dismemberment.

At some point Colonel John Wilder's two-thousand-member Illinois and Indiana Cavalry thundered by, each man carrying a brand-new Spenser repeating carbine slung across his back. It would be these rifles, much later in the battle, that would save the Union army from total destruction, as Wilder's force, operating as an independent maneuvering unit on the battlefield, drove the sixty thousand rebels back into the forest. This was the first use of the repeating rifle in the history of warfare, and Charles Evers and the rest of the riflemen in the 2nd Kentucky eyed the mounted troopers enviously. They could only fire two rounds a minute with their weapons, while the cavalrymen could squeeze off seven well-aimed rounds as fast as they could swing the lever, aim, and pull the trigger.

V.

It took less than half an hour for the 2nd Kentucky to march at double-quick time (a slow run) from Lee and Gordon's Mill to the area just south of Brock Field, where they were to be thrown into the rebel line. Just where the ranger had promised, several hundred yards south of Brock Field and five yards east of Brotherton Road, I find the cast-iron plaque commemorating its charge of 12:30 p.m. on Saturday, September 19, 1863. My son and I stand beside the weathered, century-old tablet, one of fourteen hundred placed on the battlefield by veterans when the military park (the world's first) was established on September 19, 1890. The inscription reads:

CRUFT'S BRIGADE
PALMER'S DIVISION—CRITTENDON'S CORPS
BRIG. GEN. CHARLES CRUFT
SEPT. 19, 1863, 12:30 P.M.
1ST POSITION

31st Indiana	*Col. John T. Smith*
1st Kentucky	*Lieut. Col. Alva R. Hadlock*
2nd Kentucky	*Col. Thomas D. Sedgewick*
90th Ohio	*Col. Charles H. Rippey*
Battery B, 1st Ohio	*Lieut. Norman A. Baldwin*

This brigade advanced as the center echelon of Palmer's Division from the vicinity of the Poe House, having Hazen's brigade to its left and Grose's to its right. This brigade came into action on ground encountering the line of Cheatham's division, and pushed forward into position south of the road to Brotherton's where it was severely engaged for nearly two hours. After four o'clock most of the brigade was moved to the right to the assistance of Grose's brigade which was being forced rapidly to the rear, and a little later, being joined by a portion of Turchin's brigade of Reynold's division, the advance of the enemy on this part of the field was checked.

Thick woods prevail on this part of the battlefield, the flood plain of Chickamauga Creek. Buttemut and beech trees. Sassafras and sycamore. Southern magnolia and Catawba rhododendron. Honey locust and sweet gum. Black tupelo and swamp cypress. Even the names are beautiful. At ground level there is a tangled confusion of blackberry patches, wild rose thickets, thistles, beaked hazel, serviceberry, sumac, and various other brambles. Everywhere there is poison ivy, hanging like green curtains over the living and the dead and the decaying.

It is an ideal ground to defend, a hellish place to attack.

Just as Evers marched into the forest, at 12:30 p.m., General Palmer sent a rider to General Crittendon, his superior, with the following note: "My division is just going in. The enemy seems to be in heavy force. Fight is raging, but more on the left flank."

This message arrived back at Rosecrans's headquarters at 12:50 p.m. By that time Charles Evers and his platoon were well into the woods, moving slowly toward Brock Field. It was difficult to preserve alignment in the forest, and some men fell behind or advanced too far. It is unlikely that the soldiers noticed the beauty of the autumn forest that day. They saw only concealing cover, avenues of approach, lines of retreat, a strange bit of color and movement in the leaves.

Two hundred yards in they struck the enemy line.

Eight of thirty-seven men in Evers's platoon were killed or wounded in the first volley.

For thirty minutes there was fierce fighting.

At that point the 2nd Kentucky could not take it any longer and fell back, leaving its wounded, including Evers, in the field. After regrouping it rallied forward, but by that time the wounded had either been killed by the Union artillery assault or captured.

A quarter of a century after the battle, Charles Evers described what happened to those left behind, as only a participant could:

> We were but a skirmish line left there to stubbornly hinder the
> enemy until our main line could fall back to a better position,
> where the batteries could be used to advantage. I felt that we
> were lost, sacrificed, so to speak. Visions of death and
> Andersonville prison stayed in our eyes; no one gave command; I
> wished for mother earth to swallow me up out of sight, soul, and
> body. Just when the tension was greatest and the enemy was
> almost on us a voice of command said, "Fire low and fall back."
> I never knew whether that order came from Major Hurd, who
> commanded our skirmish line, Lieut. Parkhurst, or your dear
> old self, who was next in rank. It was a welcome command,
> though it brought us lots of trouble; the enemy, thinking no
> doubt it had struck the Yankee line, gave us a volley in return.
>
> When I fired I stood behind a friendly sapling and my
> musket when I brought it to my shoulder happened to range up
> the rebel line to the left, it seemed to me not more than forty or
> fifty paces away. You can bet I was in a hurry and the first thing
> that came in range of the barrel was an infantry officer with
> blue pants and a gray coat carrying a sword in one hand and a

musket in the other. He was a gallant fellow, leading and encouraging his men like a hero, and I hope in all sincerity is living today in peace and plenty under the protection of the government we poor Yanks were then trying to keep on its legs, and he was trying equally hard to destroy. But I got my pay for shooting at him, and just as I brought my gun down preparatory to some of the best retreating that ever a Yank did, their volley came. I made one spring and went down. Oh, my leg! It was for the instant numb and useless. And my gun—you remember that beautiful Springfield, with the bands and barrel and lock always like burnished silver and its dark black walnut curl stock. That was the prettiest army gun I ever saw, and it was my solemn intention to bring it home at all hazards. But alas! for it was ruined; worse than my leg; some rebel missile had struck it at the upper band and cut it half off and bent it, and my face was so near that some splinters struck me and set my cheek and eye to bleeding.

I left the dear old gun and scrambled away on all four like a groundhog, but the rebels were upon us, and their commands of "halt, halt" to the fleeing Yankee skirmish line came from both flanks. I halted as they swept past, sitting on the ground like a miserable trapped wolf. An officer with a sword passed quite near me, and at first I thought he intended to strike me, for he seemed in a fury of excitement, but he passed with a profane command to "go to the rear." I knew that the place would, within a very few minutes, be swept by the Federal cannon, repelling the rebel advance, which had just passed over us, and I tried to crawl to a place of less exposure. A few feet away I came upon Sergeant McFadden in an effort to rise from the ground, his face covered with blood from an ugly scalp wound; but luckily the bullet had not broken his skull, only knocked him silly and totally blind for the time. I told him if we did not get away from there we would be killed by our own friends, and that very soon.

We had moved less than twenty steps when we came on poor Tom Hamilton, orderly sergeant of our company, covered with

*blood and as pale as death. A bullet had entered his left breast
and gone out at his back. While we were hastily trying to
staunch the blood from Tom's wounds, Corporal Delahaunty
staggered up with a bloody head and disabled arm, and he told
us Ed Ballou and some other I don't recall lay close. I tell you, I
was afraid to move. It seemed to me that half the company was
lying there, dead or wounded; I could not bear to find any more
of the poor fellows—to know the worst.*

*But in such times there is no room for sentiment. All is
brutality and savagery. That instant the roll of musketry and
roar of cannon told plainly that the rebel advance had reached
the Federal battle line, and that the fight was on hot and
furious. The artillery range was such that it seemed as if no
living thing could escape, on that ground. Torn begged us to
leave him and seek safety, which we did, after first laying him
behind a tree. Soon we knew the result of the fighting. The
Confederates came streaming back and the whole field seemed
covered with skedaddlers. It put me in mind of our own army a
few months before at Stone River, when Bragg turned our right
wing. But the rebel officers were active in heading off the
stragglers and especially some staff officers, who rode out from a
little mot of timber nearby, regardless of the storm of Federal
shells that was sweeping the field in every direction.*

*After the storm subsided a little an officer came to where we
were sitting in the protection of a tree, Mac and I, and told us
to follow him, as the general wished to have a word with us. You
remember what a fine-looking soldier Mac was, six feet two,
broad shouldered, and with a fine soldierly, dignified reserve of
manner.*

*Well, they put Mac through a military inquisition to beat the
band, and I was proud of him, for he was wisely deceptive in
giving "straight" information about the Federal situation as a
trained diplomat. He was grave and intelligent in his answers to
their numerous inquiries; told them of Granger's reserve corps of
23,000 men at Chattanooga and of the camp rumor of the
previous day that Burnside was hastening for Knoxville to join*

Rosecrans, all of which seemed to interest them and cause anxiety. While this was going on an orderly came and said that the general would like to borrow my Harper's Weekly, *the end of which protruded from my blouse collar, where I had stuck it in the morning, and which I had borrowed from Fred Enderly. I noticed he handed it to an officer who sat on a horse and carried his arm in a sling. I was told that it was General Hood and that his arm was hurt at Gettysburg. A few hours later he lost his leg you remember. He was a brave and reckless soldier. Some years later I had the pleasure of donating to a memorial fund for the benefit of the general's orphan children left at his death in New Orleans. One of those sons, I am told, is now an officer, fighting under the old flag in the Philippines.*

I spent the night near a little creek where the whole space seemed filled with Confederate wounded. I tore off one leg of my underdrawers and bandaged my wound, which by that time had become very painful and I was dizzy from loss of blood and through the night consumed with pain and thirst. It was one of the saddest nights of my life. Besides the tragedy and pathos of the surrounding was the torturing anxiety as to the fate of Company H comrades and the final issue of the battle, which I felt would be continued next day with unabated fury and loss of life. Then, too, I saw before me the prospect of prison, hunger, disease, and probably the amputation of my leg.

Fortunately, human nature is so constituted that when we see others about us very much worse off than ourselves, we temporarily, at least, forget our own misery in sympathy with them. It was so in my case. I can convey to you no idea of the charnel of suffering and death in that place, though all was done that seemed possible. A young Confederate lay near me, dressed in the almost new uniform of a lieutenant, delirious from a mortal wound. His low moans and muttered prayers for friends he was never to see again were pathetic at times. I crept to him several times to see if he could have a swallow of water from my canteen, but he was unconscious to all my efforts. Later in the night he grew quiet, and when it was light I went to him again. His brown hair was white with the frosty dew of the chilly night; someone had kindly spread a handkerchief across his face. I lifted it a little. His half-open blue eyes and the peaceful expression of his pale face denoted that his last moment had been quiet. He had fought his last battle. Yet, poor fellow, he was only one of the hundreds who lay strewn over that scene of strife.

vi.

The losses that day were staggering on both sides. The 2nd Kentucky, a unit of around four hundred men, suffered a total of 92 casualties (1 officer and 9 enlisted men killed, 5 officers and 59 enlisted men wounded, 18 enlisted men missing in action). By the end of the day Confederate General Bragg held seven thousand prisoners (two thousand of whom were wounded) and had captured 26 unit colors and guidons, 365 pieces of artillery, and over fifteen thousand rifles and revolvers.

The most unusual casualty was a woman from Brooklyn who had disguised her gender and enlisted as a drummer boy in a Detroit regiment. She had marched with the Michigan infantry all the way through the Tullahoma campaign in Tennessee but received a fatal bullet wound at Chickamauga. Only upon being examined by surgeons was her true identity discovered. As she lay dying she dictated the following letter to her father: "Forgive your dying daughter. I have but a few moments to live. My native soil drinks my blood. I expected to deliver my country, but the Fates would not have it so. I am content to die. Pray, Pa, forgive me. Tell Ma to kiss my daguerreotype. Emily. P.S. Give my old watch to little Eph."

The mourning extended to the White House, where President Lincoln lost his brother-in-law, who had been fighting for the South. When told of the death, Mary Todd was inconsolable and Lincoln wrote, "I feel like David of old when he was told of the death of Absalom."

President Lincoln followed the battle closely from the war room, monitoring every telegraph message as it came in, placing pins on the maps and consulting with his senior staff officers. His telegraph messages to Rosecrans are a revelation of Lincoln's character and humanity. Despite his outrage at Rosecrans's disgraceful performance, Lincoln realized the personal agony Rosecrans was experiencing and sent the following message:

> *Be of good cheer. We have unabated confidence in you and in your soldiers and officers. In the main you must be the judge as to what is to be done. If I was to suggest, I would say save your army by taking strong positions until Burnside joins you, when I hope you can turn the tide. I think you had better send a courier to Burnside to hurry him up. We cannot reach him by telegraph. We suppose some force is going to you from Corinth, but for want of communication we do not know how they are getting along. We shall do our utmost to assist you. Send us your present posting.*

The major disaster would occur the next day, on Sunday, when Rosecrans would mistakenly order Brigadier General Wood to move his regiment to the left, thus opening a 400-yard gap in the Union line, through which the Confederates literally poured. A board of inquiry later established that Rosecrans's order included no escape clause permitting the recipient to exercise discretion and that Rosecrans had a reputation for insisting that his orders be strictly obeyed. The board also established that Rosecrans had fled the battlefield for Chattanooga while there were still men fighting. A month later, Rosecrans was relieved of command. To this day, he remains the only Union general for whom no monument has ever been raised.

vii.

Next stop is Brotherton Cabin, where Charles Evers was taken on Sunday, September 20, with the other prisoners of war. Remarkably, the ancient log cabin still stands today, on the edge of an expanse of grassy hills edged on all points by thick forest. It is a sturdy structure, measuring twelve feet by sixteen feet, with tongue-and-groove logs set neatly in the corners and a well-made stone fireplace on the western wall, facing the weather. The builders of the cabin were craftsmen who took pride in what they did, and constructed their home to last. It evokes other vintage American cabins—the birthplace of Lincoln, Thoreau's retreat on Walden Pond, the cabin of Margaret Murie in Jackson Hole. From Brotherton Cabin, Charles Evers had a front-seat view of the battlefield on Sunday, with rebels pouring out of the forest and Union troops retreating toward Missionary Ridge. Years later, General Bushrod R. Johnson, a Confederate brigade commander, wrote this description of the scene:

> Our lines now emerged from the forest into open ground, on the border of long, open fields, over which the enemy were retreating, under cover of several batteries, which were arranged along the crest of a ridge on our right and front, running up to the corner of a stubble-field, and of one battery on our left and front posted on an elevation in the edge of the woods, just at the corner of a field near a peach orchard and southwest of Dyer's house. The scene now presented was unspeakably grand. The resolute and impetuous charge, the rush of our heavy columns sweeping out from the shadow and gloom of the forest into the open fields flooded with sunlight, the glitter of arms, the onward dash of artillery and mounted men, the retreat of the foe, the shouts of the host of our army, the dust, the smoke, the noise of fire-arms—of whistling balls and grape-shot and of brusting shell—made up a battle schene of unsurpassed grandeur. Here General Hood gave me the last order I received from him on the field. "Go ahead and keep ahead of everything."

From Brotherton Cabin, Naoki and I drive a short distance through the fields to Dyer's house, near where General Hood was wounded that day. There is a fine prospect of the countryside beneath a towering red oak, and I pull over to take in the scene. We step from the car and sit down in the grass. To the north and west is Snodgrass Hill, where General George Thomas gathered up the gragments of the Union army and stubbornly held the salience from repeated Confederate assaults. For his tenacity he was given the moniker "Rock of Chickamauga."

In 1886, visiting Chickamauga as a tourist, Charles Evers stayed with Dyer at his farm. Although they had fought on opposite sides during the war, the two men walked together that day as newfound friends. Evers reported that "the scars of war are still plainly visible on the large trees; cannonball often, and musket balls by the score and frequently a dozen scars in a single tree. Many of the trees show marks of the relic hunter's hatchet." No evidence of the battle is visible around the Dyer home today. Through the years an army of souvenir collectors has carried off the cannonballs and musket shot.

Evers wrote of his walk with Dyer:

> *As we tramped over the battlefield Dyer pointed out to me the ravine up which General Preston led the Confederate flank attack on Thomas' right on Snodgrass Hill. It was here I believe that a portion of the 21st Ohio boys were cut off and captured. He then showed me the empty trenches from which kindly hands had removed the dead, Federal and Confederate. As I stood looking into those empty graves, while the wind breathed a solemn requiem through the scrubby pines I felt such an inexpressible sadness that I was glad when Dyer led the way to another part of the hillside where a tornado, a few years ago, finished what was left of the smitten woods after the battle, and he had this fall seeded the land to wheat, now green and beautiful. It was in the leaden rain of death in this field that General Hood fell from his horse, shot through the thigh.*
>
> *One is reminded here of that stanza of Byron's beginning:*
>
>> *Stop! thy tread is on an Empire's dust,*
>> *An earthquake's spoil is sepulchured below.*
>> *As the ground was before, thus let it be;*
>> *How that red rain hath made the harvest grow.*

As we lie there beneath the red oak tree—the time now mid afternoon—my son indicates that he is ready for his daily nap by yawning, closing his eyes, and falling asleep. I study his face, angelic in repose. His mother is Japanese, and his features are a mixture of features Asian and American. He snores just like my father and his father. Will my father one day tell Naoki of that other war, the one in which he dropped from the sky under a camouflaged parachute, with explosives for German bridges strapped to his legs? Or of his father, my grandfather, and those nights without days in the trenches, and the time when the gas mask did not work and he thought he would never see Ohio again?

The child sleeps on.

I take this opportunity to read the facsimile issue of *Harper's Weekly* purchased earlier at the park visitors' center. The pages instantly transport me back to September 1863. "A Journal of Civilization," it calls itself, an unintentional irony, with a price per copy of six cents. The cover features an engraving of the Union attack on Brazos, Texas. Major articles report on pay for "colored" soldiers, the cascade of events in the Deep South, the petty politics of the day. For escapists, there is Chapter 47 of a serial novel by Charles Read, Esquire, entitled "Meave, Schoolmistress." The centerpiece consists of a portrait of Major General Washburne and a sketch of Chattanooga, Tennessee. The back pages feature classified advertisements for clothes, bibles, photographs, revolvers, binoculars, playing cards, stomach medicines, furniture, microscopes, music boxes, billiard balls, swampland real estate in New Jersey, get-rich schemes, and various lotions that can be used to cure baldness or remove women's facial hair. On the last page is a political cartoon of "Dr. Lincoln" dispensing medicine for "The Confederate Rash."

Truly, there is nothing new under the sun.

Sometime later, Naoki awakens with a start, demands water, and asks me what I am doing.

I tell him and he looks at the paper and decides it has no value and asks me why the soldiers fought in this place.

How do you explain Henry Clay and Daniel Webster, Slavery and Abolitionism, Frederick Douglas and John Brown, the Compromise of 1850 and the Kansas-Nebraska Act of 1854, the Dred Scott Decision and the Fugitive Slave Law, Fort Sumter and Appomattox, Abraham Lincoln and Jefferson Davis, Matthew Brady and John Wilkes Booth to a child not quite five?

"Well, one group of people made another group of people work for nothing. They were their prisoners."

"Like when Joker trapped Batman?"

I sigh in relief. "Something like that." The winter days are short, and we return to the car, a mode of travel that could not have been imagined in 1863, and to the road, which is the same as it was in 1863, with the added advantage of asphalt.

The shadows lengthen from Missionary Ridge to the west.

As a boy, traveling east from Ohio with my parents on vacation each summer, I always thought the view from the top of the Washington Monument, looking out over the Potomac River at the various monuments and state buildings of the capitol, was the finest in America. Later, when the family moved west to Denver, I added two more: the view of the Tetons from the oxbow bend on the Snake River and the view of San Francisco from the Marin County headlands. Still later, on moving to Alaska, I added a fourth: the view of Denali from the headwaters of Moose Creek on the far side of Thorofare Pass. To that list I find I must now add a fifth: the view of the Chickamauga battlefield from that red oak on Dyer's field. No massive peaks rise here, no marble monuments, and yet all that America ever was or ever will be is conjured up by these grounds.

Driving back from the mountains to Atlanta, down the highway toward the city that Sherman sacked one year after Chickamauga, my thoughts turn to the gravesite of Martin Luther King, in downtown Atlanta, where Naoki and I spent some time earlier in the week. The white marble tomb rests in a pool of water that is forever refilled by a fountain at the other end. On the tomb are chiseled the words "Free at last, free at last, thank God almighty I'm free at last." The burial site, part of an entire city block administered as a historic site by the National Park Service, is not far from the Ebenezer Baptist Church, where Reverend King's father and grandfather preached earlier in the century, teaching him the philosophy that unmerited suffering is redemptive, a belief at the core of King's life. The neighborhood, now largely run down, consists of rambling Victorian homes, built in the Queen Anne style popular in the Roaring Twenties. King was born six doors up the street from the church in 1929, just a few months before the Stock Market Crash and the Dust Bowl—twin emblems of national greed and excess—brought the nation to its knees in a way even the Civil War had not.

As Naoki and I stood there, silently paying our respects, an elderly black man, pushing his wordly belongings before him in a grocery cart, stopped beside us and asked me if I could spare some change.

'Thanks a lot, brother," he said, "That's a mighty fine-looking son you've got there."

I thanked him, turned to the tomb, and said, "That's really moving. What's written up there."

"Oh yeah, it is. That's a fact. But I always liked that other thing he said."

I asked him what it was.

"If a man don't have somethin' worth dyin' for, he ain't fit to live."

viii.

In December 1863 Charles Evers was released from Libby Prison in Richmond (its commander would later be the first person ever tried for war crimes) and put on a train for Kentucky. Family in Ohio had purchased his freedom. Evers was permanently crippled in the leg that had been shot, but he did not let the handicap prevent him from leading a full life. After the war, he was elected county sheriff of Wood County, Ohio. In this capacity, he oversaw twenty townships, fifty towns, and sixty thousand residents. He was known for his arrests, and one of his obituaries mentions the time he jumped from a moving train, reinjuring his war-crippled leg, to capture a dangerous suspect. For many years, Evers published the *Bowling Green Sentinel* and used the newspaper as a vehicle for his progressive political views. About Wood County he was known as the founder of the Bowling Green Literary Society and as the citizen who was always fighting for civic projects such as school funding and public parks. Sometime in the early 1890s he drilled the first natural gas wells in his part of Ohio, which provided him with financial independence. Evers spent the rest of his life traveling on the new train system and writing about the changing landscape of America.

It would be his second daughter, Lena, wed to John A. Murray of Kenmore, Scotland, who would give birth in 1894 to the man who would one day tell me the stories on the sunny back porch.

The old soldier died on July 29, 1909, less than two years after his wife Sarah and during the same summer former president Theodore Roosevelt was off collecting specimens for the national collection in what was then British East Africa. Although the year was 1909, the twentieth century had not really been born. Mark Twain was the leading

American writer, and Ernest Hemingway had yet to write his first article for the grade-school newspaper in Oak Park, Illinois. The young Spanish artist Picasso, experimenting freely in his early Cubist period, was still regarded with considerable disdain by the artistic establishment. The Wright brothers had only recently invented the airplane, and people were still wary of the strange new piece of technology called the telephone. In southeastern Europe, at a place called Sarajevo, the government of Serbia would shortly recognize the Austrian annexation of Bosnia and Herzegovina.

Much change would soon come to the world.

History is most often written in terms of generals and colonels, presidents and kings. We read of regiments and battalions, strategies and tactics, orders and actions, proclamations and treaties. Tolstoi said as much in *War and Peace*, describing how the personality of Napoleon decisively influenced events in the War of 1812, even as he was being borne along by those events. "Great men," observed Tolstoi, "lead humanity toward the attainment of certain goals." A few have gone further and said that all history is the biography of great men and women. That may be partially true. Sometimes, though, there is merit in regarding history through the eyes of Everyman. The perspective at the bottom provides a wide-angle view of events that is sometimes lost by those at the top, concerned as they are with the minutiae of governance and blinded as they ultimately become by personal bias and self-interest. In either case, we see quite clearly in the end that history is the continual struggle of the human spirit for freedom.

Of all the books I've read on Chickamauga, the best description I've found is in a letter written by Sergeant Charles Evers. Its clarity and forcefulness bring to mind the line from Ambrose Bierce, who also served at Chickamauga: "[It is] a simple story of a battle; such a tale as may be told by a soldier who is no writer to a reader who is no soldier." Who else but one who had lived through it could reduce a complicated conflict involving one hundred thousand men on a battlefield covering ten square miles over two days to a few sentences?

> *General Bragg, in the Chickamauga campaign, practiced some of the best strategy of the war. He completely out-witted Rosecrans. He made Rosey believe he had gone out of*

Chattanooga by three different roads on a dead run, so to speak, and Rosecrans divided his army into three parts and went gunning for Bragg. Then was Bragg's opportunity. His army lay near Lafayette intact. Rosecrans had fallen into his trap and all Bragg had to do was to precipitate his whole force on either part of the Federal Army and crush it before the other could come up. McCook was three days march away. This was a critical juncture for the Federals. Had Bragg's performance been equal to his strategy, salt would not have saved the Union Army.

Had we not had Charles Evers, and many others like him, salt would not have saved the United States of America.

First publication

Notes on Contributors

Bruce Berger divides his time between a summer home in Aspen, Colorado, and a winter residence in Baja. He is the author of a critically acclaimed book, *The Telling Distance* (University of Arizona, 1994) and has recently published *Almost an Island* (University of Arizona, 1998) on human and wild nature on the Baja peninsula.

Franklin Burroughs, an English professor at Bowdoin College in Maine, is the author of *The River Home: A Return to the Carolina Low Country* (University of Georgia, 1994) and *Billy Watson's Croker Sack* (University of Georgia, 1998).

Peter A. Christian holds a master's degree in northern studies from the University of Alaska, Fairbanks. He worked for many years as a seasonal ranger for the National Park Service in the Brooks Range of northern Alaska and is currently writing a book about his backcountry experiences.

Barbara Drake is the author of *Peace at Heart* (Oregon State University Press, 1998), in which the essay of the same title appears, and has previously published several collections of poetry and a college textbook (*Writing Poetry*, Harcourt Brace, 2nd edition 1994). She teaches creative writing and literature at Linfield College in Oregon.

Marybeth Holleman, a graduate of the MFA program in creative writing at the University of Alaska, lives with her small son in Anchorage, Alaska. Her work has been widely published in literary journals, and she is currently writing a collection of essays about Prince William Sound.

Carolyn Kremers is an English professor at Eastern Washington University in Spokane. She is the author of *Place of the Pretend People: Gifts from a Yup'ik Eskimo Village* (Alaska Northwest Books, 1997). Kremers maintains a log cabin home near Fairbanks, Alaska, where she lived for many years, and returns to Alaska every summer to travel and write.

Ken Lamberton is a graduate of the creative writing program at the University of Arizona, Tucson, where he helped edit the *Sonora Review.* He is the author of *Wilderness and Razor Wire* (Mercury House, 1999) and his work has been published widely in literary journals, including *Cimarron Review, Southwestern American Literature* and *Sonora Review.*

Gretchen Legler, who received her doctoral degree from the University of Minnesota, is an English professor at the University of Alaska, Anchorage. In 1997 the National Science Foundation sponsored her half-year residency at the U.S. base in Antarctica and she is currently writing a book about her experiences there. Previously she authored *All the Powerful Invisible Things: A Sportswoman's Notebook* (Seal Press, 1996).

Natasha Ma (pseudonym), whose educational background is in psychology, has worked across Asia, from a Cambodian refugee camp in Thailand to a school in Tibet. She hopes to return to work in Tibet soon and so uses a pseudonym to conceal her identity from the Chinese government.

Susan Marsh writes from Jackson, Wyoming, where she works as a wilderness and recreation manager for the Bridger-Teton National Forest. Her writing has appeared in *Orion, Sierra, North Dakota Quarterly, Wyoming, Northern Lights,* and other magazines and anthologies. She is at work on a collection of essays about the Yellowstone region and a memoir about Montana.

John Noland lives and teaches in Coos Bay, Oregon. His work has appeared in such journals as *Orion* and *Petroglyph.*

David Petersen is the author of such acclaimed works as *Ghost Grizzlies* (Henry Holt, 1996), *Among the Aspen* (Northland Publishing, 1992) and *The Nearby Faraway: A Personal Journey Through the Heart of the West* (Johnson, 1998). Several years ago he edited the journals of Edward Abbey (*Confessions of a Barbarian*, Little Brown, 1995). He and his wife Carolyn live in a cabin in the San Juan Mountains of southwestern Colorado.

Jeff Ripple is the author of several nature books, including *Feast of Flowers, Essays on Florida's Wildlands* (University Press of Florida, 1998). Ripple, a former artist, is also an accomplished large-format photographer. He and his wife Renee live in Gainesville and, whenever opportunity presents itself, they love to kayak in the Everglades and surrounding salt waters.

Susan Tweit is the author of such popular works as *Pieces of Light* (Roberts Rinehart, 1990), *Seasons in the Desert: a Naturalist's Notebook* (Chronicle, 1998), and *Barren, Wild and Worthless: Living in the Chihuahuan Desert* (University of New Mexico Press, 1997). She and her husband Richard Cable, an economist, live in Salida, Colorado.

Glen Vanstrum is a physician in La Jolla, California, where he also owns a nature photography business specializing in underwater photography. He has traveled widely around the world—including Greenland, the Canadian High Arctic, and New Guinea—and is working on a book of essays about his experiences. His nature essays have appeared in the *Los Angeles Times* and *The New Yorker*.

Louise Wagenknecht worked for many years as a firefighter for the U.S. Forest Service and the Bureau of Land Management in northern Idaho. She and her husband maintain a sheep ranch near Leadore, Idaho. She is currently writing a memoir about her life growing up in Pacific Northwest logging towns. Her work regularly appears in *High Country News*.

Kathryn Wilder edited the anthologies *Walking the Twilight: Women Writers of the Southwest* (1994) and *Walking the Twilight II: Women Writers of the Southwest* (1996), both by Northland Publishing. She teaches English at a community college in northern California, where she can be close to the wild rivers she loves.

Permissions

Bruce Berger: "Under the Cypress" from *Almost an Island* by Bruce Berger. Published by the University of Arizona Press. Copyright 1998 Bruce Berger. Reprinted by permission of the publisher and the author.

Franklin Burroughs: "Of Moose and a Moose Hunter" from *Billy Watson's Croker Sack,* published by the University of Georgia Press. Copyright 1996. Reprinted by permission of the University of Georgia Press.

Peter A. Christian: "Grabbing the Bull by the Antlers." Copyright 1998 by Peter A. Christian. Reprinted with permission of the author.

Barbara Drake: "Wild Apples" from *Peace at Heart,* published by Oregon State University Press. Copyright 1998 by Barbara Drake. Reprinted with permission of the author.

Marybeth Holleman, "Heating with Wood." Copyright 1998 by Marybeth Holleman. Reprinted with permission of the author.

Carolyn Kremers: "Shishmaref" from *Place of the Pretend People: Gifts from a Yup'ik Eskimo Village*, published by Alaska Northwest Books. Copyright 1997 by Carolyn Kremers. Reprinted with permission of the author.

Ken Lamberton: "Raptors and Flycatchers" from *Snowy Egret.* Copyright 1997 by Ken Lamberton. Reprinted with permission of the author.

Gretchen Legler: "All the Powerful Invisible Things" from *All the Powerful Invisible Things: A Sportswoman's Notebook*, published by Seal Press. Copyright 1996 by Gretchen Legler. Reprinted with permission of the author.

Natasha Ma (pseudonym): "Saving Tibet." Copyright 1998 by Natasha Ma. Reprinted with permission of the author.